User Experience
Questionnaires

User Experience Questionnaires

How to use questionnaires to measure the user experience of your products?

Martin Schrepp

Preface

In today's highly competitive market, a good user experience is important for the long-term success of a product. User experience describes a person's subjective impression of a product. Different persons can have very different opinions in this regard. Therefore, we need to survey larger samples to measure the user experience.

There are many facets of human-computer interaction that are summarized under the term user experience. Which of these facets are important to the users of a product and should therefore be measured in a study depends on the type of product being evaluated. Therefore, a deep understanding of the concept of user experience is a prerequisite for developing appropriate strategies to measure this characteristic.

Given the importance of user experience for the success of a product, it is important to be able to measure it accurately. The result can be used, for example, to check whether a new product version has improved the user experience compared to previous versions, whether a product is better or worse than the competition on the market, or whether investments in the user experience have paid off.

Since user experience describes a person's subjective impression, the use of questionnaires is a very popular method for quantifying this characteristic. Questionnaires make it possible to collect data from large samples of users with little effort. If the questionnaire is started directly online in a product, data can be collected from real end users during their daily work with the product. In addition, there are many standard questionnaires that can be used by researchers in their projects. In most cases, such standard questionnaires are based on solid scientific research, are published in journals, and can be used free of charge.

Using a questionnaire to gain insights into the user experience of a product looks simple at first glance. In practice, however, mistakes in the selection of a suitable questionnaire or in the collection, analysis and interpretation of the data are not uncommon. If important and possibly expensive decisions for the further development of a product should be derived from the results of the questionnaire, such errors can have serious consequences.

This book is intended to help user experience researchers to use questionnaires in their research activities and to get the best out of the data. The suggestions are based on several scientific papers I have published on this topic in recent years and on my own experience as a user experience researcher working with different questionnaires in my own projects.

Parts of this book are based on an earlier book I published on this topic. The title is *User Experience mit Fragebögen messen* (only available in German). However, new topics were added to the material and thus the content was largely restructured.

This book contains an introduction to the basic concepts of user experience measurement. Several popular user experience questionnaires are discussed in detail. It is described how such questionnaires can be used and extended with study-specific questions.

Selecting an appropriate questionnaire for a study requires a deeper understanding of the aspects of user experience that are to be measured. Therefore, a special focus of this book is on the semantic meaning of the term user experience. We discuss various aspects or facets of user experience in detail. Furthermore, typical questions regarding the measurement of user experience are discussed, e.g. empirical dependencies between semantically different aspects, or inter-individual differences in the perception of user experience.

The book also includes tips on data collection, data analysis and presentation of results to help researches avoid some pitfalls and get the most out of their data. Sometimes it is not sufficient to reuse and extend an existing standard questionnaire. Therefore, in a separate chapter, we describe how to develop your own questionnaire.

We refer to existing questionnaires by their short name to keep the text short and readable. Appendix 1 list for the used short names the full name and the reference to a publication describing the questionnaire in detail. Appendix 2 describes the basic structure, scales, and application areas of a larger list of user experience questionnaires. This should help researchers to find the most suitable questionnaire for their projects.

Table of Contents

About the author

Dr. Martin Schrepp finished his diploma in mathematics in 1990 at the University of Heidelberg (Germany). In 1993 he received a PhD in Psychology (also from the University of Heidelberg). Since 1994 he works as a user interface designer and researcher for SAP SE.

His research interests are the application of psychological theories to improve the design of software interfaces, the application of Design for All principles to increase accessibility of business software, measurement of usability and user experience, and the development of general data analysis methods. He has published several research papers concerning these fields.

He has extensive experience concerning the development of user experience questionnaires (UEQ, UEQ+) and in their practical application in the evaluation of interactive products.

1 User Experience

If you try to measure a property, then you should have a pretty good conceptual understanding of this property. Otherwise it is difficult to judge if your measurement method provides the expected results. In this chapter we will clarify our understanding of the term *user experience*.

Before we clarify the meaning of *user experience* we start with the simpler and well-established concept of *usability*. A generally accepted definition of this concept is provided in the ISO 9241-110. This norm defines the usability of a product as *the extent to which a product can be used by specified users to achieve specified goals with effectiveness, efficiency, and satisfaction in a specified context of use*.

The mentioned criteria of usability have the following meaning:

- *Effectiveness:* Are users able to achieve their goals accurately and completely?

- *Efficiency:* Are users able to achieve their goals with reasonable effort?

- *Satisfaction:* Are users comfortable using the product?

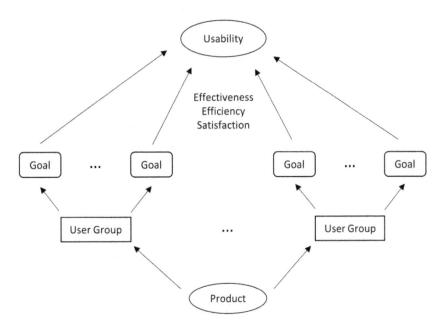

Figure 1: The usability of a product depends on the user group and the goals of the users.

This definition contains some important points. First, usability is not a property of a product. It is defined with respect to a given context of use and a given user group. Second, it stays unclear if usability is an objective or subjective concept. Let us have a closer look at these two points.

The dependency between the usability of a product and the user group respectively the context of use can be explained using simple examples. MS Power Point is a quite effective and efficient tool to create simple visualizations for business or scientific presentations. But it does clearly not offer enough functionality (i.e. is not effective) to be used by professional graphic artists for the creation of highly sophisticated visualizations. Another recent example is the German booking procedure for vaccination appointments against Corona viruses. Booking is possible over a web page. When users try to register, they must enter a phone number. After submission of the data a text message containing a registration code is sent to this number. The user must then enter this code in the web page to proceed and finish registration. For younger people this works quite well. It is a typical pattern used by many web services and they are familiar with such procedures. For the elderly, this was a disaster (and people over 80 were the main target group when this action started) as they were often unfamiliar with such text messages and could not register without help.

Clearly satisfaction of a user with a product is purely subjective, i.e. we must ask users about their personal view. There is no objective method to measure user satisfaction. For effectiveness and efficiency this is not true.

Of course, we can ask users if they think that they could reach their goals with a product effectively and efficiently. Thus, effectiveness and efficiency can be measured by capturing the subjective opinions of users in a questionnaire. But it is also possible to measure parts of these criteria objectively. For example, it is a common practice to count in usability tests the number of solved and failed tasks per participant. The task completion rate over all participants can then be interpreted as a measure for the effectiveness of the product. In addition, the time required to perform tasks or formal modelling techniques like GOMS (Card, Moran & Newell, 1983) analysis can be used to estimate the efficiency of a product objectively.

Effectiveness, efficiency, and satisfaction are quite abstract principles. These are not helpful as concrete suggestions for designers. Therefore, the ISO 9241 defines in addition 7 more detailed and concrete *dialog principles*. We describe the dialogue principles through a series of questions. The positive or negative answers to these questions indicate whether a product fulfils the principle or not. The questions are only examples, i.e. do not fully cover the principles.

- *Suitability for the task:* Does the product offer all functionality that is required for users to achieve their goals? Do users need to perform unnecessary steps to complete their work? Does the product display just the required information, or is it distracting users with unnecessary information?

- *Self-descriptiveness:* Does the product provide all the necessary information? Is there suitable feedback on the current system status, e.g. success or error messages and status displays? Is the navigation structure of the product obvious?

- *Controllability:* Does the user feel in control? Is the product forcing users to take steps they don't want to take? Is it possible to interrupt work at any time and continue at a later point without losing data? Does the product react as expected to user input or user actions?

- *Conformity with user expectations:* Does the user interface design meet the user's expectations? Are common interaction patterns used? Is the product design consistent? Are similar functions implemented in a similar way throughout the product?

- *Error tolerance:* How does the product react to incorrect entries? Does it provide enough help or information for the user to easily resolve such error situations? Does it correct simple errors automatically? Is it designed in a way that helps to avoid errors?

- *Suitability for individualization:* Can users adapt the product to suit their personal work style or preferences? Is it possible to hide unnecessary elements on the user interface (menus, buttons, fields, or textual information)? Is it possible to automate routine tasks?

- *Suitability for learning:* Is It easy for the user to learn how to use the product? Does the product support the user to get familiar with the interaction, for example through available documentation, consistent placement of elements on the user interface, wizards, or design principles, such as progressive disclosure?

These dialog principles played an important role in the early development of usability questionnaires. Some questionnaires, for example, ISONORM or ISOMETRICS measure usability with the help of these dialog principles. They contain one scale for each of the seven principles. The items in this

3

scale cover aspects relevant to this design principle. In addition, many other questionnaires contain items that map to these seven dialog principles.

The dialog principles are, on the one hand, concrete enough to formulate questions about a product that can be easily answered by users, for example *Was it easy for you to learn how to use the product?* On the other hand, they are still abstract enough to be applicable to a wider range of products.

Usability in the sense of ISO 9241 is a well-established and well-understood concept. The term *user experience* (we use in the following the abbreviation UX) is much more difficult to describe.

Again, there is a definition in ISO 9241-210. Here UX is defined as a *person's perceptions and responses that result from the use or anticipated use of a product, system or service.* Similar to the definition of usability, the UX of a product depends on the user group and the context of use. But there are several important differences compared to the definition of usability.

Perceptions and responses cover emotions, beliefs, physical and psychological reactions, behaviours, or accomplishments. While usability focuses on a user's tasks and goals, UX has a much broader scope.

In addition, UX is a completely subjective quality. In the centre of the definition is the impression of the user. Thus, we need to ask the user about his or her subjective impressions concerning the product in order to measure UX.

Another important point is that user experience is not only influenced by the actual use of the product. The concept also covers the time before the user uses the product (anticipated use). User expectations towards a product they want to use but have not yet used affect the UX.

Since it is a subjective quality it is also clear that UX depends on the user group and context of use, i.e. concerning these dependencies it is similar to usability.

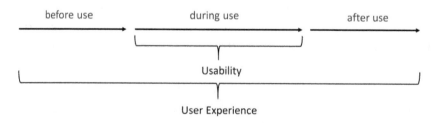

Figure 2: UX spans the time before and after using a product.

The ISO 9241-210 definition of UX is not very concrete. For a UX designer who wants to know what to do to create a good UX for a product the definition is not helpful at all. In contrast to the usability concept, where the dialog principles describe desirable elements of an interaction with a product, there is no link to detailed design properties or interaction qualities of a product. The same is true concerning the measurement of UX. While the dialog principles provide a good basis to formulate questions, the UX definition lacks the necessary level of detail.

However, there are alternative approaches. Preece, Rogers & Sharp (2002) distinguish between two types of product qualities related to UX:

- *Usability goals:* These are qualities that relate to the tasks users must complete in order to reach their goals. They correspond to the classic dialog principles described above.

- *User Experience Goals:* These are qualities related to the subjective impression concerning the overall interaction with the product, for example fun of use or aesthetic appeal of the user interface.

A similar distinction is described by Hassenzahl (2001). He distinguishes between:

- *Pragmatic qualities:* Qualities that influence how well users can complete their tasks and thus achieve their goals with the product.

- *Hedonic qualities:* Qualities that are not related to tasks and goals.

Thus, in both approaches there is a binary classification of UX related qualities. One class corresponds to the usability concept, the other contains UX quality aspects that are not related to working on specific tasks.

Both approaches list specific qualities that fall into the category of hedonic quality or user experience goals.

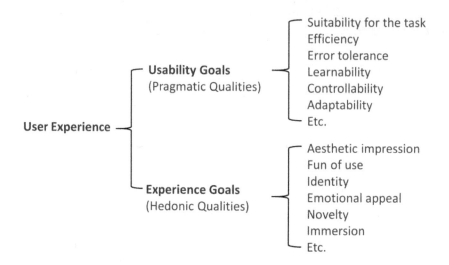

Figure 3: UX as a set of distinct qualities.

Thus, if we follow this approach then UX is described by a set of quality aspects. It contains the classical usability criteria, for example the dialog principles described above, and some additional qualities. For the creation of UX questionnaires this concept of user experience is quite helpful, since the discussed hedonic qualities are on a detail level that allows to formulate concrete questions to measure them.

Another approach that follows a similar logic but considers some additional components is the CUE model (CUE stands for *Components of User Experience*). This model (Thüring & Mahlke, 2007) also distinguishes between task-related (pragmatic) and non-task related (hedonic) qualities. But it sets a strong focus on emotional aspects.

The basic assumption in the CUE model is that the perception of the task-related and non-task-related qualities during an interaction with a product triggers (positive or negative) emotional reactions. These emotional reactions together with the perceived qualities then determine the overall impression of the product and the formation of *consequences*, for example the intention to use the product more (or less) intensively. Thus, with respect to this model it is also of interest to measure emotions and consequences, for example loyalty or overall impression.

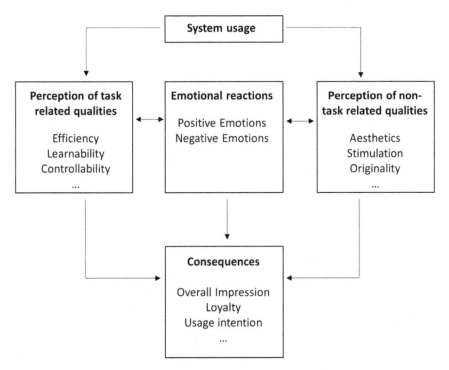

Figure 4: Basic structure of the CUE model (simplified and terminology adjusted) accordingly to Thüring & Mahlke (2007).

The distinction of UX qualities into pragmatic and hedonic qualities has some inherent problems. First, the pragmatic qualities share some common underlying concept. They are all related to the ability of the product to support the user while working on tasks. But what is the common concept behind the hedonic qualities? They are simply the rest after the pragmatic qualities are grouped. Thus, they do not share a common concept or idea. This immediately raises the question whether these hedonic qualities can be further split into some sub-groups. Second, for some UX qualities it is quite difficult to decide if they are pragmatic or hedonic. As a simple example we look at the *content quality* of a web page. Good content quality of a web page means that the information is relevant to the user, written in an interesting and motivating style, contains nice visualizations, is reliable, etc.

Is content quality a pragmatic or a hedonic quality? This somehow depends on the motivation of the user to visit a page:

- Suppose a user is looking for a specific piece of information. The user navigates to a page that seems to contain this information. The user finds the content interesting to read and reliable, i.e. has the

7

impression that the page has a high level of content quality. In this scenario content quality is more a pragmatic quality in the sense that it helps the user to reach his or her goal, since finding the information was the primary intention to visit the page.

- Suppose a user is reading an article on a news site. The user finds by chance (without a clear goal in mind) a link to a page with interesting, relevant, and reliable content. In this view content quality is more a hedonic quality since it is not related to a clear task.

Thus, content quality is a UX quality that makes semantically a lot of sense (if you run a web page you will be of course interested to improve the content quality and therefore you will find a scale that measures it useful) but that cannot be classified as pragmatic or hedonic. The context of use defines if content quality is more a hedonic or pragmatic quality.

There is another group of UX qualities for which it is a bit questionable how to classify them. Household appliances (vacuum cleaners, washing machines, etc.) are clearly used to reach certain goals with maximal comfort. Some of these household appliances have a more or less complex user interface and thus classical usability criteria play a role for the satisfaction of the users with the product. Nobody wants to spend a lot of time reading the manual to be able to operate the new washing machine. In addition, typical hedonic UX qualities play a role, for example the visual appearance of the machine.

But for such household appliances there are at least two other typical qualities that influence UX. First, they generate some operating noise. If this is too loud or the frequency of the sound is unpleasant for the user, this can create quite strong feelings against the product. Second, you need to operate some of these household appliances (such as a vacuum cleaner) in your hands. Thus, the feeling when you touch the device is important (haptics). It is important for the user experience that touching the device generates a pleasant feeling and that you have the impression that it fits comfortably in your hand. Scales to measure acoustics and haptics for household appliances were, for example, developed by Boos & Brau (2017).

But are haptics and acoustics pragmatic or hedonic UX qualities? In some sense they cover aspects of both categories. If a tool creates a pleasant haptic feeling this is of course a hedonic aspect. But such a pleasant haptic feeling enables the user to work for longer periods of time comfortably with the tool, thus also increases the pragmatic quality.

2 UX Quality Aspects and Psychological Needs

An UX quality aspect describes the subjective impression of users towards a semantically clearly described aspect of product usage or product design. In this sense, learnability, efficiency, fun of use or visual appeal are clearly UX quality aspects. Satisfaction with product price or service quality is not considered a UX quality aspect.

In the previous chapter, we showed that UX describes the subjective impression of users regarding their interaction with a product. Thus, measuring UX requires to ask users about their opinion. There is no objective method to measure UX!

But what should we ask? A high-level question like *How do you rate the user experience of the product?* does not make sense (the same is true if we replace *user experience* with *usability*). We as UX professionals understand what UX means, but this is not true for typical users of a product. Different users may understand the term quite differently.

But users can typically answer questions like *Does the system react fast enough to your inputs?*, *Was it easy for you to learn how to use the product?*, *Is the user interface visually appealing?*, or *Is it fun to use the product?* Such questions are specific enough and users can relate them to their personal experiences using the product.

Thus, to measure UX we need to define UX aspects that are concrete enough to be understood by users. In fact, all UX questionnaires do just that. They select a couple of UX aspects as scales and formulate several items (questions) per scale that relate to the underlying aspect.

In this sense, each questionnaire defines by the selection of the scales which UX aspects are most important for the application scenario in which the questionnaire is to be used. Thus, each UX questionnaire implements a different UX concept.

Of course, there is a huge number of possible UX aspects that may be of interest in UX research. This variety of UX aspects can also be found in existing UX questionnaires. We show this with a small example.

Schrepp (2020) analysed a list of 1248 items from 40 UX questionnaires. The items were reduced to adjectives (all other words are removed). For example, the item *Does the system react fast enough to your inputs?* was reduced to *fast*. Items for which such a reduction to an adjective was not possible were ignored for the further analysis. The extracted adjectives were unified concerning spelling and their frequency was counted.

The following word cloud (generated with the free word cloud generator www.wortwolken.com) shows the word cloud resulting from the final list of 291 different adjectives. Font sizes represent frequency, i.e. the bigger the font is, the more frequent was the attribute. Shades of grey of the word are used only for decoration and have no meaning.

Figure 5: Word cloud of adjectives used in the analysed questionnaires.

The pure number of different adjectives and the word cloud in Figure 5 show how heterogenous UX is. However, in practice it is possible to define a reasonable number of scales, i.e., groups of semantically similar items, that can be used to measure UX for many different types of products. There is some common understanding what is worth measuring and what is not. But which aspects of an interaction with a product are good candidates for such UX scales? We will try to clarify this in the rest of this chapter.

New interactive products and new interaction paradigms appear quite frequently. They also create the need to consider new UX aspects. Thus, the list of relevant UX aspects is not static, but changes over time. Let's look at some examples.

30 years ago, interactive products were merely used in a professional environment by trained users. Typically, the employer was responsible for operating and maintaining the system. Trust in the system therefore meant that it was expected that the data entered would be stored correctly. The

aspect of security of the personal data entered was not important at this time and therefore does not appear in older UX questionnaires.

When ATM's, social networks or e-commerce offerings starts to emerge this aspect of trust became quite important. These systems process sensitive data and thus the aspect of whether they store personal data securely is very important. If people have the impression that this is problematic, they will not trust the product and may refuse to use it. Therefore, trust is a highly relevant UX aspect for many types of modern products. For this reason, trust related items are quite common in newer UX questionnaires.

It was in the past also commonly accepted that users need to spend some time to learn how to use interactive systems. The existence of handbooks or extensive learning material was an important UX quality aspect. The expectation that products should be intuitive to use or that users could learn the system by trial and error was simply not there. Thus, older UX questionnaires contain many questions concerning the availability and quality of textual help or documentation. In more recent questionnaires, such items are not frequent or often not present at all.

In addition to new usage scenarios we have also to consider new ways to interact with a product. Older products offered only command line or graphical user interfaces. New interaction paradigms, such as touch or voice interaction, require the creation of new scales to capture users' subjective experiences with these new products.

If we want to figure out which aspects of an interaction with a product are good candidates for scales in UX questionnaires, we need to understand why people use products.

A first important distinction is between *extrinsic* and *intrinsic motivation*:

- *Extrinsic motivation:* Extrinsic motives are set by others. For example, in a business context there are tasks that users must perform as part of their daily work. Or personal administrative tasks that require interactions with a public service on the web (request a new ID card, submit your tax declaration). These are tasks that you need to do as part of your work or personal life and that require you to use a product or system.

- *Intrinsic motivation:* Humans have basic psychological needs. To fulfill them, people take actions that sometimes result in the interaction with a product. Thus, in this case the intention to use a product does not come from an external source, but from the person itself. For example, people use a social network to fulfill the need of relatedness to others.

Let us have a deeper look at these intrinsic motivations. The concept of basic psychological needs has its origin in self-determination theory (Ryan, 1995 or Deci & Ryan, 2000). This theory focusses on the intrinsic motivation behind people's behavior, i.e. the motives that are not based on external influences. The theory describes the three basic psychological needs of *competence*, *autonomy* and *relatedness* (a more detailed explanation of this concepts is given below) as the main forces behind intrinsically motivated behavior. It is assumed that these needs are universal (present in all cultures) and innate.

Based on these concepts additional psychological needs are described (Sheldon, Eliot, Kim & Kasser, 2001). Some studies link these needs to the use of interactive systems. In Lallemand, Koenig & Gronier (2014) a selection of 7 psychological needs is used as a basis for an expert review process. The psychological needs are described on cards and these cards are used like heuristics in a classical heuristic evaluation (Nielsen & Molich, 1990) of a product.

The following list of seven psychological needs relevant for the interaction with a product is taken from Lallemand, Koenig & Gronier (2014):

- *Relatedness:* Fulfilled if a person feels in close contact with other people important for him or her. Not fulfilled if a person feels lonely, isolated or uncared for.

- *Competence:* Fulfilled if a person feels competent and effective in his or her role (for example at work). Not fulfilled if a person feels incompetent or ineffective concerning what he or she is doing.

- *Autonomy:* Fulfilled if a person thinks that he or she can decide what to do on his or her own. Not fulfilled if a person feels concerning his or her decisions controlled by external forces.

- *Security:* Fulfilled if a person feels save and in control of his or her own life. Not fulfilled if a person feels uncertain and threatened by external forces he or she cannot control or influence.

- *Pleasure:* Fulfilled if a person feels fun, enjoyment and pleasure. Not fulfilled if a person feels bored or under-stimulated.

- *Meaning:* Fulfilled if a person feels that he or she can develop own potentials to make a positive impact. Not fulfilled when a person feels that their own life is meaningless and that it is not possible to fully develop his or her personal potential.

- *Popularity:* Fulfilled if a person feels liked and respected by others. Not fulfilled if a person feels that nobody is interested in his or her opinion or advice.

We can give now a first answer to the question of which aspects of an interaction with a product make sense as scales in a UX questionnaire. These are of course all aspects of the interaction that relate to the fulfillment of external goals (and in fact these are the typical usability aspects) and aspects that relate to the fulfillment of psychological needs.

External goals and psychological needs overlap. For example, if a product enables users to perform their tasks efficiently while working on external goals and the product is intuitive to use, this also supports the feeling to being competent.

But there are some other factors that must be considered for UX measurement. When we interact with products, sensory qualities also play a role. If we have to operate a product with our hands, the haptic quality is important. If operating a device causes noise, then it is important that the sound is not annoying. If we interact through a graphical UI, then the colors or contrast settings are important. If a product provides voice output, then it is important that the speaker's voice sounds pleasant and is easy to understand.

Depending on how we interact with a product, a number of aspects related to the stimulation of our senses affect our perception of the interaction. There are special scales for such sensory qualities available, for example for haptics and acoustics (Boos & Brau, 2017) or voice output (Klein, Hinderks, Schrepp & Thomaschewski, 2020).

The UX aspects related to fulfillment of external goals, psychological needs and sensory qualities are all related to requirements of users. They are all important for the overall impression of users towards the UX of a product.

There is another group of UX aspects that may not be relevant to the users of a product but are relevant to the manufacturer of the product or the provider of a service in order to achieve business-related goals. For example, that the product will arouse interest through a new and innovative design and thus increase the customer base. Or that certain values are communicated through the product design in order to strengthen one's own brand impression. Such UX aspects, which relate to the marketing requirements of a product, should therefore also be measured in UX questionnaires.

Thus, aspects of an interaction between a user and a product are relevant to be measured by scales in UX questionnaires for the following reasons:

- They relate to the external goals of users.
- They relate to basic psychological needs of the user.
- They describe sensory qualities.
- They are important for the manufacturer or provider to promote the product.

Of course, an UX aspect can relate to several of these reasons.

3 Some popular UX questionnaires

The goal of this chapter is to provide a deeper insight into the structure of some popular UX questionnaires. For each questionnaire we describe the format of the items, the way results are calculated, and the interpretation of the scales. This should help to gain some insight into of the different approaches currently being used to measure UX with questionnaires.

Of course, we cannot provide a complete list of all available UX questionnaires. We selected the questionnaires that we describe in this chapter based on a few criteria. First, they are available in English. Second, there is enough material, for example some scientific papers, describing how the questionnaire was constructed and validated and how it should be used. Third, they have some visibility in the UX community. In addition, the selection of questionnaires in this chapter is intended to show the various options for implementing a UX questionnaire. A more extensive list of questionnaires is contained in Appendix 2.

3.1 Net Promotor Score (NPS)

The Net Promoter Score is a single item questionnaire that measures customer loyalty or satisfaction. The single question is typically formulated as (deviations occur caused by the context of the study):

How likely is it that you would recommend our company/product/service to a friend or colleague?

Not at all likely O O O O O O O O O O O *Extremely likely*

The answer possibilities are scored from left (*Not at all likely*) to right (*Extremely likely*) with the values 0 to 10. Depending on their answer participants are classified into three categories. A participant answering with 0 to 6 is classified as a *detractor*. A participant answering with 9 or 10 is classified as a *promotor*. All other participants are classified as *passives*.

The NPS score is calculated by a simple formula:

NPS = *Percentage of promotors – Percentage of detractors*

Thus, the NPS score ranges from -100 (worst case) to 100 (best case).

What is the idea of this scoring scheme? The underlying assumption is that promotors are extremely impressed by a product or service (therefore only participants answering with 9 and 10 are classified as promotors) and thus positively influence other people. Of course, positive comments from people you know personally have a huge impact on your personal buying decisions (much higher than any other form of marketing). Thus, a high rate of promotors is an effective marketing for a product, will most likely help to increase the number of customers and is a sign of a high customer loyalty (it is unlikely that you lose a promotor to competitors). On the other hand, detractors are at least not very happy with the service or product. If they talk about their experience to others, this will decrease the likelihood that these persons converge to customers. Thus, a high NPS should in the long run increase the number of customers and thus revenue.

Reichheld (2003) made the NPS quite popular. His paper suggests a positive influence of the current NPS score on the further growth of a company relative to its competitors in the market. However, some replications (Keiningham, Aksoy, Cooil & Andreassen, 2008) failed to reproduce these results. In addition, purchasing decisions for quite complex or very expensive products are not always based on feedback from people you know personally.

The NPS is a general measure of customer loyalty and satisfaction. It is not influenced solely by the UX of a product, but by various factors of product experience. However, it is currently quite popular and can be used in situations in which there is not enough time to apply a more extensive questionnaire.

The calculated NPS score is quite sensitive against sampling effects. This results from the mapping of the 11 answer categories into the three categories detractors, passives and promoters that are used for the NPS calculation. Don't be surprised if your NPS score changes massively between studies for the same product when you only have 100 participants. Stable estimations of the NPS score require sample sizes of several hundred participants.

3.2   Customer Satisfaction (CSAT)

This is a single item questionnaire measuring overall customer satisfaction. The item is typically formulated as *How satisfied are you with <product name>?* (small deviations of this formulation depending on the research context occur frequently).

The participant can answer the CSAT question by the predefined answer categories *Very satisfied, Satisfied, Neither Satisfied nor Dissatisfied, Dissatisfied,* and *Very Dissatisfied.*

The CSAT Score is calculated as the relative frequency of satisfied participants or customers, i.e.

$$\frac{\text{No. of participants who answered } \textit{Very Satisfied} \text{ or } \textit{Satisfied}}{\text{No. of all participants}}$$

The CSAT score is an easy to interpret metric that represents the overall satisfaction with a product. It gives quite stable results, even with small samples.

Overall customer satisfaction depends on many facets of an interaction between a customer and a manufacturer, for example the buying experience, the customer service, the available functionality in the product, the user experience and potential other product features. Thus, a CSAT score is a general satisfaction measure that does not allow to infer the UX quality of a product directly. But due to its rather simple form it can be an interesting option in many situations that do not allow to apply a more detailed questionnaire.

3.3   Usability Metric for User Experience (UMUX)

Usability Metric for User Experience (UMUX) is a short questionnaire containing just 4 items (Finstad, 2010). The items are short statements that can be rated on a 7-point answer scale.

Example of a UMUX item:

> *I have to spend too much time correcting things with this system.*
>
> *Strongly disagree* O O O O O O O *Strongly agree*

Since the UMUX is short, we show all the remaining items:

- This system's capabilities meet my requirements.
- This system is easy to use.
- Using this system is a frustrating experience.

The four items form a single scale, i.e. the UMUX provides just a single score that represents overall satisfaction with the UX of the product. The UMUX score ranges from 0 to 100, which is achieved through a scoring procedure similar to the System Usability Scale (this questionnaire is described at a later point in this chapter in detail).

For the first and fourth item, agreement with the statement represents a bad experience. For these items the answers of a subject are scored as 0 to 6 starting from right to left. For the other two items, agreement represents a good UX. Answers to these items are scored as 0 to 6 starting from left to right. Thus, the answers of a participant to an item range from 0 to 6, with 0 being the most negative and 6 being the most positive evaluation. The scores are then simply added up for each participant. This results in a participant score between 0 and 24. This score per participant is then divided by 24 and multiplied by 100. The average across all participants is the UMUX score for the product.

There is an even shorter version containing just 2 items (*This system's capabilities meet my requirements* and *This system is easy to use*), which is called UMUX-LITE. UMUX and especially the UMUX-LITE realize a concept similar to the *Technology Acceptance Model* (Davis, 1986). This model assumes that user acceptance of a new technology is based on its perceived usefulness (items 1 and 2 of the UMUX) and perceived ease of use (items 3 and 4 of the UMUX).

It is reported that the UMUX and UMUX-LITE correlate highly with the System Usability Scale (SUS). There is even a formula published that allows to predict a SUS score from an UMUX-LITE score (Lewis, Utesch & Maher, 2013).

The UMUX and especially the UMUX-LITE provide a high-level measurement of overall UX. They can be used in research situations that allow to present a small number of questions to the participants but not a full UX questionnaire.

3.4   After Scenario Questionnaire (ASQ)

After Scenario Questionnaire (ASQ) is a short three item questionnaire that is designed to be used as part of usability testing sessions (Lewis, 1991).

A *scenario* is defined as a sequence of related tasks that are performed during such a usability test. The ASQ measures the usability of a product concerning such a scenario. The ASQ should be filled out immediately after a participant finishes a scenario. If a usability test contains several scenarios, the participant needs to fill out the ASQ several times during a test. Due to the small number of items this is usually not a problem, at least if the number of scenarios is in a reasonable range.

The three items of the ASQ are short statements that cover classical aspects of usability. Test participants can express their agreement respectively disagreement with these statements on a 7-point answer scale.

Example of an ASP item:

Overall, I am satisfied with the ease of completing the tasks in this scenario.

Strongly disagree O O O O O O O *Strongly agree*

The ASQ allows to mark such a statement as not applicable, i.e. there is a special answer alternative that allows to express that the item does not fit to the scenario.

The answers to the three items are simply summed up to form a score per scenario. Thus, the ASQ allows to compare different scenarios concerning their usability.

The other two items are:

- Overall, I am satisfied with the time it took to complete the tasks in this scenario.

- Overall, I am satisfied with the support information (on-line help, messages, documentation) when completing the tasks.

The ASQ is useful to find out how well a product supports different use cases (scenarios). It is short enough to be repeatedly filled out in a usability test. The ASQ is designed to be used as part of usability testing sessions and should not be used as a standalone questionnaire sent to users of a product.

3.5   System Usability Scale (SUS)

System Usability Scale (SUS) is a relatively short questionnaire containing 10 items (Brooke, 1996, 2013). The items are short statements describing usability related aspects of a system. The participants can express their disagreement or agreement to a statement on a 5-point answer scale.

Example for a SUS item:

I think that I would like to use this system frequently

Strongly disagree O O O O O *Strongly agree*

The original publication (Brooke, 1996) introduces the SUS as *a quick and dirty usability scale*. Despite of this modest description the SUS is clearly the most used and popular usability questionnaire at present. In addition, there is a large body of research dealing with the psychometric properties of the SUS, so it is quite well understood.

Since the SUS is quite short, we show in the following all 10 items:

- I think that I would like to use this system frequently.
- I found the system unnecessarily complex.
- I thought that the system was easy to use.
- I think that I would need the support of a technical person to be able to use this system.

- I found the various functions in this system were well integrated.
- I thought there was too much inconsistency in this system.
- I would imagine that most people would learn to use this system very quickly.
- I found the system very cumbersome to use.
- I felt confident using the system.
- I needed to learn a lot of things before I could get going with this system.

The items of the SUS focus on classical usability criteria. They cover mainly the overall impression concerning ease of use and usefulness, perceived complexity, consistency, and ease of learning.

The SUS does not group the items to scales. It only provides an overall usability score. This score ranges between 0 and 100.

The calculation is a bit complicated. For half of the SUS items (1, 3, 5, 7, 9 in the order shown above), *Agreement* semantically describes a positive evaluation (items with positive polarity). For the other half, *Disagreement* represents a positive evaluation (items with negative polarity).

For the items with positive polarity answers are from left to right coded as 0 to 4, for the items with negative polarity from 4 to 0. Thus, a 4 always represents the most positive evaluation and a 0 the most negative evaluation. If we sum up these values over the 10 items per participant we get a value between 0 and 40. This value is multiplied by 2.5 to scale it up to a range between 0 and 100 (the argument for this rather strange scaling is that such a range is easier to communicate, since it reminds to a percentage range). The SUS score for a product is then simply the average over all participant scores.

A strong point of the SUS is the availability of a benchmark that helps to interpret the results. In fact, several versions of such a benchmark are published. We refer in the following to the benchmark described in Lewis & Sauro (2018). This benchmark contains data from 241 industrial usability studies.

Category	Score Interval		Percentile
A+	84.10	100.00	96-100
A	80.80	84.00	90-95
A-	78.90	80.70	85-89
B+	77.20	78.80	80-84
B	74.10	77.10	70-79
B-	72.60	74.00	65-69
C+	71.10	72.50	60-64
C	65.00	71.00	41-59
C-	62.70	64.90	35-40
D	51.70	62.60	15-34
F	0,00	51.60	0-14

Table 1: The SUS benchmark accordingly to Lewis & Sauro (2018).

You can compare your measured SUS score for a product with the scores of the products in the benchmark data set. Category is the classification scheme. First, find the score interval in which your measured SUS score is located. The percentile *x-y* can be interpreted as follows: *x* percent of the 241 products in the benchmark data set showed a result lower than your score, 100-*y* of the products showed a better result. This provides an easy way to interpret a single SUS score.

Thus, if you measure for example a SUS score of 82.00 for your product you are in category A and your result is better than the results of 90% of the products in the benchmark data set. Therefore, the usability of your product is pretty good compared to an average product. If you score is 66.00, then your product is in category C, i.e. 40% of the products in the benchmark data set scored worse, but 41% scored better, i.e. the usability of your product is pretty much average.

The SUS is limited to measure classical usability aspects, with a strong focus on learnability and efficiency. Thus, it can be successfully used to evaluate products that are mainly used to achieve clearly defined goals. The SUS does not consider hedonic or non-task-related UX aspects. Therefore, it may be a good idea to use it for the evaluation of a business application or a programming environment. It is maybe not a good idea to use it to evaluate a social network or an app that is used mainly for fun or leisure activities.

3.6 Software Usability Measurement Inventory (SUMI)

Software Usability Measurement Inventory (SUMI) is a 50-item questionnaire that measures 5 different aspects of usability. The scales of the SUMI are named *Efficiency, Affect, Helpfulness, Control,* and *Learnability.*

The items of the SUMI are statements that describe positive or negative aspects of the interaction with a software product. The participant can answer with *Agree, Disagree* or *Undecided* to each of these statements, i.e. a 3-point answer scale is used.

Examples of some items:

- There are too many steps required to get something to work. (1)
- This software responds too slowly to inputs. (2)
- The software allows the user to be economic of keystrokes. (3)
- It takes too long to learn the software commands. (4)
- Learning how to use new functions is difficult. (5)
- I have to look for assistance most times when I use this software. (6)
- If this software stops, it is not easy to restart it. (7)
- I feel in command of this software when I am using it. (8)
- The software hasn't always done what I was expecting. (9)
- The software documentation is very informative. (10)
- The instructions and prompts are helpful. (11)
- The software has a very attractive presentation. (12)
- Working with this software is mentally stimulating. (13)
- Using this software is frustrating. (14)
- I would recommend this software to my colleagues. (15)

The assignment of the items to the scales and the scoring procedure are not published. You need to buy a license to get this information. However, for many items (they are available in the publications concerning SUMI) it is not hard to guess to which scale they belong. The SUMI provides a benchmark that allows to compare a measured SUMI score to results of other products in a larger benchmark data set. This information is also not available without a license.

What do the scales of the SUMI measure? As mentioned above the connection between items and scales is not published. Thus, the following description is based on my personal assumptions.

Efficiency items cover aspects of technical response time (2) and the impression that the product does not cause unnecessary effort to complete typical tasks (1, 3).

Learnability items focus on the effort (4) and difficulty (5) to learn how to use the product. It also covers if users have the impression that they can use the product intuitively or at least acquire the required skills without help by others (6).

Control items describe if the users feel that they can adequately control (7, 8) and predict the behavior of the product (9).

Helpfulness items describe if the supporting information material or documentation (10) is adequate or if the product provides helpful hints during interaction (11). For some items it is a bit unclear if they belong to control or helpfulness, i.e. the distinction seems to be a bit fuzzy.

Affect is a quite heterogenous scale. It covers aspects like fun of use (13), visual design (12), emotional responses (14) and loyalty (15).

The SUMI was developed 1993. Of course, the items were formulated to cover usability aspects of products that were popular at the time. If we look at today's standards and user expectations some of the items (7, 10) look a bit old-fashioned. Like other questionnaires developed in that period of time the focus of the SUMI is clearly (4 out of 5 scales) on classical usability criteria. Remarkably, the *Affect* scale contains already several items (for example, 12 and 13) that look quite modern (in the sense that they already cover hedonic aspects of the interaction).

Because of the huge number of items, participants need to spend some time to complete the SUMI. This restricts the usage to professional evaluations, for example after usability tests or surveys with paid participants. Due to the focus on pragmatic aspects the SUMI is somehow restricted to evaluate products used in a working environment. But in such situations the SUMI provides due to the higher number of items and the five scales much more insights into the strengths and weaknesses of a product than the SUS or UMUX.

3.7 ISOMETRICS

This questionnaire was built to measure the usability criteria defined in the ISO 9241 norm. The ISOMETRICS (Willumeit, Gediga & Hamborg, 1996) contains 75 items which are grouped into the 7 scales *Suitability for the task, Self-descriptiveness, Controllability, Conformity with user expectations, Error tolerance, Suitability for individualization,* and *Suitability for learning*. The interpretation of these scales matches the definition of the ISO 9241 dialog principles described in Chapter 1.

The items are short statements describing aspects of the interaction with a product. The items can be rated on a 5-point answer scale with the end points *Predominantly disagree* and *Predominantly agree*. In addition, it is possible to skip an item by the option *No opinion*.

Below each question, the participants are asked to rate how important the aspect described by the item is for their overall impression of the product. Therefore, for each item two separate judgements are required. The basic idea behind the second question is that the response can be used to weight the rating given to the first question. It also provides insight into which aspects of usability are most important to the participants and helps to decide which improvements to the product will have the highest impact on the overall impression.

In addition, the participant can provide some comments concerning the item (*Can you give a concrete example where you cannot agree with the above statement?*).

An example of an ISOMETRICS item is shown below:

	Pre-dominantly disagree		So - so		Pre-dominantly agree		No opinion
The functions implemented in the software support me in performing my work.	1	2	3	4	5		

	Unimportant		So - so		Important		No opinion
Please rate the importance of the above item in terms of supporting your general impression of the software.	1	2	3	4	5		

Some examples of other items:

- The way in which data is entered is suited to the task I want to perform with the software.

- The software provides me with enough information about which entries are permitted in a particular situation.

- The software allows me to interrupt functions at any point, even if it is waiting for me to make an entry.

- I have no difficulty in predicting how long the software will need to perform a given task.

- If I make a mistake while performing a task, I can easily undo the last operation.

- The software lets me change the names of commands, objects and actions to suit my personal vocabulary.

- I feed encouraged by the software to try out new system functions by trial and error.

There is a short version that contains only the statements and their rating scale. The question concerning the importance of a statement and the comment field are not contained in this short version.

Some of the items describe very specific potential problems in a product. In some sense the list of items in the ISOMETRICS is therefore a kind of checklist of aspects relevant to usability. Since the participant is also asked to give concrete examples for situations in which he or she cannot agree to a statement, this can provide very concrete indications of usability problems.

The length of the ISOMETRICS restricts the possible application scenarios. It can be used with professional testers to collect very detailed feedback concerning potential problems in a product, but not for getting feedback by users on a voluntary basis. Due to the focus on the ISO dialog principles the ISOMETRICS only covers task-related UX aspects. Thus, the application area is restricted to products that are mainly used in a work context.

A similar, but with 35 items much shorter questionnaire, is the ISONORM (Prümper, 1997). It covers, with slightly different scale names, the same seven ISO 9241 dialog principles.

3.8   Questionnaire for User Interaction Satisfaction (QUIS)

Questionnaire of User Interaction Satisfaction (QUIS) contains 27 items that are grouped into the scales *Learning*, *Terminology & System Information*, *System Capabilities*, *Screen*, and *Overall Reaction* (Chin, Diehl & Norman, 1988).

An item consists of a short text that explains a usability related property of an interactive system and two attributes with opposite meanings that describe the extreme positive respectively negative evaluation concerning this property. The rating can be performed on a 10-point answer scale. In addition, there is a *No Answer* option to skip some items.

Example of an item:

Computer informs about its progress:

never O O O O O O O O O O *always*   NA O

This answer format is somehow a mixture between statements that set a context and a semantic differential. This format is quite unique in the field of UX questionnaires.

Some other items:

- Characters on the computer screen: hard to read / easy to read
- Sequence of screens: confusing / very clear
- Usage of terms throughout the system: consistent / inconsistent
- Exploring new features by trial and error: difficult / easy

Some of the items of the QUIS look quite outdated (which is not a surprise for a questionnaire developed in 1988). In addition, it is not so easy to interpret the scales of the QUIS, since the items associated with a scale sometimes cover quite different semantical aspects.

The scale *Overall reaction* is a valence dimension, i.e. simply measures if a user has a bad or good impression towards the system. *Learning* measures how easy it is to learn how to use the system and if this is possible by pure exploration (trial and error). *Terminology & System Information* mix two not directly related aspects. First, if the terminology is easy to understand and fits to the tasks. Second, if the system feedback concerning user actions is adequate. *Screen* measures the impression concerning the overall information architecture and navigation.

The scale *System Capabilities* is very difficult to interpret.

Examples of items in *System Capabilities*:

- System speed: too slow / fast enough (1)
- Designed for all levels of users: never / always (2)
- Correcting for mistakes: difficult / easy (3)

Thus, items concerning efficiency or system speed (1), controllability (3) and required expertise (2) are contained in a single scale.

The QUIS is not available for free, some license seems to be required (see the homepage of the QUIS).

3.9 Purdue Usability Testing Questionnaire (PUTQ)

This questionnaire is designed to be used at the end of a usability test (Lin, Choong & Salvendy, 1997). It is with 100 items and a quite complex scoring scheme a very time-consuming questionnaire. The 100 items are grouped into the scales *Consistency, Minimal Memory Load, User Guidance, Learnability, Compatibility, Flexibility, Minimal Action,* and *Perceptual Limitation*.

The items of the PUTQ are short statements that describe desired behaviors of an interaction with a product or system. For each statement an evaluator needs first to judge if the statement is *applicable* to the system or not, i.e., if the behavior described by the statement makes sense for the product or if it is completely irrelevant. Items judged as *non-applicable* are skipped.

For the applicable items, the evaluator needs to make two further decisions. First, he or she needs to judge if the property is available in the system or not. For the available properties it must be judged on a 7-point answer scale how well the system supports this property and how important this property is for the overall satisfaction with the system (on a 3-point scale for *low (1), medium (2)* and *high (3)* importance).

Let us try to explain this by an example, since it is a bit complicated. We look at the item *Are erroneous entries displayed?*. If the evaluated system is used to access information, but does not require any data entry, this item would be classified as *non-applicable*. There can be no erroneous entries, thus the statement does not make any sense for this system. If the evaluated system allows data entry, but completely fails to visualize any errors in input fields, then the item would be classified as *applicable* and *not available*. If the system somehow indicates errors in input fields (the item is then classified as *applicable* and *available*) then the evaluator will rate on a scale from 1 (worst) to 7 (best) how well this is realized in his or her opinion.

Examples for PUTQ statements (corresponding scale in brackets):

- Is the cursor placement consistent? (Consistency)
- Does it provide index of commands? (Minimal Memory Load)
- Are erroneous entries displayed? (User Guidance)
- Is the data grouping suitable for easy learning? (Learnability)
- Is the wording familiar? (Compatibility)
- Can users assign command names? (Flexibility)
- Will the required data be entered only once? (Minimal Action)
- Does it provide visually distinctive data fields? (Perceptual Limitation)

The PUTQ allows to calculate an overall usability index over all scales. The calculation is also a bit complicated. To make it easier to understand we deviate here a bit from the description given in Lin, Choong & Salvendy (1997).

The index can be calculated for each evaluator. The non-applicable items are simply ignored in the calculation.

For an applicable item i (i between 1 and 100) we have the rating of importance w_i (scored as 1, 2, or 3, see above). Thus, we can calculate the maximal possible score for this evaluator if we sum up $w_i * 7$ (7 is the best possible score) over all applicable items i. We call this sum in the following *MaxScore*. Now we calculate the real score for this evaluator. For applicable items we have two cases. First, the item is available and thus we have a score s_i ranging from 1 (worst) to 7 (best). In this case we set $e_i = w_i * s_i$, i.e. importance multiplied by score. Second, the item may be evaluated as not available, in this case we do not have a score and set $e_i = - w_i$. Since the non-availability of an applicable feature is of course not desirable, this acts as a penalty term. We now sum up e_i over all applicable items to calculate the real score *RealScore*. The index for the evaluator is then simply calculated as (*RealScore* / *MaxScore*) * 100, i.e. ranges between 0 and 100. A score for the complete product evaluation is then reached by averaging the index over all evaluators.

The huge number of items and the complex decision procedure (this require some special instructions to evaluators) makes an application of the PUTQ extremely time consuming. Thus, it is clearly restricted to be used as part of a usability test with paid testers who can be appropriately

28

instructed how to score the items. On the other hand, the PUTQ describes a very detailed list of usability properties, i.e. provides clear and detailed feedback concerning the usability of a product.

3.10 Post-Study System Usability Questionnaire (PSSUQ)

The Post-Study System Usability Questionnaire (PSSUQ) is a 16 item questionnaire that should to be used at the end of a usability test (Lewis, 1992). There is also a version available (sometimes called CSUQ) that can be used as a questionnaire for end users. Both versions differ only in the details concerning the wording of the items. The 16 items are grouped into the 3 scales *System Usefulness*, *Information Quality* and *Interface Quality*.

The items are short statements concerning positive aspects of the interaction with the product. The participant can rate these statements on a 7-point answer scale with the end points *Strongly Agree* (scale value 1) to *Strongly Disagree* (scale value 7). Since all statements describe positive usability aspects *Agreement* stands for a positive impression, i.e. small item values are an indicator for good usability and high values are an indicator for bad usability. It is possible to skip items intentionally by crossing a *No answer* alternative.

Example for an item:

The system gave error messages that clearly told me how to fix problems

Strongly agree O O O O O O O *Strongly disagree*   N/A O

Some other items (corresponding scale in brackets)

- It was simple to use this system. (System Usefulness)
- It was easy to learn to use this system. (System Usefulness)
- I was able to complete the tasks and scenarios quickly using this system. (System Usefulness)
- Whenever I made a mistake using the system, I could recover easily and quickly. (Information quality)
- It was easy to find the information I needed. (Information quality)
- The organization of information on the system screens was clear. (Information quality)
- I liked using the interface of this system. (Interface Quality)
- Overall, I am satisfied with the system. (Interface Quality)

System usefulness covers ease of learning, ease of use, and the impression that tasks can be performed quickly with the product. *Information quality* describes recovery from errors, how easy it is to find the required information in the screens, and how useful this information is. *Interface Quality* refers to an overall impression of the interaction with the product (do users like the interface, are they satisfied, is the interaction pleasant). The PSSUQ provides an overall score by averaging over all 16 items and three sub-scores for the scales.

Compared to the PUTQ the items of the PSSUQ are less concrete and focus more on the subjective impression concerning more general aspects. In addition, it is much shorter than the PUTQ. Another nice feature is that the PSSUQ can be applied at the end of a usability test and also to directly access end users (with the CSUQ version). This allows to compare the results obtained in usability test with user feedback from the product, which is for many scenarios quite helpful.

3.11 AttrakDiff2

The AttrakDiff2 (Hassenzahl, Burmester & Koller, 2003) is a questionnaire that sets a strong focus on the measurement of non-task-related (hedonic) aspects of an interaction with a product. It contains 28 items that are grouped into the 4 scales *Attractiveness*, *Pragmatic Quality*, *Hedonic Quality Stimulation* and *Hedonic Quality Identity*.

Items have the form of a semantic differential, i.e. an item consists of a pair of terms with opposite meaning. The two terms span a semantic dimension. Participants can decide which of the two terms describe the product better on a 7-point answer scale. It is randomized if the term describing the positive end of the dimension is placed left or right. For the scoring the polarity of the items is considered. If the positive term is right the responses are coded as 1 to 7 from left to right. If the positive term is left responses are coded from 7 to 1 from left to right. Thus, 7 always corresponds to the best and 1 to the worst rating of an item.

Example of an item:

human O O O O O O O *technical*

Other examples of items:

- *Attractiveness:* pleasant / unpleasant, ugly / pretty, good / bad, repulsive / pleasing
- *Pragmatic Quality:* practical / impractical, simple / complex, predictable / unpredictable, confusing / clear

- *Stimulation:* original / conventional, harmless / challenging, dull / absorbing, bold / cautious

- *Identity:* brings me closer to people / separates me from people, poor quality / high quality, not presentable / presentable, isolates / connects

Attractiveness is a pure valence dimension, i.e. measures the overall impression of the product on a good/bad dimension, without any reference to concrete properties of the interaction. *Pragmatic Quality* represents the classical usability aspects of an interaction. *Stimulation* measures if a product catches the attention of a participant, i.e. if the design is original and innovative and if the interaction with the product is challenging and stimulating. *Identity* covers the impression that using or owning a product improves prestige or social influence of the user.

Since only 7 of the 28 items represent classical usability criteria, the AttrakDiff2 is not a good choice to evaluate products that are mainly used to work on defined tasks (for example, business software, programming environments, word processors, spreadsheets, etc.). It is more suitable for products that are used for fun or leisure activities.

The items of the scale *Identity* can sound strange in some contexts. For example, *brings me closer to people/separates me from people* works well if a new expensive smart phone or a social network is evaluated, but sounds very strange in the context of a news website. The scale *Identity* is problematic for products that the user is forced to use, i.e., where the decision to use or purchase the product is not made by the user.

3.12 User Experience Questionnaire (UEQ)

The User Experience Questionnaire (UEQ) is designed to allow a quick assessment of UX (Laugwitz, Schrepp & Held, 2006, 2008) concerning a broader set of different task-related and non-task-related UX aspects. It contains 26 items which are grouped into the 6 scales *Attractiveness, Efficiency, Perspicuity, Dependability, Stimulation* and *Novelty*.

The item format and scoring scheme is the same as in the AttrakDiff2, i.e. a semantic differential with a 7-point answer scale, where the positive term is in half of the items placed in the right and in the other half in the left position.

Example of an item:

attractive O O O O O O O *unattractive*

Examples of other items:

- *Attractiveness:* unpleasant / pleasant, good / bad, friendly / unfriendly
- *Efficiency:* efficient / inefficient, fast / slow, organized / cluttered
- *Perspicuity:* not understandable / understandable, easy to learn / difficult to learn, clear / confusing
- *Dependability:* unpredictable / predictable, secure / not secure, obstructive / supportive
- *Stimulation:* boring / exciting, not interesting / interesting, motivating / demotivating
- *Novelty:* conservative / innovative, usual / leading edge, creative / dull

Attractiveness is a pure valence dimension. It measures whether users like or dislike the product. *Efficiency* tries to capture whether users think they can perform tasks in the product fast and without unnecessary effort. *Perspicuity* covers whether users have the impression that the usage of the product is easy to understand and easy to learn. The scale *Dependability* tries to measure whether users feel in control of the interaction. *Stimulation* captures whether users feel that it is exciting and motivating to use the product. *Novelty* covers whether the design of the product is perceived as inventive and original and thus catches the interest of users.

Thus, *Efficiency*, *Perspicuity* and *Dependability* measure UX quality aspects related to solving tasks with the product (pragmatic quality aspects), while *Stimulation* and *Novelty* measure non-task-related UX qualities (hedonic quality aspects).

Filling out the UEQ does not require much time (around 3 minutes). The questionnaire is short enough to be used as an online questionnaire but can also be used at the end of a usability test. Because of the quite abstract formulation of items and the balanced choice of pragmatic and hedonic scales, it can be applied for a wide range of products.

The UEQ offers a large benchmark data set (Schrepp, Olschner & Schubert, 2013 or Schrepp, Hinderks & Thomaschewski, 2017), that contains data from 452 studies with different products. The benchmark is included in the data analysis Excel that can be downloaded from www.ueq-online.org. The benchmark provides per scale a grouping into 5 categories (*Excellent, Good, Above Average, Below Average, Bad*). Each category is linked to a percentile of products from the benchmark data set. If a product falls, for example, for a scale into category *Excellent* this means it is amongst the 10% of the best products. If it falls into category *Above Average*, then 25% of the products from the benchmark data set have better results and 50% have worse results concerning this scale.

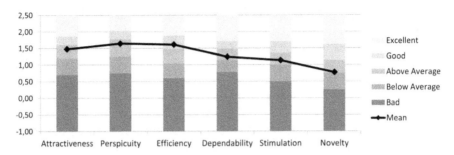

Figure 6: Example for a comparison of a product evaluation to the UEQ benchmark.

There are two variations of the UEQ available. A short version, called UEQ-S, with just 8 items (4 from the pragmatic scales and 4 from the hedonic scales) is available for scenarios requiring very short completion times. This short version does not allow to measure the 6 UEQ scales. It contains only two scales for pragmatic and hedonic quality (Schrepp, Hinderks & Thomaschewski, 2017).

The UEQ in its original form does not allow to calculate an overall score, only the result of the 6 individual scales are provided. The reason is that we cannot assume that these scales are equally important for the overall judgement of the UX quality of a product (see Winter, Hinderks, Schrepp & Thomaschewski, 2017 for a more detailed discussion). For this reason, the KPI extension of the UEQ contains per scale an additional question (see Hinderks, Schrepp, Domínguez Mayo, Escalona & Thomaschewski, 2019) concerning the importance of this scale for the overall impression. Scale values of the 6 scales can then be weighted with their importance ratings to compute a single value representing the overall impression concerning UX.

3.13 Modular User Experience Questionnaire (UEQ+)

The UEQ+ is a modular extension of the User Experience Questionnaire (Schrepp & Thomaschewski, 2019). It contains a larger list of UX scales (including the 6 scales from the UEQ) that can be combined by UX researchers to build a concrete UX questionnaire adapted to their concrete research questions. In this sense the UEQ+ is not a UX questionnaire, it is a tool to build questionnaires optimized for special evaluation scenarios.

Since the list of scales will potentially grow (currently there are 20) we will not discuss them here in detail (the available scales are described at ueqplus.ueq-research.org) and just refer to the basic concept behind the UEQ+.

To allow an arbitrary combination of scales a special format is used. As an example, we show the UEQ+ scale *Efficiency*:

To achieve my goals, I consider the product as

slow ○○○○○○○ fast

inefficient ○○○○○○○ efficient

impractical ○○○○○○○ practical

cluttered ○○○○○○○ organized

I consider the product property described by these terms as

Completely irrelevant ○○○○○○○ Very important

A short sentence is used to set a common context for the 4 items of a scale. These items have, similar to the UEQ, the form of a semantic differential. In contrast to the UEQ the negative term is always placed left and the positive term always placed right.

Similar to the KPI extension of the UEQ the question concerning the importance of the scale is used to weight the scale values by the importance rating and to calculate a value representing the overall UX impression. The question concerning the importance is optional, i.e. can be dropped if the calculation of an overall value is not required.

The UX researcher can pick from the available scales those that he or she wants to consider. The item blocks corresponding to the chosen scales are then simply displayed below each other.

What is the idea behind this modular approach? Let us explain this with an example. Assume a researcher gets the task to evaluate a business software product with a UX questionnaire. The product is heavily used during a workday. Of course, for such a product efficiency will be a key factor of a good UX. For such types of applications users typically accept some learning, i.e. intuitive use is here in general not expected. If the researcher should evaluate a self-service application (for example, used by employees to change the bank account to which their salary should be paid) the main criterium will be intuitive use (user do not change that too often, so they cannot remember how they did it last time and nobody will accept to spend a long learning curve for this). Efficiency is not important for such an infrequently used application. Thus, which scales are important for the overall UX evaluation depend on the type of product being evaluated. A more systematical investigation of this dependency is given in Winter, Hinderks, Schrepp & Thomaschewski (2017) or Santoso & Schrepp (2019).

Thus, if you try to find a UX questionnaire that measures exactly the scales that are important for a product under evaluation, this can be difficult. Often it would require more than one questionnaire to cover all relevant aspects. And in such cases the different item formats make such an approach difficult and time consuming for participants. In addition, it may also be difficult for the researcher to combine the different scale values from different questionnaires into a common format.

This is where the idea of the UEQ+ comes into play. It simply offers a large list of UX scales, all of which have the same response format. The researcher can simply pick what is relevant for the creation of a questionnaire adapted to his or her research goals.

3.14 Visual Aesthetics of Website Inventory (VISAWI)

Visual Aesthetic of Website Inventory (VISAWI) is designed to measure the visual aesthetics of websites on 4 dimensions (Mooshagen & Thielsch, 2010). In fact, the VISAWI is not really limited to websites. It can be used to evaluate all products with a graphical user interface concerning visual aesthetics.

The VISAWI contains 18 items that are grouped into the scales *Simplicity*, *Diversity*, *Colorfulness* and *Craftmanship*.

Items are short statements that describe perceptions concerning the visual design. Participants can express their level of agreement to the statements on a 7-point answer scale with the endpoints *Strongly disagree* and *Strongly agree*.

Example for items (corresponding scale is shown in brackets):

- Everything goes together on this site. (Simplicity)
- The layout is pleasantly varied. (Diversity)
- The color composition is attractive. (Colorfulness)
- The layout appears professionally designed. (Craftmanship)

Simplicity items describe whether the user interface is well-structured, looks clear and is easy to scan. *Diversity* describes whether the user interface looks interesting, inventive, and inspired. The scale *Colorfulness* measures whether colors in the user interface are attractive and the color composition is harmonic. *Craftmanship* covers the impression that the design looks up-to-date and professional.

There is a short version of the VISAWI with just 4 items available (Mooshagen & Thielsch, 2013). These are the 4 items shown above as examples. The short version does not allow to measure the sub-scales and only returns one overall score representing the visual quality of the evaluated product.

The VISAWI provides a benchmark (integrated in the data analysis Excel that can be downloaded from the web site https://visawi.uid.com) that contains measurements for several categories of web sites. For each category the mean and standard deviation of several website evaluations in this category are listed. Thus, the benchmark allows mainly to decide if an evaluated product is better or worse than an average website from this category.

The VISAWI gives a very detailed measurement of the visual impression concerning a product. Especially if a new visual design is rolled-out or if two versions of the design should be compared, the full version of the VISAWI provides a very detailed information concerning the strength and weaknesses of the design. If visual design is just evaluated as one out of several relevant UX aspects the full version may be too time consuming. In this case the short version provides enough insights to decide whether the visual aesthetic of the product is of good quality or not.

3.15 Product Reaction Cards

The Product Reaction Cards (Benedek & Miner, 2002) are a collection of 118 attributes that describe positive or negative properties of an interaction with a product. The attributes are presented as cards containing one attribute per card. Participants can select those attributes that fit to the evaluated product. Thus, each attribute can be either selected or not selected by a participant.

Examples for attributes: attractive, boring, busy, clean, comfortable, consistent, creative, dull, efficient, engaging, familiar, fragile, fun, impersonal, motivating, novel, inconsistent, powerful, rigid, secure, slow, sterile.

The 118 attributes cover a wide range of UX related properties of a product. They are not grouped into scales. Data analysis is done by simply counting how often each card is selected. This can then be nicely visualized by a word cloud. Such a visualization offers an efficient way to derive semantical interpretations about the perception of a product by users and concerning the weak or strong points of the product.

The Product Reaction Cards are not a UX questionnaire in the classical sense. They do not provide some numeric scale values and the results are mainly qualitative. But they are an interesting, innovative, and easy to perform method to get a first impression how a product is perceived by its users.

A practical problem in the application of the method is the huge number of cards. In fact, depending on the type of the evaluated product some of these cards may not make much sense. So, it seems to be possible to reduce the number of cards by some expert judgement before the evaluation is done and thus to reduce the required completion time.

4　Structure of UX Questionnaires

In the previous chapter we described several common UX questionnaires in detail. In this chapter we will focus on the main differences between questionnaires concerning item format, length, and measurement philosophy.

4.1　Item format

The most common item format within UX questionnaires are short statements describing an aspect of interaction with a product or a feature of the product design. The items allow participants to express their level of disagreement or agreement with the statement on an answer scale.

For example, an item from the SUS:

I think that I would like to use this system frequently

Strongly disagree O O O O O *Strongly agree*

Prominent examples of UX questionnaires that use this item format are the SUS, SUMI, PSSUQ or VISAWI. A review of 40 common UX questionnaires (Schrepp, 2020) found that 35 of them used this answer format. Thus, this is clearly the dominant format.

Another item format used in some recent questionnaires (4 out of 40 questionnaires in the examined list from Schrepp, 2020) are semantic differentials. Here an item consists of a pair of adjectives with opposite meanings. Thus, participants can express their impression regarding the product on a semantic dimension.

For example, an item from the UEQ:

attractive O O O O O O O *unattractive*

Well-known examples of questionnaires that use this format are UEQ and AttrakDiff2.

What are the advantages and disadvantages of these formats?

Semantic differentials allow to express subjective impressions concerning product experience quite directly. The response time is short, since the participant needs just to read and understand two terms instead of a complete sentence. Not much analytical thinking is required to decipher the meaning of the item.

On the other hand, semantic differentials do not allow very concrete or specialized questions. Look, for example, at the statement *Is the cursor placement consistent?* (PUTQ). How would you express this in a semantic differential?

Thus, semantic differentials are less flexible than statements. But if a fast and immediate subjective response should be measured, they have some benefits.

4.2   Length of the answer scale

Different questionnaires use different answer scales for their items. For example, SUMI uses 3, SUS 5, UEQ 7, QUIS 10 and NPS 11 categories.

Again, we have a trade-off. A higher number of response categories allows a more fine-grained response. Small differences in the perception of different items can be expressed, which may not be possible with a smaller number of categories.

But on the other hand, the cognitive effort of a participant increases with an increasing number of alternatives.

Look for example on the following variations of a sematic differential:

attractive O O O unattractive

attractive O O O O O unattractive

attractive O O O O O O O unattractive

attractive O O O O O O O O O unattractive

attractive O O O O O O O O O O O unattractive

Clearly, the variant with just three categories is quite restrictive. It forces participants to decide between *attractive, undecided* or *unattractive*. For some participants this will be difficult. For example, if they perceive the product to be somehow more attractive than unattractive, but still far away from being perfectly attractive. But the longer the list of options is, the harder it is to decide. At some point it is random which of the neighboring options a participant tick. In the example above (perceive the product as more attractive than unattractive, but not perfectly attractive), will a participant cross option 2, 3, or 4 (from left to right) in the example with 11 options?

There are several studies concerning the optimal number of response categories (a good summary can be found in Lewis & Erdinc, 2017). Such studies typically vary the number of response options for a given questionnaire and then examine the extent to which the results of the variations differ. The conclusion of the research on this topic is that there are no practically significant differences as long as one stays within the range of more than 5 response categories. For example, the mentioned work by Lewis & Erdinc (2017) compared response scales with 7-, 11-, and 101-levels (a scale visualized as a continuous line with a slider) but could not really find any practically significant differences in the quality of the results.

In the study cited above (Schrepp, 2020) 21 of the 40 investigated UX questionnaires used 7 answer categories and 13 used 5 answer categories. Obviously, the authors of these questionnaires assumed that the best trade-off between cognitive effort for the participant and ability to express differences is somewhere in the region between 5 to 7.

Nearly all UX questionnaires use an odd number of alternatives. This has the advantage that it allows the participant to express quite naturally that he or she is undecided concerning an item by ticking the middle category. Being undecided concerning some aspects of an interaction with a system is quite natural. Thus, it is typically not a good idea to force a decision in such cases.

4.3 Detailed versus abstract statements

The items in UX questionnaires differ concerning their level of abstraction. Some items describe very concrete properties of a product design or interaction with a product. Other questionnaires use items that describe more abstract impressions concerning a product (all semantic differentials are of the second type).

Some examples of quite concrete item formulations:

- Is the ordering of menu options logical? (PUTQ)
- Messages always appear in the same place. (ISOMETRICS)
- The software documentation is very informative. (SUMI)

Such concrete formulations make it easier for participants to answer the items and are quite stable against misinterpretation. A problem with such formulations is that the concrete wording can be problematic. For example, in the second example in the list above there is the problematic term *always*. In fact, participants should judge on a 5-point scale if they agree or disagree with this statement. But how will you judge this statement, if according to your experience with the product most messages appear at a constant position, but there are a few exceptions. The word *always* makes the statement a binary choice, which is obviously not what is intended. Some participants may interpret the item, as intended, as a statement which can be more or less true; others may interpret it differently as a binary decision. Thus, the formulation will cause some noise in the data.

A disadvantage of concrete item formulations is that they restrict the applicability of the questionnaire to special types of products. For example, assume that a self-service application should be evaluated. A self-service must be intuitive to use and will thus have no documentation. Thus, an item like *The software documentation is very informative* will sound silly in this context.

Examples of abstract item formulations:

- useless / useful (UEQ+)
- lacking style / stylish (AttrakDiff2)
- I felt very confident using the system. (SUS)

Items formulated in a more abstract way are not directly tied to concrete elements in the user interface of a product. Therefore, they require a certain degree of abstraction on the part of the participant, since the concrete experiences with the product must be mentally mapped onto these more abstract formulations. In addition, abstract item formulations increase the probability of misinterpretations. For example, an item *insecure/secure* will not be interpreted exactly the same when rating a social network and when rating enterprise software.

But such items are not restricted to special product properties or product types. Therefore, questionnaires using more abstract item formulations can be used for a wider range of products.

4.4   Measurement philosophy

There is a dependency between the number of items in a questionnaire and the accuracy of measurement. The more items we have, the lower is the impact of random response errors in single items. In addition, a single item can typically not express the meaning of complex UX concepts, like efficiency, learnability, controllability, stimulation, or aesthetic impression. The more items are used in a scale, the better the meaning of the scale can be covered.

But on the other hand, a higher number of items cause higher completion times for the participants of a study. Thus, again there is a classical trade-off between accuracy and effort.

Several questionnaires are obviously built with the goal to measure usability or UX as exact as possible. To achieve this goal, they accept long completion times. For example, ISOMETRICS uses 75 items to measure the usability of a product in the sense of ISO 9241. PUTQ uses 100 items. Such questionnaires are usually created to be used in a usability test. Usability tests are typically performed with a limited number of testers (often around 10 to 15). The time required to fill out the questionnaire is not so crucial in such settings. But a high accuracy of measurement is required to obtain a reliable result despite of the low number of testers.

Other questionnaires are designed to capture just a rough impression of a participant towards a product. They use scales that require not much time to be filled out and can thus be applied in many practical research settings. Examples are the SUS with 10 items used to calculate an overall usability score or the UMUX with just 4 items. Some questionnaires try to achieve a shorter response time for participants by using semantic differentials, for example UEQ with 4 items per scale or AttrakDiff2 with 7 items per scale. Such questionnaires can be used either as part of usability tests or as online surveys sent to users or triggered during system use. The lower accuracy of a single response can be compensated in such scenarios by a much higher number of respondents.

4.5 Scale names and semantic meaning

If researchers try to find a UX questionnaire that fits to the needs of their projects, then the scale names are often used as a first orientation. The scale names describe which semantic UX aspect the scale measures. But you should be quite careful here. Scale names can be misleading. We will illustrate this in the following by some examples.

The questionnaires AttrakDiff2 (Hassenzahl, Burmester & Koller, 2004) and UEQ (Laugwitz, Held & Schrepp, 2008) contain both a scale named *Stimulation*.

The corresponding items in the UEQ scale are: *boring / exciting, not interesting / interesting, motivating / demotivating, valuable / inferior.* Thus, stimulation is defined here in the sense of an exciting, interesting, and motivating interaction. This concept of stimulation can also be described as fun of use.

The items in the AttrakDiff2 scale are: *original / conventional, unimaginative / creative, bold / cautious, innovative / conservative, dull / absorbing, harmless / challenging, novel / conventional.* This concept of stimulation is broader than the corresponding concept in the UEQ. It covers in addition to fun of use the perception that the design of the product is creative, unconventional in a positive sense and original.

Therefore, both conceptualizations of stimulation are similar, but of course not identical. The aspect of an original and unconventional design is captured in the UEQ in a separate scale called *Novelty*. Thus, semantically the combination of the UEQ scales *Stimulation* and *Novelty* covers the meaning of the AttrakDiff2 scale *Stimulation*.

Clearly, both ways to operationalize the concept of *Stimulation* are valid. A novel and creative design raises interest in a product and thus makes it more interesting. Thus, it is a valid approach to see *Novelty* as a part of *Stimulation*. But it is also a valid approach to keep both concepts separately, i.e., split them into two different scales.

This example already shows that you should not rely only on the scale names when you select a UX questionnaire. The true meaning of a scale is contained in the items!

As a second example we look at the concept of *Usefulness*. Scales to measure usefulness of a product are contained in several UX questionnaires. The meCUE contains a scale called *Usefulness*, a scale with the same name appears in the USE and PUEU contains a scale named *Perceived Usefulness*. Given the scale names, these questionnaires seem to measure the same concept.

But let us have a look at the concrete items. In PUEU *Perceived Usefulness* is understood in the sense of *usefulness for the job*, i.e. in a purely professional context.

Examples of PUEU items in this scale are:

- Using the system would make it easier to do my job.
- Using the system would improve my job performance.
- Using the system in my job would increase my productivity.

In the USE usefulness is understood much broader. It contains items that relate both to a personal and a professional context.

Examples for USE items in this scale:

- It gives me more control over the activities in my live.
- It does everything I would expect it to do.
- It helps me be more effective.
- It helps me to be more productive.

In the meCUE the items of the scale *Usefulness* are formulated more general, for example:

- I consider the product extremely useful.
- With the help of this product I will achieve my goals.

Thus, we see three different conceptualizations of *Usefulness* that are to some extent similar, but of course semantically not identical. If we evaluate the same product with the same target group using these three different scales, it is not unlikely that we get different results.

Another example that shows an interesting aspect is the VISAWI. This questionnaire concentrates on the measurement of visual aesthetics of websites. The questionnaire contains 4 scales that reflect different aspects of aesthetic impression or beauty of a website. Some items, for example, *The design is uninteresting* or *The layout is pleasantly varied* reflect semantical aspects that relate closely to concepts like *Stimulation* or *Fun of Use* in other questionnaires. Items like *The layout is inventive* relate to concepts like *Novelty* and items like *The layout appears professionally designed*, or *The site is designed with care* are quite similar to scales like *Value* or *Identity* in other questionnaires. It is important to note that we do not find a real one-to-one correspondence to other scales here. The items in the VISAWI scales are semantically similar to existing scales in other questionnaires, but they are combined with new items related to visual appearance to form new scales.

These examples show that UX researchers have to deal with the quite unpleasant situation that the scale names of UX questionnaires do not exactly describe what is measured by the scale. What causes this situation?

The problem results from the current practice to construct UX questionnaires by an empirical process that selects the items from larger items pools. We will describe this process in Chapter 14 in detail, and just sketch the main idea below. This process typically consists of the following steps:

1. A large pool of potential items is constructed. The potential items cover those UX aspects that should be measured in the questionnaire.
2. A larger sample of participants evaluate several products using all items from the item pool.
3. Statistical methods (typically principal component analysis) are used to extract components (hypothetical UX aspects corresponding to the scales) from the data.
4. Those items that represent the extracted dimensions best (show the highest loadings) are then selected to form the scale.

5. The scale name is chosen by the authors of the questionnaire to represent the common meaning of all the items in the scale. Different persons have of course different personal preferences and follow different conventions. This explains the missing overall consistency in scale names.

This process ensures that the items of the questionnaire cover the most relevant aspects of the products investigated in step 2. Items that are not relevant are simply removed by the empirical construction.

But there are also some disadvantages. First, the constructed scales consist of items that show high correlations with each other. However, this does not necessarily mean that these items are similar from a semantic point of view.

Second, the scale structure that is constructed depends massively on the products used in the data collection. Items in a UX questionnaire are always interpreted in the context of the evaluated product. An item *costs time/saves time* has a different meaning if a business software (for such products it will be interpreted in terms of efficiency) or if a social network is evaluated (there is an alternative interpretation here regarding the risk of wasting too much valuable time in the network). In the case of a business software the item *costs time/saves time* will show high correlations to other items that represent efficiency. In the case of a social network this correlation will be much lower. Thus, the correlations between items depend on the products used in the second step of the construction process described above. These correlations influence which scales and items from the pool are selected. This is also the reason that different products should be used when a questionnaire is constructed by such an empirical process.

5 Enhance Standard Questionnaires

In one of the previous chapters we introduced some common UX questionnaires. These questionnaires are standard questionnaires that measure specific UX aspects through their scales. They are designed to be reused by UX researchers to answer specific research questions. However, it is quite common for researchers to enrich these standard questionnaires with some additional questions that are specific to the goals of their concrete study.

First, there is usually a need to obtain some information about the participant, i.e. to ask some demographic questions. Second, there is often an interest to ask some specific product-related questions or to collect concrete information concerning possible improvements to the product.

In this chapter we give some hints concerning extensions of standard questionnaires. How to develop completely new questionnaires to measure specific UX aspects is not the focus of this chapter. How to develop a completely new questionnaire is described in Chapter 14.

5.1 Possible changes to standard questionnaires

Before we describe what can be done to enhance a standard questionnaire, we need to mention what should be avoided. As we described in the previous chapter, the main result of a UX questionnaire are the scale scores or, if available, an overall UX score averaging over all available scales.

First, you should not modify the items or scales of a standard questionnaire! If you change the text of an item, this will most likely also shift the semantic meaning of the item. Thus, such a change will influence the value of the corresponding scale. Therefore, you cannot compare the result of your modified scale with the original scale. The same applies if you add or remove items from a scale. If the questionnaire offers a benchmark, then the comparison to the scores in the benchmark is no longer possible if you modify or drop some items. Thus, if you use a standard questionnaire use the items and scales unchanged!

If a questionnaire does not provide an overall UX score or if you are only interested in the scores of single scales, then you can of course drop entire scales if they do not fit to the product or if you are simply not interested in the underlying UX aspects.

5.2 Demographic questions

In most cases researchers would like to get some additional information about the participants of their studies. Such information is often quite interesting to properly interpret the results of the UX evaluation. Let's take a look at some typical examples.

For professional tools, it is often quite interesting to find out how well the design supports users with different levels of expertise (for example, new and very experienced users). Thus, asking about the experience of a participant provides valuable insights, for example when long term users rate the UX of the tool differently than inexperienced users.

Typical questions that attempt to determine experience level are:

- How often do you use the app?
- How long have you been using the product?

Figure 7 shows the results of 5 items from a questionnaire measuring the user experience of a professional application.

Experience was captured by the question *How long have you been using the application?* with the answer options *Less than 6 months, 6 months to a year, 1 to 3 years, More than 3 years*.

User Experience was measured on the basis of some statements concerning the application. Participants could rate each statement on a 7-point answer scale with the extreme poles *Fully disagree* (1) and *Fully agree* (7).

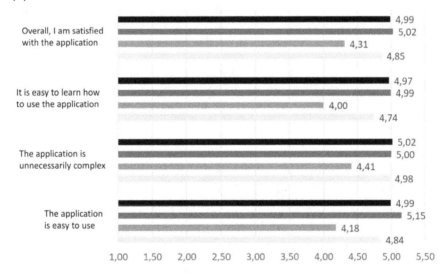

Figure 7: Mean values of the ratings of 4 items depending on the experience level of the participant. The darker the bar, the higher is the experience level.

The results show a clear trend. The ratings concerning the investigated aspects of user experience first decrease and then increase with experience. Users who have been using the application for *6 months to a year* are most critical concerning the tool.

Clearly, this is an important information about the UX of the application. The basic interpretation is that new users start working with the basic features of the application and are at least not dissatisfied (midpoint of the answer scale is 4). After the initial exploration, there seems to be a sharp drop in user satisfaction, which is most likely due to problems exploring advanced features. Once users get past this stage, their satisfaction increases again. This clearly points into a specific direction to trigger improvements. This information would not be available if the experience level was not captured in the questionnaire.

As a second example, suppose you want to evaluate the UX of a health care site that provides information about a particular disease. Of course, user expectations concerning the way content is written and presented will depend on the age and perhaps gender of the visitors. So, it is a good idea to have these as demographic questions. In addition, people may visit the site with different expectations. They may suffer from the disease themselves, a friend or relative may be affected, or they may be interested in the information for other reasons. Depending on the motive for visiting the site, satisfaction with the content can vary. Therefore, in this case, it is a good idea to ask about the motives for visiting the website.

Other typical demographic questions attempt to capture income level, education level, frequency of usage, time spent on usage, etc. However, you should try to keep the number of demographic questions to a minimum. Only add questions that you really need to interpret your data.

Many researchers try to collect as much data as possible with the idea that they might be helpful later. But each additional question increases the dropout rate for online questionnaires and the overall accuracy of answers. Don't strain participants' patience unless you have a very good reason!

Try to avoid text entry questions concerning such demographic aspects. The willingness to provide textual entries is typically low. Thus, for a question like *How often do you visit the website?* don't just offer a text entry field, but better offer meaningful categories like *Every day, Several times a week, Several times a month, Less often* and offer them either as a select field or in the form of a radio-button group.

If you have a paper-pencil questionnaire or pay your participants, then it doesn't matter if you place the block of demographic questions at the beginning or the end of your questionnaire. For online questionnaires, this is different:

- If you have only a few demographic questions (2-4) you can place them at the beginning of the questionnaire.

- If you have many demographic questions, it is advisable to place them at the end. In such cases, it is likely that some participants will drop-out if they see such a large block of non-product related questions at the beginning.

5.3   Concrete hints for potential improvements

If you launch a UX questionnaire directly in a product, it is often a good idea to ask the participants for concrete hints concerning problematic points.

To get such information, it is important to ask open-ended questions. A question like *Does the tool offer enough flexibility to organize your work?* will quite often result in a *Yes* or *No* as answer. In addition, these questions should clearly indicate what information you want to know. For example, the question *Anything to add?* does not specify what information you expect. Users will frequently skip such questions or enter irrelevant information.

Here are some good examples of questions:

- What are the strong points of <product>?

- What improvements would you like to see in <product>?

- What functions in <product> do you use the most?

- What was your overall impression concerning <product>?

- If you could change one thing in <product>, what would it be? Why?

- What one thing are you most excited in <product>? Why?

If you ask about problems, for example with the question *What improvements would you like to see?*, then it is a good idea to also ask about the strength of the product. It is not uncommon that different users have quite different opinions about particular features or design elements in a product. In such cases, the same feature may be mentioned in answers concerning the weak points, as well as in answers concerning the strong points. If you ask only for the weaknesses, such a feature will be identified as a problem and maybe eliminated or changed in further versions of the product based on that feedback. If you ask both questions, you have a chance to find out that there are different opinions about the feature.

Filling in such text entry fields requires much more effort for the participant than selecting predefined alternatives. Thus, such questions are quite often not answered. You should not force an entry by making the corresponding field a mandatory field! This is not helpful and will cause some negative effects. First, some participants will simply abandon the entire questionnaire if they feel forced to enter information they do not want to provide. Second, participants will just enter some meaningless phrase to quickly skip such questions. Just accept that only a small fraction of the participants will enter something here.

Limit the number of text entry fields in a questionnaire to a maximum of 2-3. Participants will usually not be willing to give more than two or three longer comments. Questions that require text input should be placed at the end of the questionnaire.

5.4   Test your questions

Of course, you do not need to review the questions you reuse from a standard questionnaire. This has already been done by the authors of this questionnaire. Exceptions may occur if you want to apply the questionnaire to a target group that was not considered when the questionnaire was created.

If you add some questions yourself, it is advisable to do a small test before going into a potentially costly data collection. Often it is sufficient to show the questions to some of your colleagues and ask for comments. If you have some special questions that require some knowledge (special terminology used in a certain target group) from the participants, it is always a good idea to do a small pre-test with persons from your target group.

A special problem arises if you know that the participants will not answer the questions in their natural language. For example, suppose you evaluate a tool for software developers. The tool is not translated into different languages and is only available in English (which is not that uncommon for such tools). Thus, your questionnaire will also be delivered only in English. In such cases it is crucial to test how easily your questions could be understood by non-native speakers. In this example, you should test your questions with a small number of non-native speakers, and the lower their English proficiency, the better for the test!

5.5   Control the length of your questionnaire

As mentioned above, be careful not to add too many questions to a standard questionnaire. The overall length is what counts. If you have a SUS with only 10 questions, it is less critical to add some demographic or text entry questions than if you use an already quite long questionnaire, like the SUMI.

Especially if you target volunteer participants in an online questionnaire, adding too many questions will increase the drop-out rate, cause participants to skip questions, and will decrease the overall quality of the answers. Thus, only add questions that are necessary to gain additional insights.

6   Why is it Important to Measure UX?

Measuring UX is not an end in itself. There are several typical research questions that can only be answered by a quantitative measurement of UX. UX questionnaires are an adequate and cost-effective method for deriving the desired insights for many of these questions (Schrepp, Hinderks & Thomaschewski, 2014).

6.1   Continuous improvement

Most products develop over a long period of time. An initial version is released, and then newer and enhanced versions are delivered periodically. Of course, it is an important question if the UX of the product improves over time, i.e. whether newer versions are better than older versions.

Newer versions typically fix some bugs, resolve issues found in usability tests, or generally react on the wishes and comments of customers. But quite often they also include new functionality. For example, if a lot of new options are added that are not well-integrated with the existing functionality or overall navigation, this will have a negative impact on the UX of the product.

It is a quite natural question whether the new version of the product has a better UX compared to older versions. If this is not the case, then obviously something is going wrong and some adjustments are required.

UX questionnaires can answer the question above quite easily, as they provide numeric representations of overall UX or single UX quality aspects. You just need to measure the user experience of each new product version with a representative sample of users. A simple statistical comparison of the results for different versions will clearly show whether the product improves concerning UX.

The following figure shows the results of a UEQ questionnaire (scale ranges from -3 to +3) filled out at the end of a usability test with two product versions. The newer version (dark grey) shows a slightly better result than the previous one (light grey). However, the number of participants was too small (see the big error bars) to draw decisive conclusions. But at least there is an indication that the product is developing in the right direction.

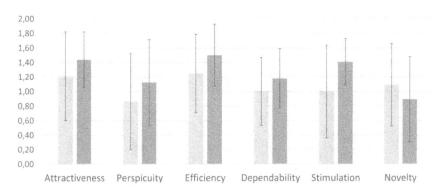

Figure 8: Comparison of two product versions with the UEQ questionnaire.

6.2   Comparison to the direct competitors in the market

Another important question is how good or bad the UX impression of a product is compared to direct competitors in the market. This question is structurally identical to the question above. You just need to measure different products with a representative sample of users and the same UX questionnaire. Again, you can compare the results using simple statistical tests.

Sounds trivial, but in practice it can be quite problematic. Of course, it's relatively easy to collect questionnaire data concerning the products your company develops. You can allow feedback directly in the user interface or you can contact customers via email campaigns.

Collecting similar data for competitor products can be practically very difficult or even impossible, especially for classic on-premise products. For modern web-based applications this if often not so difficult. In many cases, at least product demos or trial versions are available on the web. Thus, you can set up a test scenario and recruit some testers to get results in such cases.

Figure 9 shows the comparison of 4 web-based products with an UX questionnaire created with the UEQ+ framework. A simple scenario was defined that could be performed in all 4 products. Then, a number of testers performed the scenario in each product and evaluated the result at the end using the questionnaire. The results show clear differences between the ratings of the different UX aspects. If you are responsible for product A, then you can be quite relaxed. If you are responsible for product D, then you should have good arguments beside UX to convince people to use it.

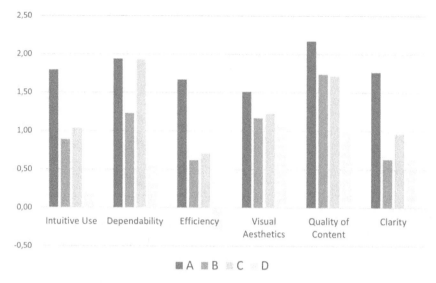

Figure 9: Comparison of four products with a UEQ+ based questionnaire.

6.3 Test if the UX of a product is sufficiently high

When a new product is launched, a typical question is whether the UX of the product is sufficiently high to meet the general expectations of users. Such general expectations are formed during their interaction with other common products that they use frequently.

The general expectations towards user experience have of course increased massively over the last 20 years. This is due to users' everyday experience with modern websites and modern devices, for example smart phones or tablets. These products have raised the general expectations concerning UX for other products, for example complex business software packages.

The question of whether the UX of a product is sufficiently high can be answered by comparing the scale scores for the product with the results of a larger sample of frequently used products. Many UX questionnaires enable such a comparison by providing a benchmark data set.

Depending on the questionnaire, different types of benchmarks are published. Let's take a look at two examples.

The VISAWI-S allows to measure the visual appeal of web sites. The VISAWI-S benchmark contains for different categories of web sites (for example, e-commerce, e-learning, news portals, information pages) the mean value and standard deviation for the visual appeal (range from 1 to 7) for a larger number of web sites in the corresponding category. Assume you measured

54

an e-commerce web site and your visual appeal score was 5.1. In the benchmark, you can see that web sites in this category have an average score of 4.6 with a standard deviation of 1.4 (based on 31 websites and 431 individual responses). This information shows that your web site is clearly above average in terms of its visual design.

As a second example, we look at the benchmark from the UEQ. The UEQ measures the UX of a product concerning the 6 scales *Attractiveness, Perspicuity, Efficiency, Dependability, Stimulation* and *Novelty*. The benchmark (based on more than 400 product evaluations) provides for each scale a classification of the measured scale value into 5 categories.

Figure 10 shows the result of a concrete product evaluation with the UEQ. Clearly, we can see that the product is rated quite positively in terms of the pragmatic quality aspects *Efficiency, Perspicuity,* and *Dependability*. In terms of the hedonic quality aspects *Stimulation* and *Novelty* the result indicates poor quality.

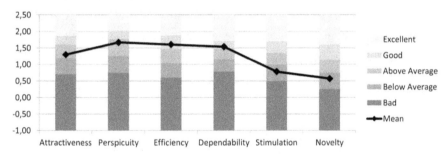

Figure 10: Example of a comparison of a product evaluation with the UEQ benchmark.

6.4   Determine areas of improvement

What should be changed in order to improve the UX of the product?

Some UX questionnaires contain quite detailed questions about specific UX features of a product. For example, *Is the cursor placement consistent?* (from the PUTQ). If you receive a negative rating for such a question, it is relatively clear what should be improved and where to search for specific problems. But because of this level of detail in the items, such questionnaires are often only applicable during or after usability tests.

Questionnaires that use more abstract item formulations are easier to apply to a wider range of products. But the results of such questionnaires do not directly indicate potential improvements. However, the scale values still point to aspects of the product that are problematic. If we look, for example, at the results of the evaluation shown in Figure 10, we see that

Stimulation and *Novelty* are rated much lower than the other scales. Thus, the product is quite weak concerning hedonic aspects. Adding elements that improve the fun of use and a more creative product design are therefore the areas where an investment has the greatest impact on the overall UX. Thus, even here the result helps to identify areas for improvement.

6.5   Evaluate return on UX investment

Investments in the development of a product or special product features can be easily quantified, for example by the development effort in days or the amount of money invested. Management will often ask whether such an investment was worth it.

If you just have some intuitive feeling that things have been improved, this is of course nice, but such a subjective impression can easily be challenged by others. If you have data from a UX questionnaire for the previous and the new version of your product, you can provide some numeric arguments. For example, if the UX investments consumed 10% of the development budget and you managed to improve the overall UX score 30% compared to the previous version, this is a good argument that your investments created a reasonable benefit.

7   Some Common UX Quality Aspects

As we have seen in the previous chapters, there are many different UX questionnaires. Each questionnaire measures a selection of UX quality aspects, i.e. each questionnaire defines its own concept of usability or user experience by the definition of its scales and items.

The results obtained by different UX questionnaires cannot be directly compared. Even if the scale names are identical or quite similar for two questionnaires, the items in these scales may still measure a slightly different semantical concept.

This makes it quite difficult for UX professionals to select a UX questionnaire that fits their research questions. We describe in this chapter some aspects of UX that are referred to in many UX questionnaires. These concepts should help to understand what UX means on a level that is suitable for the formulation of concrete items.

Of course, there are many ways to define such UX aspects, and of course there is no objectively correct solution to this problem. Others may arrive at a different taxonomy and their solution will be equally valid. This is to some extend a matter of taste and there are no objective criteria to judge if one solution is better or worse than another.

Please note that the list of UX aspects described in this chapter is not exhaustive. First, there are of course additional UX aspects that are only relevant for special products and use cases. Second, new products and new interaction techniques will lead to the formulation of new UX quality aspects, so the journey never ends.

7.1   Efficiency

Users typically do not want to spend unnecessary time and effort to complete their tasks with a product, i.e., they want to be able to work efficiently. Efficiency is a core concept in the ISO definition of usability. Thus, items related to efficiency can be found in many UX questionnaires.

Items related to this aspect:

- I am able to complete my work quickly using this system. (CSUQ)
- cumbersome/facile (ATTRAKDIFF2)
- The software forces me to perform tasks that are not related to my actual work. (ISOMETRICS)
- Efficient, effortless, fast (MS Product Reaction Cards)

- I was able to efficiently complete the tasks and scenarios using this system. (PSSUQ)
- inefficient/efficient (UEQ)
- Using it is effortless. (USE)
- I can quickly find what I want on this website. (WAMMI)

Efficiency is clearly a task-related UX aspect. When users feel that they can complete their tasks in an efficient manner, this also increases their feeling of being competent and effective in their role. Thus, efficiency of a product helps to fulfill the psychological need for *Competence*.

Efficiency can be divided into two sub-aspects. First, the *response time* of a product, i.e., the time it takes the product to respond to user commands (for example, click on a button or link). Second, the *efficiency of the interaction design*, i.e., whether the product enables the user to complete his or her tasks with a minimal physical (for example, key presses or mouse movements) and mental (for example, memory load) effort.

7.1.1 Response time

Users do not like to wait. Especially when the user is under pressure to finish some work, waiting for a system response causes mental stress and anger. Of course, this will trigger negative feelings towards the UX of the system. Thus, system response time is a rather important UX aspect (Kuroso, 2015).

Items related to this aspect:

- System speed: too slow/fast enough (QUIS)
- This software responds too slowly to inputs. (SUMI)
- fast / slow (UEQ)
- The Web site loads quickly. (WEBQUAL)
- When I use the Web site there is very little waiting time between my actions and the Web site's response. (WEBQUAL)
- This website is too slow. (WAMMI)

It is of course possible to measure system response times technically. But whether they are considered acceptable or not is a subjective judgement that depends on the specific situation and the concrete user.

However, there are some general recommendations concerning response times that we want to mention briefly. If the user triggers a simple change between two states of a product (navigation between two screens in the application, display of a message as a result of a button click), then the

58

general recommendation is that feedback should be available within less than one second (Miller, 1968 or Nielsen, 1993). Longer waiting times, exceeding 2-3 seconds, should be avoided as they interrupt the user's flow (Nakamura & Csikszentmihalyi, 2009).

If the user action results in reading a larger amount of data (for example to populate a dashboard or a long list of work items) and the user will spend some time working with the result, then longer response times are acceptable. It is hard to give clear limits here, as they depend heavily on the usage scenario. But times around 10 seconds were described as acceptable in such situation by Nielsen (1993).

For complex products, the response time to a command depends on many factors, for example the current system load caused by other users. Thus, if you repeat an action twice, the resulting response times may vary. Users will remember situations where they had to wait quite a long time. But they will typically not notice that the response time for a request was fast enough. Thus, the impression regarding response times is not so much influenced by the average response time over all tasks the user performs with the product! What remains in the memory of users and creates a negative impression towards the product are situations with very slow response times.

7.1.2   Efficient design

Sometimes products force users to enter the same data more than once or require extensive navigation steps (leading to unnecessary clicks) to complete a task. Of course, this limits the user experience. Nobody likes to waste time and resources. When a product is used multiple times during a typical workday, such efficiency issues make users quite unhappy.

Items related to this aspect:

- Too many different steps need to be performed to deal with a given task. (ISOMETRICS)
- Will the required data be entered only once? (PUTQ)
- Does it require minimal cursor positioning? (PUTQ)
- There are too many steps required to get something to work. (SUMI)
- The software allows the user to be economic of keystrokes. (SUMI)
- It requires the fewest steps possible to accomplish what I want to do with it. (USE)

A complex product, for example a business software, will not be able to support all possible tasks with the least number of steps or manual effort.

59

In order to create a good impression concerning this aspect of efficiency, it is important to support the most frequent tasks in a close to optimal way. Smaller inefficiencies in some infrequent tasks will be forgotten quickly. But users will recognize and remember even small inefficiencies in tasks they must perform several times a day.

It is possible to theoretically analyze the steps required to complete tasks and to identify unnecessary steps or even make a comparison regarding the time required to complete a task with an ideal scenario (Schrepp & Fischer, 2007), for example using tools like GOMS analysis (Card, Moran & Newell, 1983). But again, the subjective impression concerning the efficiency of the interaction varies from user to user. Thus, such objective measures can be used to find and eliminate inefficiencies, but they cannot answer the question of how actual users judge this aspect.

7.2 Intuitive Use

Intuitive use means that users can successfully work with a product without seeking advice from others and without reading documentation or going through a tutorial.

Items related to this aspect:

- I was able to use the software right from the beginning by myself, without having to ask coworkers for help. (ISOMETRICS)
- I can use it without written instructions. (USE)
- Using this website for the first time is easy. (WAMMI)
- This website seems logical to me. (WAMMI)
- Intuitive, Straightforward (MS Product Reaction Cards)
- Performing tasks is straightforward: never / always (QUIS)
- I could use the system without thinking about it. (QUESI)
- It was always clear to me what I had to do to use the system. (QUESI)
- I automatically did the right thing to achieve my goals. (QUESI)

For many products an intuitive use is a key user expectation. No one finds it natural to ask for help or read documentation before placing an order in a web shop. If it is not possible to use such a shop intuitively, customers will switch to an alternative offering.

But why can we intuitively use products we have never used before? Intuitive use means that users unconsciously apply existing knowledge to infer what they need to do (Mohs, Hurtienne, Kindsmüller, Israel & Meyer,

2006) to operate a product they use for the first time. Intuitive interaction does not require much mental effort since the user does not have to actively recall things he or she has previously learned.

This prior knowledge is derived from previous experiences with other products. If certain methods of interaction or presentation are used in common products (for example, MS Office), then designers of other products tend to adopt these interaction patterns. Over time, without any formal guidance or organization, this leads to a standardization of user interfaces across products and enables intuitive use.

Intuitive use describes the feeling that you can use a product to achieve certain goals instantly, without help from others or the need to learn something. Thus, it is a task related UX aspect. When they are able to work intuitively with a new product, users attribute this experience not only to the superior design of the product, but also to their own knowledge and cleverness. Thus, intuitive use clearly supports the psychological need for *Competence*. In addition, the psychological need for *Autonomy* is supported by an intuitive design (you can use it without consulting other people or external sources of information).

In the next section, we describe the UX aspect of *Learnability* or *Perspicuity*. Is *Intuitive Use* not a part of this concept? If you can use a product intuitively, i.e., directly without the help of other persons or without reading any documentation or tutorial, then there is obviously no need to learn how to use it. So, in a sense, intuitive use describes an optimal level of learnability. This example shows that other categorizations of UX aspects are of course possible.

We decided to consider intuitive use and learnability as two separate aspects. The reason is that from a user researcher's perspective, it is quite unlikely that one would want to measure both for the same product. Typically, the product defines whether intuitive use is expected or not. For complex business software, intuitive use is typically not possible and not expected. In any case, user must learn how to map the specific business processes of their company to actions in the product. Thus, in any case, some learning will be required, and in such scenarios a researcher will attempt to measure learnability. For a simple web-based service, no user will accept that he or she must learn something to use the service (there are plenty of alternatives if the user does not immediately understand the service). Therefore, for such services a researcher will measure intuitive use rather than learnability.

There are two specialized UX questionnaires that measure intuitive use. Both questionnaires distinguish some sub-aspects or components of intuitive use.

The QUESI (Hurtienne & Naumann, 2010) is a short questionnaire with 14 items that can be used to measure 5 sub-aspects of intuitive use. These sub-aspects describe the following subjective impressions of users:

- I do not need to concentrate or think to use the product.
- I can reach all my goals with the product.
- How to use the product was clear and easy from the start.
- The interaction with the product felt familiar.
- I did not encounter any problems or errors during usage of the product.

The INTUI questionnaire (Ullrich & Diefenbach, 2010) distinguishes 4 sub-aspects of intuitive use. These sub-aspects describe the following subjective impressions of users:

- Using the product feels natural, easy, and effortless?
- I can use the product without thinking just guided by my intuitive feelings.
- The interaction is inspiring, fascinating, like a magical experience.
- It is hard to explain in retrospect how I did things.

Thus, despite minor differences in the wording and grouping of the sub-aspects, the semantic concept of intuitive use is quite similar in these two questionnaires.

7.3   Learnability (Perspicuity)

Of course, when we start using a new product, some learning may be required, at least if the product is not completely intuitive to use. And of course, users do not want to spend too much time and effort learning how to use a product. They want to start working with the product as quickly as possible. The time and effort required to learn how to use a product is therefore an important UX aspect.

Items related to this aspect:

- It was easy to learn to use this system. (CSUQ)
- It is quickly apparent how to use the product. (meCUE)
- It was easy to learn to use this system. (PSSUQ)
- It would be easy for me to become skillful at using the system. (PUEU)

- Learning how to use new functions is difficult. (SUMI)
- easy to learn / difficult to learn. (UEQ)

Learnability describes the feeling that it is easy to acquire the knowledge required to use a product in order to achieve certain goals. It is therefore a task-related UX aspects. Similar to intuitive use, people attribute the fact that they are able to learn something quickly to some degree to their own intelligence or skills. Thus, a good learnability supports the psychological need for *Competence*.

We can distinguish several sub-aspects of learnability. A product is *self-explanatory* if the user can learn how to use it by trial and error. The product thus supports users in exploring new features and it is therefore not necessary to read the documentation or to go through tutorials. A second sub-aspect is the *time required to learn*. Of course, users do not want to waste time in a lengthy learning process. For example, simple interaction concepts and a good match between the elements visible in a user interface and the users' mental models obviously help to reduce learning time. *Consistency* means that similar elements and functions are presented in the same way in all parts of the product. Thus, users learn certain things once and can then apply that knowledge in other parts of the product. This, of course, also speeds up learning. *Availability of help or documentation* is especially relevant for more complex products. Here the users often need to learn how to map their mental concepts of a task to the capabilities of the system.

The distinction of items into these sub-aspects is not always clear. Some items cover more than one of these sub-aspects.

7.3.1 Self-descriptiveness

This UX aspect describes the user's impression that the product supports exploratory learning. How to perform certain tasks with the product does not have to be intuitive, but it is possible to figure it out while using it. Therefore, the user may get it wrong a few times. But in the end, he or she can find the right path through the system. Another aspect of self-descriptiveness is that the terminology used in the product is easy to understand.

Items related to this aspect:

- Exploring new features by trial and error: Difficult / Easy (QUIS)
- Are the command names meaningful? (PUTQ)
- Is the wording familiar? (PUTQ)

- The terminology used in the software reflects that of my work environment. (ISOMETRICS)

- Understandable, Meaningful (MS Product Reaction Cards)

- The Web site labels are easy to understand. (WEBQUAL)

- Learning to operate this software initially is full of problems. (SUMI)

- The way that system information is presented is clear and understandable. (SUMI)

- Learning to find my way around this website is a problem. (WAMMI)

There are several design elements that support the impression of a self-explanatory system. For example, short explanatory texts that are displayed on the user interface to provide guidance in difficult situations. Or animations that guide the user, for example when a deleted object does not simply disappear but flies into the trash can. This animation provides an immediate feedback that deletion was successful and gives the user an idea where to look if the object should be restored.

7.3.2   Learning time and effort

This aspect refers to the time and effort required to learn how to use a product. For many complex products, users will expect and accept a certain amount learning effort. Typical examples are complex business management systems, or interfaces for complex technical or medical devices. With such products, it is necessary to teach not only how to operate the product itself, but also the process behind it. In other words, it is usually not possible to use such systems without some training or instructions. But it is important that the effort required to learn such systems is not unnecessarily high, i.e., that the user does not feel that he or she must encounter any unnecessary difficulties.

Items related to this aspect:

- It was easy to learn to use this system. (CSUQ)

- I believe I became productive quickly using this system. (CSUQ)

- Learning to operate the system: Difficult / Easy (QUIS)

- I quickly became skillful with it. (USE)

- There is too much to read before you can use the software. (SUMI)

- In order to use the software properly, I must remember a great many details. (ISOMETRICS)

- I needed a long time to learn how to use the software. (ISOMETRICS)

7.3.3   Consistency

If a user can apply knowledge acquired in one part of a product to other parts, this naturally facilitates learning. If similar functionality is implemented in a consistent way throughout the product, this will of course improve the time it takes to learn how to use the product. For example, if the same element (input field, menu entry or button) is labelled differently on multiple screens in an application, this is a clear consistency issue.

Items related to this aspect:

- The software is inconsistently designed, thus making it more difficult for me to do my work. (ISOMETRICS)
- Is the feedback consistent? (PUTQ)
- Use of terms throughout system: inconsistent / consistent (QUIS)
- Position of messages on screen: inconsistent / consistent (QUIS)
- I thought there was too much inconsistency in this system. (SUS)
- I think this software is inconsistent. (SUMI)
- Is the data display consistent with user conventions? (PUTQ)
- Consistent, Inconsistent (MS Product Reaction Cards)

We can distinguish two types of consistency. Of course, users expect that different parts of a product behave consistently. This is sometimes called *internal consistency*. It is an obvious requirement, but not so easy to realize for larger products that are developed over a longer period of time. The second aspect is consistency with quasi-standards (*external consistency*). Users are usually happy to reuse knowledge they have acquired in other product they frequently use. Some interaction elements occur in quite a few products (for example, the shopping cart metaphor or the recycle bin) and thus users expect a similar behavior in other products. Items in UX questionnaires refer to the aspect of internal consistency. External consistency is more related to the concept of intuitive use.

7.3.4   Availability of help and documentation

This aspect describes whether the product offers supporting information material, for example easy access to documentation.

As long as people used only a few interactive products, it was acceptable to spend some time to get familiar with each product. Older UX questionnaires therefore include a lot of questions about the availability and quality of help and documentation. These expectations have changed drastically in recent years. We all use a huge number of interactive products in our daily lives. If we had to read lengthy documentation to use them, it obviously wouldn't work. Thus, except for very complex products used exclusively for professional purposes, users expect that products can be used intuitively, or at least that they can learn how to use the product quickly by trial and error.

Items covering this aspect were quite common in older usability questionnaires and are rather rare in more recent questionnaires.

Items related to this aspect:

- The information (such as online help, on-screen messages, and other documentation) provided with this system is clear. (CSUQ)

- Overall, I am satisfied with the support information (online-line help, messages, documentation) when completing the tasks. (ASQ)

- The software documentation is very informative. (SUMI)

7.4   Controllability (Dependability)

When users interact with a product, they want to have the feeling that they are in complete control of the interaction with the system, even though this may not be the case. In other words, the user should always believe that he or she controls the system, not the other way around.

Let's take autonomous driving as an example. Many people still have major reservations about this technology. The feeling of handing over control to a software they do not fully understand triggers unease. However, drivers already no longer have full control over the driving behavior of modern cars. Assistance systems already intervene in various situations. However, these interventions are often not recognized or even advertised as increasing control for the driver.

Controllability is an aspect that is already mentioned in ISO 9241 and on which older UX questionnaires place a lot of emphasis. In newer questionnaires, this aspect is often rather weakly represented.

Items related to this aspect:

- Controllable, Uncontrollable (MS Product Reaction Cards)

- I would find it easy to get the system to do what I want it to do. (PUEU)

- Is the sequence control user initiated? (PUTQ)

- It is easy to make the software do exactly what you want. (SUMI)

- The software hasn't always done what I was expecting. (SUMI)
- I feel in control when I'm using this website. (WAMMI)

Control is understood in UX in the sense that the user controls the process to achieve certain goals. Thus, controllability is a task-related UX aspect. When users feel that they are in complete control of the interaction with a product, this supports the psychological need for *Security*.

It is possible to distinguish between different sub-aspects of controllability. *Feeling in control* describes the user's impression that he or she has full control over the behavior of the product. *Predictability* means that the responses of the product to user actions confirm to the user's expectations. *Transparency* describes that the user is always informed about the current status of the processing. *Error prevention* refers to the product's ability to help the user to avoid errors or, if this is not possible, to correct them quickly. The boundaries between these sub-aspects are not always clear.

7.4.1 Feeling of control

We usually operate interactive products to achieve specific goals. In doing so, it is of course important that we have control over the processes and the results of our actions.

Typical examples for a lack of control are missing possibilities to undo actions, processes that cannot be interrupted by the user, or forms that do not allow saving incomplete data.

Items related to this aspect:

- The software allows me to interrupt functions at any point, even if it is waiting for me to make an entry. (ISOMETRICS)
- I feel in command of this software when I am using it. (SUMI)
- I feel in control when I'm using this website. (WAMMI)
- obstructive / supportive (UEQ)
- Does it provide CANCEL option? (PUTQ)
- Does it provide UNDO to reverse control actions? (PUTQ)

7.4.2 Predictability

Most people like surprises more in the context of private relationships (gifts or other nice things) and not in relation to their work with interactive systems (let's exclude games). When they trigger an action in a system, users assume that the result matches their expectations or predictions.

A very typical and annoying problem is automatic updates. Such updates are downloaded in the background and then installed automatically when the computer is shut down or booted. Who is not happy about the nice message *Updates are being installed. Do not turn off your computer!* What always annoys me about this is the fact that I don't get any information how long this process really takes. Should I wait or should I do something else first? I am being deprived of control over my computer and it is not even communicated when control will be returned to me.

Items related to this aspect:

- Predictable, Reliable (MS Produkt Reaktion Cards)
- unpredictable / predictable (UEQ)
- I have no difficulty in predicting how long the software will need to perform a given task. (ISOMETRICS)
- Are the results of control entry compatible with user expectations? (PUTQ)

7.4.3   Transparency of system state

I think we all know the unpleasant situation of having triggered an action in a software and not being informed by the product whether it has produced the desired result or not. Another example for a non-transparent system state is the lack of feedback (waiting indicator, progress bar) for long processing times for certain operations.

Items related to this aspect:

- Is completion of processing indicated? (PUTQ)
- I sometimes don't know what to do next with this software. (SUMI)
- Computer informs about its progress: never / always (QUIS)

7.4.4   Error tolerance

Of course, nobody is happy to make mistakes. First, we usually feel stupid when we do something wrong. Second, mistakes cost time, since they must be corrected. A system that easily lets users run into error situations and that offers little help to correct these errors will most likely not leave a very positive impression regarding UX.

Items related to this aspect:

- If I make a mistake while performing a task, I can easily undo the last operation (ISOMETRICS)
- Are erroneous entries displayed? (PUTQ)
- Error messages: unhelpful / helpful (QUIS)

- I can recover from mistakes quickly and easily. (USE)

- Error prevention messages are not adequate. (SUMI)

7.5 Adaptability (Suitability for individualization)

We all have personal preferences, habits and working styles, and we are usually very reluctant to give them up. Thus, if we have to use a new product, we still want to process tasks in a way we are used to.

Such personal preferences can be very general in nature or relate to very specific requirements. For example, users often have a preference regarding the amount of information to be displayed on a screen. If too much information is displayed, the user feels overloaded with details; if too little information is displayed, the user feels bored. But the concrete amount of information that is comfortable varies between different users. Other examples for very concrete requirements concerning adaptability are the desire to control the font size in a screen or to hide screen elements that are not of interest.

Adaptability describes whether the user feels that he or she can adapt a product to his or her own working style. Again, it must be mentioned that this as a purely subjective assessment. Even if a product is full of customization options, users may still feel that it is not adaptable, for example, because the customization options are too hidden or because they simply do not meet their needs.

Adaptability is clearly a task-related UX aspect. If adaptability is sufficient, this supports the psychological need for *Autonomy*.

Since *adaptability* or *suitability for individualization* was already included in ISO 9241, this aspect is quite prominent in older usability questionnaires, for example ISONORM and ISOMETRICS.

Items related to this aspect:

- The software lets me adapt forms, screens and menus to suit my individual preferences. (ISOMETRICS)

- I am able to adjust the amount of information (data, text, graphics, etc.) displayed on-screen to my needs. (ISOMETRICS)

- I can adjust the attributes (e.g. speed) of the input devices (e.g. mouse, keyboard) to suit my individual needs. (ISOMETRICS)

- I can adjust the software's response times to my own personal working speed. (ISOMETRICS)

- Customizable, Flexible (MS Product Reaction Cards)
- Can users name displays and elements according to their needs? (PUTQ)

Every adaptation of a product to personal preferences requires a certain amount of effort. Of course, we only invest this effort if it is worthwhile, i.e., if we believe we can benefit from the personalization. Most people work today with many different products, both professionally and privately. The willingness to adapt these products to personal preferences is therefore decreasing. This is obviously also reflected in the development of UX questionnaires, and therefore this UX aspect is hardly represented in more recent questionnaires.

7.6   Clarity (Visual Complexity)

The amount of information presented in a user interface and the way this information is organized or grouped obviously has an impact on UX. The more information is shown on a display and the more confusing it is arranged or grouped, the more difficult it is for the user to find the relevant information. A clear and concise display of information therefore has a positive impact on UX. We refer to this UX aspect as *clarity*. Another common term is *visual complexity* (high clarity corresponds to low visual complexity).

The perception of visual complexity is influenced by several factors. For example, Roberts (2007) identified the number and organization of different elements and the asymmetry of the layout as the three main factors that influence the perception of visual complexity in images. In a study on the perception of web pages (Müller & Schrepp, 2013), the number of elements and alignment lines on the page (which corresponds to the organization of elements and asymmetry of the layout in the study of Roberts, 2007) were identified as main factors for perceived visual complexity.

Items related to this aspect:

- The organization of information on the system screens is clear. (CSUQ)
- Clear, Clean, Organized (MS Product Reaction Cards)
- The website has a clean and simple presentation. (SUPR-Q)
- organized / cluttered (UEQ)
- Organization of information: confusing / very clear (QUIS)
- The layout is easy to grasp. (VISAWI)

- The layout appears well structured. (VISAWI)
- The layout appears too dense. (VISAWI)
- The organization of information on the system screens was clear. (PSSUQ)

Perceived clarity of a user interface shows a correlation to usability related UX aspects. Of course, clarity helps users to find things faster and creates the impression of simplicity. Thus, perceived clarity will typically also create a good impression about the efficiency or learnability of a product.

On the other hand, clarity also refers to visual aesthetics. In Lavie & Tractinski (2004) two factors of visual aesthetics are distinguished. *Classical aesthetics* describes aspects like symmetry, clarity, and order. *Expressive aesthetics* focuses of creativity and originality of the design. Thus, terms like clear, clean, symmetrical, organised, and ordered represent classical aesthetics, while terms like creative, original, or sophisticated represent expressive aesthetics. Thus, the UX aspect clarity obviously is semantically very close to the concept of classical aesthetics.

Schrepp, Otten, Blum & Thomaschewski (2020) describe two empirical studies that show a strong mediator effect of clarity on the dependency between perceived aesthetics and perceived usability. Thus, clarity is a mediator variable that can explain the often-reported dependency between perceived beauty and perceived usability of a user interface (Kuroso & Kashimura, 1995 or Tractinsky, 1997).

Is clarity a UX quality in its own right? This is certainly debatable. It would be entirely possible to see it as a sub-aspect of efficiency or aesthetics. However, clarity is somehow the link between some of the classic usability aspects and visual aesthetics. In addition, for some products it may be of interest to measure clarity in detail. Therefore, I decided to list this as an independent UX aspect.

Since clarity is to some extent a mediator between usability and aesthetics, it cannot be classified as a pure task-related UX aspect. Indirectly, it supports the psychological needs of *Competence* (relation to efficiency) and *Pleasure* (relation to aesthetic impression).

7.7 Stimulation (Fun of use)

Products should be designed in such a way that it is as interesting as possible for the user to work with them. Stimulation describes if the design of the product is interesting, mentally stimulating and thus motivating.

This criterion is also often referred to as fun of use. However, we have decided to use the somewhat more neutral term stimulation, since *fun* is a too strong requirement for many products. An enhancement of stimulation is immersion, which we will discuss in detail later.

Items related to this aspect:

- boring / exciting (UEQ)
- not interesting / interesting (UEQ)
- It is fun to use. (USE)
- motivating / discouraging (AttrakDiff2)
- dull / absorbing (AttrakDiff2)
- The product exhilarates me. (meCUE)
- Engaging, Entertaining, Motivating, Inspiring (MS Product Reaction Cards)
- dull / stimulating (QUIS)
- Working with this software is mentally stimulating. (SUMI)

The impression that interaction with a product is interesting or exciting is not directly related to the user's goals. Thus, stimulation is not a task-related UX aspect. Clearly, stimulation or fun of use supports the psychological need for *Pleasure*.

In recent years, there has been a hype about gamification, i.e., the attempt to enrich classic products with design elements familiar from games. The goal is obviously to make such gamified applications more interesting to use. However, it is important to understand that stimulation should not be confused with adding game mechanics or creating fun. A product can also be stimulating if it allows users to develop their skills, for example, if they feel that they are learning something new or developing new insights by using it.

As an example, consider a development environment for web application developers. It is a strong motivator for developers that their applications are used by many people. A finished application is published and launched, and from time to time the developer will check if the application is running without errors and with good technical performance. It is therefore usually a good idea to include usage statistics or user ratings in the monitoring tool. If the application has a problem, this provides valuable information. If everything is going well, such information is good for the developer's ego and makes the purely routine monitoring more interesting (*Let's see how many users we had today?*).

7.8   Novelty (Originality)

Products usually compete with other products for the attention of potential users or buyers. In order to position a product successfully, it is thus usually helpful to be perceived as original and novel.

New and surprising design elements arouse the interest of people and thus attention is drawn to the product. Originality is an example of a UX aspect that users often do not assess as important for a product (Winter, Schrepp, Hinderks, Thomaschewski, 2017), but is often seen as central by the provider of the product. The goal of an original design is to attract attention and therefore stand out from competing offerings. This can be done through novel functions or through an original visual design that is clearly different from other products.

The aspect of novelty or originality does not appear in the older usability questionnaires. However, it can be found in many of the more recent UX questionnaires.

Items related to this aspect:

- unimaginative / creative (AttrakDiff2)
- novel / conventional (AttrakDiff2)
- inventive / conventional (UEQ)
- The product is creatively designed. (meCue)
- Unconventional, Novel, Creative, Cutting edge (MS Product Reaction Cards)
- The design is uninteresting. (VISAWI)
- The layout is inventive. (VISAWI)
- The Web site design is innovative. (WEBQUAL)
- The Web site is creative. (WEBQUAL)

Novelty has a connection to the concept of expressive aesthetics in the sense of Lavie & Tractinsky (2004), thus there is some relation between the perception of originality and visual aesthetics.

The perception of a product as novel and creative is independent of the tasks users are trying to accomplish using the product. Thus, novelty is clearly a non-task-related UX aspect. Novel and original designs attract the interest of potential users. Thus, novelty supports the psychological need for *Pleasure*.

The more similar the products in a product category ultimately become, the more important it is for the success of an individual product to attract attention through original design. However, it should also be noted that a high degree of originality does not necessarily mean that a product will always be preferred to other, more conventionally designed products. There are some well-studied psychological mechanisms that indicate that too much novelty can be a problem.

A well-studied effect is the preference for prototypes (Whitefield, 2000). Studies show that consumers tend to prefer typical examples of a product category to more atypical examples. The MAYA (Most Advanced Yet Acceptable) principle of the American designer Raymond Loewry (1951) is also well known in this context (see also Hekkert, Smelders & van Wieringen, 2003). This principle states that successful products or designs should stand out through their design but should not deviate so far from the established or typical appearance that they are no longer acceptable. Designers should look for a balance between new and established design elements.

Thus, unlike other UX qualities, higher originality or novelty is not always desirable. With criteria such as efficiency, it is obvious that a higher score is associated with a higher overall preference for the product. With originality, this is not always to be expected. If the originality of a product exceeds a certain level, this can reduce the attractiveness of the product due to the effects mentioned above.

7.9   Usefulness

Usefulness plays a central role in the *Technology Acceptance Model* (TAM) of Davis, Bagozzi & Warshaw (1989) or Venkatesh & Davis (2000). The central assumption of this model is that a person's willingness to use a technology depends on the subjectively perceived usefulness of the technology and the subjectively perceived usability (perceived ease of use). The higher the perceived usefulness and the perceived usability are, the greater the willingness to use a new technology or product.

In the case of products that are primarily used to achieve specific goals in the professional or private context, usefulness naturally plays an important role in the overall evaluation of UX.

Items related to this aspect:

- practical / impractical (AttrakDiff2)
- I consider the product extremely useful. (meCUE)
- Powerful, Useful (MS Product Reaction Cards)
- Using the system in my job would increase my productivity. (PUEU)
- I would find the system useful in my job. (PUEU)
- It gives me more control over the activities in my life. (USE)
- It makes the things I want to accomplish easier to get done. (USE)
- It is easier to use the Web site to complete my business with the company than it is to telephone, fax, or mail a representative. (WEBQUAL)

In the sense of the Technology Acceptance Model and concerning the typical interpretation inside UX questionnaires, usefulness is clearly a task-related UX aspect. A product is perceived as useful if it helps to achieve productive goals or simply saves resources. There is some overlap with the UX aspect of efficiency. If users think that a product help to improve their productivity, this will support the psychological need for *Competence*. Some items that cover usefulness go in the direction of having control about activities in one's live or being able to do things without the help of others. Thus, also the psychological need for *Autonomy* may be supported by a product that is perceived as useful. But this dependency may not exit for all use cases.

7.10 Trust

We transfer money via banking apps, we shop via e-commerce sites, we maintain contacts via social networks, and we sometimes disclose very personal details in messengers or e-mails. Our trust that the information we provide to such services will not be used to harm us is a prerequisite for their usage.

Who will order something on an e-commerce site if the site seems suspicious? In other words, trust is an essential prerequisite for the success of many products. For example, an early study on e-commerce showed that the most important reason that prevents consumers from buying online is a lack of trust in the corresponding website (Doney & Cannon, 1997).

The design of a website or service has an impact on the perception that the site is trustworthy. Everard & Galetta (2003), for example, identified three factors of design that are important with respect to trust. These are graphic and visual design, completeness of expected information, and freedom from errors. Similar factors are also described in Nielsen (1999). Intuitively, this dependency between design and the perception of trust is evident. Would you shop in a web store whose visual design looks like the first work of an amateur designer, where important information about the availability of goods and delivery conditions is missing, and where every second click produces an error? Probably not, unless you like risk and gambling.

In older UX questionnaires, which are based on the classic concept of usability, trust does not play a role. However, newer questionnaires and especially questionnaires intended for e-commerce strongly consider this aspect.

Items related to this aspect:

- Confident, Not Secure, Secure und Trustworthy (MS Product Reaction Cards)
- I feel safe in my transactions with the Web site. (WEBQUAL)
- I trust the Web site to keep my personal information safe. (WEBQUAL)
- I feel confident conducting business on the website. (SUPR-Q)
- insecure / secure (UEQ+)
- unreliable / reliable (UEQ+)
- non-transparent / transparent (UEQ+)

The feeling that a product can be trusted is somehow independent from performing tasks. But there is some connection with controllability. If the user has the impression that he or she cannot control the interaction, this can damage the perception of trust. Especially if errors occur and the user is not informed what went wrong and how to resolve the situation. Thus, trust is more a non-task related UX quality, but this classification is potentially controversial. Clearly, trust in a product supports the psychological need for *Security*.

Trust is especially important for products that deal with sensitive personal data (social networks, messengers, etc.), commercial aspects (banking apps, web shops, etc.) or storing of important and private data (dropbox, web storage, etc.).

7.11 Identity and Value

Sometimes people assume that owning a product (or in the case of an online service the ability to access it) improves their prestige. The corresponding UX quality is often called identity (Hassenzahl, Burmester & Koller, 2003).

The basis of this perceived gain in prestige is the perception that a product is valuable or stylish. The owner or user hopes to use the product to improve his or her self-presentation and to establish contacts with other people more easily. Identity is thus closely related to the perception of value.

Semantically, identity and value are different aspects of the perception of a product. But a high value of a product is a prerequisite for believing that ownership of the product improves the personal prestige or popularity. If you perceive a product as unprofessional, inferior, or tasteless you will of course not be proud to own it. Because of this close interdependence, we discuss these two aspects together.

Items that relate more to identity:

- brings me closer to people / separates me from people (AttrakDiff2)
- The product would enhance my standing among peers. (meCUE)
- By using the product, I would be perceived differently. (meCUE)
- isolates / connects (AttrakDiff2)

Items that relate more to value:

- stylish / lacking style (AttrakDiff2)
- The layout appears professionally designed. (VISAWI)
- The site is designed with care. (VISAWI)
- inferior / valuable (UEQ+)
- not elegant / elegant (UEQ+)
- tasteless / tasteful (UEQ+)

The first questionnaire that included this aspect as a separate scale was the AttrakDiff2. However, items that can be assigned to identity can also be found in other UX questionnaires, for example the meCUE.

Clearly, identity and value are non-task-related UX aspects. Since the main motivation behind the desire for identity and value is to increase prestige, these UX aspects clearly support the psychological need for *Popularity*.

Identity or value are only relevant if the user can personally decide to buy or use the product. A typical example is smartphones or other exclusive products such as an Apple Watch. A business management system provided by the employer will not evoke a sense of identity or value.

7.12 Visual Aesthetics (Beauty)

When buying or superficially evaluating a product, we often decide purely on the basis of its appearance, i.e. the visual appeal of the product. Thus, for the positioning and financial success of a product, it is advisable to pay attention to its visual aesthetics or beauty of product design.

Several studies, e.g. Kurosu & Kashimura (1995), Tractinsky (1997) and Tractinsky, Katz & Ikar (2000), showed a positive influence of the aesthetics or beauty of a product on the perceived usability, which is often succinctly formulated as *What is beautiful is usable*.

The VISAWI is a specialized questionnaire that exclusively measures the visual appeal of web pages (or more general products that offer a graphical user interface). Other questionnaires also contain individual items that measure this aspect.

Items related to this aspect:

- ugly / pretty (Attrakdiff2)
- The software has a very attractive presentation. (SUMI)
- The Web site is visually pleasing. (WEBQUAL)
- The pages on this website are very attractive. (WAMMI)
- The Web site displays visually pleasing design. (WAMMI)
- The colors are appealing. (VISAWI)
- The color composition is attractive. (VISAWI)

Visual Aesthetics is, of course, a non-task-related UX aspect. An attractive design will naturally make users a bit happier and improve their mood (Norman, 2003). Thus, a visually aesthetic product will support the psychological need for *Pleasure*.

7.13 Immersion

Immersion occurs when the user is strongly fascinated by his or her activity and this activity is mentally very demanding. Thus, there is little capacity left for the perception of the outside world. This is a very important UX quality for games, but not so relevant for other types of products.

Immersion is rarely considered in UX questionnaires. However, there are game experience questionnaires, e.g. Jennett, Cox, Cairns, Dhoparee, Epps, Tijs & Walton (2008) or Ijsselsteijn, de Kort, & Poels (2013) (Game Experience Questionnaire, short GEQ), that measure this aspect.

Immersion is, in a sense, stimulation increased to the maximum level.

Items from GEQ related to this aspect:

- If someone talks to me, I don't hear them.
- Things seem to happen automatically.
- I lose track of time.
- I lose track of where I am.
- I play without thinking about how to play.

Clearly, immersion is a non-task-related UX aspect. It supports the psychological need for *Pleasure*. Immersion is certainly only relevant for special products. Of course, as already mentioned above, for games. But the aspect also plays a role for video portals or social networks.

7.14 Valence (Attractiveness)

Valence describes the general satisfaction or dissatisfaction with a product, i.e. a general assessment on a good/bad dimension. Thus, it does not measure any concrete semantically delimited properties of a design or interaction with a product. But for concrete research situations, it is often of interest to separately measure users' valence towards a product. Valence items are quite common in UX questionnaires.

In questionnaires, this aspect often appears as a scale under the term attractiveness.

Items related to this aspect:

- good / bad (AttrakDiff2, UEQ)
- Overall, I am satisfied with how easy it is to use this system. (CSUQ)
- Overall, I am satisfied with this system. (PSSUQ)
- The website is easy to use. (SUPR-Q)
- It is user friendly. (USE)
- frustrating / satisfying (QUIS)
- Usable, Satisfying (MS Product Reaction Cards)

As an overall assessment, valence is a non-task-related UX aspect. Obviously, valence develops as a consequence of a longer lasting satisfactory experience with a product. Thus, in the terminology of the CUE model (Thüring & Mahlke, 2007), it is a consequence of product interaction. It is not possible to assign it to concrete psychological needs.

7.15 Loyality

We all have our favorite products, i.e. products that we use over a longer period of time and that we do not like to replace with other products, even if the alternatives may be better or cheaper. These are exactly the products that we also like to recommend to friends.

It is precisely this feeling of loyalty that a manufacturer of a product most urgently needs to establish. It simply ensures a stable customer base and recurring purchases or the permanent use of a product.

Loyalty takes time to develop and requires that a user is satisfied with a product over a longer period of time. If you buy a new product and it appears to you to have an inferior UX, then it is quite unlikely that you will develop any loyalty.

In UX questionnaires, this aspect is rather underrepresented. However, in some questionnaires (especially in meCUE, which has a separate loyalty scale) there are items that depict this aspect.

Items related to this aspect:

- I would not swap this product for any other. (meCUE)
- I would get exactly this product for myself (again) at any time. (meCUE)
- I could not live without this procduct. (meCUE)
- How likely are you to recommend the website to a friend or colleague? (SUP-RQ)
- I would recommend it to a friend. (USE)

Like valence, loyalty is non-task-related and is formed during a longer interaction with a product, so it is also a consequence in terms of the CUE model (and therefore does not correspond to concrete psychological needs).

7.16 Haptics

For products that are held in the hand during use, the haptic impression (feeling when the device is touched) is of course an important aspect of UX. Typical examples are smartphones or household appliances. A smartphone should fit well into one hand. A hair dryer should have a reasonable weight and should create a stable and slip-resistant feeling.

Haptic perception is influenced by various factors, e.g. shape, size, weight, and the surface properties of the product (hardness, warmth, friction, roughness, see Okamoto, Nagano & Ho, 2016).

Regarding surface properties, there is a scale developed by Boos & Brau (2017) with the items (in the form of a semantic differential with a 7-point answer scale):

- unstable / stable
- unpleasant to the touch / pleasant to the touch
- rough / smooth
- slippery / slip-resistant

Originally, this sensory scale was developed for household appliances. It covers only a part of the haptic properties that affect UX. The scale is available within the UEQ+ framework.

7.17 Acoustics

Some products produce sounds or noises when they are operated. These sounds can be pleasant or unpleasant for the user. A super intuitive and efficient user interface for a kitchen appliance is quickly forgotten if the device produces an annoying noise when operated.

This aspect is very important for household appliances. In this context, not only the pure volume is important, but also the sound in general, e.g. sharpness and rhythm (Hulsmeier, Schell-Majoor, Rennies & van de Par, 2014).

A scale for the assessment of acoustic impression was developed by Boos & Brau (2017). This scale contains the following 4 items (in the form of a semantic differential with a 7-point answer scale):

- loud / quiet
- dissonant / melodic
- booming / dampened
- piercing / soft

The items above were originally designed for household appliances. This sensory scale is available within the UEQ+ framework.

7.18 Content Quality

Why do people visit a website several times? Probably because the content or information offered there is interesting, important, and up to date (Thielsch & Jaron, 2012). This aspect is called content quality. Of course, it is mainly relevant for products that mainly convey content to the user. For example, the web presence of a club (where members can find current events or where non-members simply want to obtain information), an online magazine, the web presence of a city, or learning platforms.

This UX aspect does not make sense for products that are used to generate information or to process some routine tasks, for example, a word processor or a programming environment.

However, content quality is also important for some business applications. For example, if these implement tax or other legal requirements as content. The quality of this implementation, or whether the functionality implemented in the application complies with the current legal requirements, can certainly be interpreted as content quality.

The WEBCLIC is a specialized questionnaire for measuring content quality of websites. Two scales concerning different aspects of content quality (trustworthiness of the content and interest in the content) are contained in the UEQ+.

Items related to this aspect:

- The Web site adequately meets my information needs. (WEBQUAL)
- The information on the Web site is pretty much what I need to carry out my tasks. (WEBQUAL)
- The text on the Web site is easy to read. (WEBQUAL)
- I can trust the information on the web site. (WEBCLIC)
- The information is of high quality. (WEBCLIC)
- The content of the web site are clearly presented. (WEBCLIC)
- I enjoy reading the web site. (WEBCLIC)

Content quality is included in our list as representative or example of a special type of UX aspects. If we look at the items in the list above, we see that they have a close semantical connection to more general aspects that we have already discussed. For example, usefulness (items 1 and 2), trust (item 4), value (item 5), clarity (item 6), or stimulation (item 7). Thus, items that are related to these more general principles are just reformulated for a special use case.

Such items are of course only usable for very special types of applications. They are useful, since the specialization to a particular use case allows to formulate the items in a very concrete and thus easy-to-interpret form. Since they are a mixture of different more basic UX aspects, it is usually not possible to classify them as task-related or non-task-related.

7.19 Emotions

According to the CUE model (Thüring & Mahlke, 2007) emotions during an interaction play an important role for the overall impression regarding a product. Thus, it is not surprising that some UX questionnaires try to measure emotional UX aspects.

A questionnaire with a strong emphasis on measuring emotions is the meCUE. But other questionnaires also contain items that point in this direction.

Items related to this aspect:

- The product annoys me. (meCUE)
- The product frustrates me. (meCUE)
- The product makes me feel euphoric. (meCUE)
- The product angers me. (meCUE)
- The product calms me. (meCUE)
- I felt angry. (PLEXQ)
- I felt stressed. (PLEXQ)
- frustrating / satisfying (QUIS)
- Using this software is frustrating. (SUMI)

From my personal experience in the field of UX evaluation, I see two problematic points concerning the measurement of emotions. First, emotions are not very persistent. Of course, working with a product can trigger anger or frustration. But these emotions either have to be very strong or must be triggered very often to be remembered after some time. Second, in many cases, the interaction with a product does not really cause strong emotions. Users can be quite unhappy or quite happy with a product without feeling angry or euphoric. In most cases, the evaluation of the product is done rather on a rational basis. Thus, in my opinion the influence of emotions on the overall evaluation of the UX of a product is somewhat overestimated.

8 Why are UX Aspects not Independent?

In the previous chapter, we described various UX aspects in detail. Each of these UX aspects represents a semantically different facet of UX. But you should not confuse this with statistical independence.

When several UX aspects are measured in a UX questionnaire, we typically observe quite substantial correlations between these aspects. We will describe several reasons for this phenomenon in this chapter. In practice, these reasons share some similarities and, depending on the product and usage scenario, any of them or even all of them together can be responsible for an empirical correlation between semantically different UX aspects.

8.1 HALO effects and impact of the general impression

Not every participant who fills out a questionnaire has a clear opinion on every UX aspect measured in the questionnaire. Different users perform different use cases or have different levels of expertise with a product. If a participant cannot judge a specific aspect based on his or her experience, then there is a tendency to infer the judgement from general impressions about the product.

Let's assume, for example, a relative inexperienced user of a product who has a positive impression regarding the visual design or beauty of the product. Regarding controllability, he or she may not yet have a clear opinion. But it is quite likely that the items in the controllability scale will not be rated neutrally. The positive impression with regard to visual design may lead to a positive judgement concerning controllability.

Such an effect is known from social psychology under the term *attractivity stereotype* or *HALO-effect*. It describes the tendency to infer from directly visible characteristics of a person (an attractive appearance) to characteristics that are not directly observable (intelligence, social competency). See, for example, Dion, Berscheid & Walster (1972) or Dick, Dipankar & Gabriel (1990).

From marketing research, a similar phenomenon is known as *evaluative consistency*. This describes the tendency to infer missing information about a product from the general brand or other known information about the product. For example, consumers often infer superior quality from a high price (Ford & Smith, 1987).

If we transfer this to user interfaces, then missing information concerning some UX aspects should be derived from the impression on other aspects for which the user has some information from previous experiences with the product or which are directly visible (for example, the visual design). This explanation is especially convincing when users have not interacted intensively with a product at the time of the evaluation, since they have not much information about the quality of the interaction design in this state (Ilmberger, Schrepp & Held, 2009).

Another assumption that points in the same direction is the *general impression model* (Lance, LaPointe & Stewart, 1994). This model assumes that the overall impression of an object influences individual aspects of the impression. Thus, if a user has a good overall impression of a product, he or she will also judge individual aspects positively, e.g., efficiency or controllability.

8.2 Mediator effects of external variables

A high correlation between two UX aspects can also result from the influence of a mediator variable. Let us explain this with a well-known example.

Several studies (for example, Kurosu & Kashimura, 1995, Tractinsky, 1997 or Tractinsky, Katz & Ikar, 2000) found that the perceived aesthetics or visual beauty of a user interface has an impact on the perceived usability of the product, i.e., semantically clearly different UX aspects such as efficiency, learnability or controllability. This finding is often condensed in the statements *What is beautiful is usable* or *Attractive things work better*.

A popular explanation by Don Norman (2003) assumes that the mood or emotional state of the user is responsible for this dependency. It is known from psychological research (Isen, 2000) that a positive emotional state of a person improves his or her creativity and flexibility in problem solving. A negative emotional state favours systematic, inflexible and analytical problem-solving behaviour (Schwarz, 2002).

When interacting with a product, according to Norman (2003), a user in a good mood should overcome problems with creative ideas more easily than a user in a bad mood. Thus, a user in a good mood will judge problems as less severe. As a consequence, a user in a bad mood should judge the usability of a user interface worse than a user in a good mood.

The basic idea behind Norman's explanation is that a beautiful design of a product causes a positive mood, while an ugly design causes a negative mood. Several papers have shown that the design of a product can influence the mood of its users (Kim & Moon, 1998 or Rafaeli & Vilnai-Yavetz, 2004). The mood or emotional state of the user acts in this explanation as a mediator variable between perceived aesthetics and perceived usability.

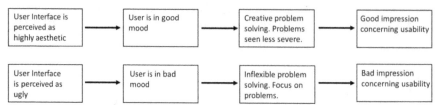

Figure 11: Mood as mediator variable influencing aesthetic impression and perceived usability.

Thus, to generalize this example, a positive correlation between semantically different UX aspects A and B can occurs if A influences a third variable C (which may not itself be a UX aspect, like the mood of users in the example above) and this variable C then influences UX aspect B. Thus, there is an indirect dependency through a mediator variable.

8.3   Semantic overlap

Of course, the simplest explanation of an empirical correlation between two semantically distinct UX aspects is that they have an overlap that is not so directly visible.

Let us look again on the dependency between aesthetics and usability. At first glance, beauty and usability seem to be unrelated quality aspects of a user interface that can be designed and developed independently of each other. But is this true if we look a little bit deeper into these concepts?

Lavie & Tractinsky (2004) distinguish two components of visual aesthetics. The concept of *classical aesthetics* describes design aspects such as symmetry, clarity and order. *Expressive aesthetics* focuses of creativity and originality of the design. Thus, terms like *clear, clean, symmetrical, organised,* and *ordered* represent classical aesthetics, while terms like *creative, original,* or *sophisticated* represent expressive aesthetics.

A study by Ngo & Byrne (2000) shows that balance and symmetry of a user interface improve the aesthetic impression of the product. A measure for the complexity of typographic layouts (Bonsiepe, 1968) is based on the alignment of elements and the variety of element sizes. Results in Deng & Poole (2012) demonstrate that visual complexity and perceived order of the layout have an impact on perceived aesthetic impression and preferences for websites. These results are also in line with the well-known fluency effect (Reber, Schwarz & Winkielman, 2004), which describes the observation that objects that are cognitively easier to process are perceived as more aesthetic. A very basic formulation of this idea actually dates back to the middle of the last century. In Birkhoff's *aesthetic measure* (Birkhoff, 1933), the ratio of order and complexity is used to measure the aesthetic value or appeal of an object.

In the previous chapter, we defined this notion of clear, clean, structured, organised layout as a separate UX aspect called *Clarity*.

But items that cover this aspect of product perception can be found in many UX questionnaires as representations of classic usability dimensions. For example, the UEQ contains an item *organised/cluttered* representing the dimension *Efficiency* and an item *clear/confusing* representing the dimension *Perspicuity*. The AttractDiff2 contains an item *confusing/clear* in the scale *Pragmatic Quality* (which is a representation of classical usability aspects). There are many other examples of this type in other UX questionnaires. For example, the PSSUQ contains an item *The organisation of the information on the systems screens was clear* as an indicator for the scale information quality. A similar statement *The website seems clearly arranged and not cluttered* is used in the NRL as part of the scale aesthetics.

Intuitively, it is quite natural that the visual clarity of a user interface influences usability judgements. Of course, a clear and structured user interface that contains only a small number of elements is easier to scan than a complex and cluttered user interface. Thus, the time to detect elements on the user interface that are important for a task, and thus efficiency, is also influenced by visual clarity. In addition, high visual clarity creates the impression that the user interface is of low complexity and thus easy to learn.

Thus, in this explanation the UX aspect *Clarity* acts as a mediator between classical usability aspects and visual aesthetics. It describes a not so obvious but existing common factor of these two UX aspects that look so different at first glance. In a series of empirical investigations this mediator effect of clarity on the dependency between aesthetic impression and usability could be confirmed (Schrepp & Müller, 2015 or Schrepp, Otten, Blum & Thomaschewski, 2021).

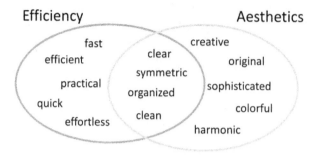

Figure 12: Dependency caused by shared semantic aspects.

Is this just an exotic example or are there other hidden dependencies? We discussed the close connection between *Identity* and *Value* in the previous chapter. Identity describes the user's impression that processing or using a product will increase his or her personal prestige. Value describes the impression that a product is professionally designed, stylish, and valuable. Of course, these are semantically different concepts and we need different items to measure them. But it is intuitively clear that we will hardly see a product that scores high on an identity scale but low on a value scale. This would mean that participants of the study assume that owning or using an inferior, unprofessionally looking product that lacks style will improve their social prestige. This is not very plausible.

If you take a closer look at the UX aspects described in the previous chapter, you will probably find many more of such hidden dependencies. Two UX aspects can describe two semantically different concepts of product design. Both can be of interest for UX researchers in different contexts. Thus, we need different sets of items to measure them, i.e. different scales in questionnaires. But this does not imply that these UX aspects are somehow statistically independent. As a rule, they are not!

9 Interindividual differences

Different users can have quite opposite feelings about UX qualities of a product. We will discuss in this chapter how participants in a UX questionnaire arrive at their ratings and what causes different impressions regarding a product.

But first, we will use a small example to illustrate how massively ratings for the same product can vary between different participants.

Figure 13 shows the distribution of SUS ratings for three products. The example is taken from Rummel & Schrepp (2018). In this paper you can find a more detailed description of the data.

The SUS is a 10-item questionnaire that mainly covers usability-related UX qualities. It provides an overall score ranging from 0 (worst) to 100 (best). The overall scores are 44 for product X, 69 for product Y and 80 for product Z. Thus, accordingly to the SUS benchmark (Lewis & Sauro, 2018, see Table 1 in Chapter 3) product X falls into category F (corresponding to an extremely bad usability), product Y into category C (medium usability) and product Z into category A (excellent usability).

We can, of course, calculate the rating per participant (the overall score is simply the average of the scores of all participants). As we can see from Figure 13, the participants' ratings (we grouped them into intervals of length 10) span for product X (blue) the entire range, i.e. there are participants that have a score in the range from 0 to 10 (a really bad impression) and participants with a score in the range from 91 to 100 (a really enthusiastic impression). This also applies to the other two products, but here the response range is obviously shifted somewhat to the right.

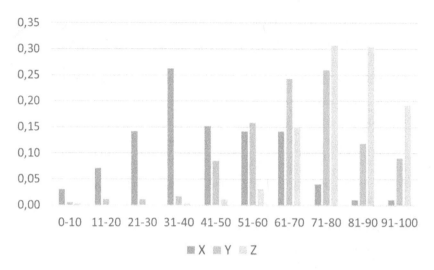

Figure 13: Relative frequencies of individual SUS scores for three different products.

Despite using the same product, some users have a very positive impression, while others have a very negative impression. What causes such strong interindividual differences in the perception of UX?

Of course, users differ in terms of demographic factors (gender, age, cultural background, etc.). Such differences can influence the perception of UX.

However, from my experience with the evaluation of professionally used products, the differences in the perception of UX resulting from these demographic factors are usually rather small. This is also confirmed by some empirical studies. For example, Aufderhaar, Schrepp & Thomaschewski (2019) showed that there were no substantial systematic differences between women and men in the evaluation of UX for three common German websites.

The impact of cultural background on the subjective importance of various UX aspects was investigated in Santoso & Schrepp (2019). The study compared ratings of German and Indonesian participants. Participants had to rate how important different UX aspects (a subset of the UX aspects described in Chapter 7) are for several types of products (messengers, video conferencing tools, text editors, programming environments, social networks, etc.). The results showed that the impact of culture is considerably lower than the impact of interindividual differences between people of the same culture. In addition, both samples show quite similar rankings of the importance of UX aspects. Product type has a much greater influence on the importance of a UX aspect than cultural differences.

Users rate products based on experiences with the product they can remember. When asked to rate a UX aspect, they must recall episodes from their past interactions with the product that are related to that aspect.

Let's consider two examples. We ask a user about the performance (time the product needs to react on user input) of a product. If he or she has no memories of negative experiences (he or she had to wait a long time for a response from the system), this is likely to be perceived as positive. That is, a good rating results from the absence of memories regarding negative experiences on system speed. The pragmatic UX aspects are all of this type.

Now suppose we ask the user if using the product is fun (stimulation). Let's assume that the user cannot remember any positive experiences. In this case it is unlikely that the user gives a good rating on this aspect. That is, the absence of appropriate memories is negative here. This is essentially the case with hedonic UX aspects.

Of course, the episodes that can be remembered when a participant answers items in a questionnaire varies from person to person. First, of course, users have an individual history of product usage. The tasks they perform in a product will vary. For example, with complex business software, the usage scenarios for a product will vary greatly between different customers or even by different departments within a single company. Thus, different users are simply performing different tasks and that naturally leads to different impressions regarding the UX of the product. Second, no one has a perfect memory. Thus, the episodes a person remembers when filling out a questionnaire will be random to some degree. This alone will cause some variation in the answers.

Different users may also have very different prior experiences with similar products. These experiences set a certain expectation for the UX. Depending on how well these expectations are met, the UX judgment varies.

Such prior experience can have a massive impact on a UX evaluation. If a new product A works similar to an already known product B, then the user naturally gets the impression that this product A is easy to learn and understand. The user has usually already forgotten that he or she had many problems when learning B, e.g., because this product was poorly designed with respect to this quality aspect.

Users have in addition a different expertise with the content area in which the product is located. This can massively affect learning or intuitive understanding and thus the UX impression. If the user only has a nebulous idea of what he or she needs to do, they will have difficulties (which they may then blame to the product design), no matter how well the product design supports the task.

Of course, personal likes and dislikes also play a role here. Especially with regard to more hedonic qualities, e.g. aesthetic design or novelty, every user has his or her own taste, to which the design of the product more or less corresponds.

Because of these factors, different people come to completely different assessments when evaluating the UX of a product. If you only survey a very small group of users of a product, you can easily come to the wrong conclusions. The higher the interindividual differences in users' impressions concerning the UX of a product are, the more participants are required to fill out a questionnaire in order to measure UX accurately.

10 Importance of UX Aspects for Product Categories

In Chapter 7 we described several common UX quality aspects. However, it is intuitively clear that not all UX quality aspects are of equal importance for a given product. In this chapter, we will take a closer look at the dependency between the type or category of a product and the importance of certain UX aspects for the overall user satisfaction.

10.1 Differences between products

Suppose we have a business software that is frequently used by employees of a company during a typical workday. For example, to create sales orders or to send out invoices to customers. For such an application scenario efficiency is an extremely important UX aspect for the overall satisfaction with a product. If, for example, the response time to user commands is slow or if the user is forced to perform some unnecessary interactions to complete a task, this will reduce productivity and satisfaction with the application. For tasks that may need to be performed 50 times a day, even small inefficiencies hurt a lot. The fact that such an application can be used intuitively, on the other hand, is nice, but much less important than efficiency.

Now let's assume that the employees of the same company can perform some infrequent administrative tasks via some self-service applications. For example, they can create leave requests. Such self-service applications are rarely used, maybe once a month. Intuitive use is therefore quite important for such applications. We cannot assume that the user will remember how to use the application if he or she last used it four weeks ago. Efficiency is of much less importance here due to the infrequent use.

Such differences in the importance of UX aspects have an impact on the design of an application. Let's assume that a new feature is planned for a new release of the frequently used business application from our example above. The idea is to introduce a wizard to increase intuitive use. However, as a side effect, this wizard will replace some more flexible screen flows and thus require some additional clicks to complete typical tasks. Since efficiency is much more important than intuitive use for this application, it would be a bad idea to implement this feature. If a similar feature is planned for the self-service of the second example, things would be different. Here, it would be a good idea to implement such a feature, as it would support intuitive usage and the few additional clicks would not hurt since the application is rarely used.

For measuring UX, the importance of UX aspects is obviously an important information. When selecting a questionnaire for a UX evaluation, it is important that the scales of this questionnaire cover the UX aspects that are most important for the overall user satisfaction with the product. We will present in the following some research that tries to identify the most important UX aspects for typical product categories.

10.2 An empirical study

In the examples above, it is clear how the importance of the UX aspects varies between the two different example applications. However, in many cases, this is less obvious. We describe below a study by Winter, Hinderks, Schrepp, & Thomaschewski (2017) that investigated this dependency in a more systematic way.

Sixteen UX aspects were used for the study. These are largely identical to the UX aspects covered in Chapter 7. Each UX aspect was explained to the participants in the study with a short text:

- *Content Quality (CQ):* The information provided by the product are actual and of good quality.
- *Customization (CU):* I can adapt the product to my personal preferences or personal work style.
- *Perspicuity (PE):* It is easy to understand and learn how to use the product.
- *Efficiency (EF):* I can achieve my goals with minimal time and minimal physical effort. The product responds quickly to my input.
- *Immersion (IM):* When I deal with the product, I forget the time. I completely sink into the interaction with the product.
- *Intuitive Usage (IN):* I can use the product directly without any learning or help of other people.
- *Usefulness (US):* Using the product brings me advantages. It saves me time and effort and makes me more productive.
- *Novelty (NO):* The design of the product is interesting and unusual. The design catches my attention.
- *Beauty (BE):* The product is beautiful and attractive.
- *Identity (ID):* The product helps me to make contacts and to present myself positively.
- *Controllability (CO):* The product always reacts predictably and consistently to my input. I have full control over the interaction.

- *Stimulation (ST):* I find the product stimulating and exciting. It's fun to deal with the product.

- *Clarity (CL):* I find the user interface of the product looks tidy and clear.

- *Loyalty (LO):* Even if there are other equivalent products for the same tasks, I would not change the product.

- *Trust (TR):* My given data is in safe hands. The data will not be misused to harm me.

- *Value (VA):* I find the product makes a high-quality and professional impression.

Participants were asked to rate the importance of these quality aspects for several product categories. To give participants a clear idea of the categories, they were described with some examples of well-known products (participants of the study were German students, thus the examples were chosen with this target group in mind) from the category.

The following product categories and examples were provided:

- *Word Processing:* Word, MS PowerPoint, Latex, Writer (OpenOffice)

- *Spreadsheet:* Excel, Calc (OpenOffice)

- *Messenger:* WhatsApp, Facebook Messenger, Snapchat

- *Social Network:* Facebook, Xing, LinkedIn

- *Video Conferencing:* Skype, Facebook Video Call

- *Web Shops:* Amazon, Conrad, Redcoon, ebay

- *News Portals:* Spiegel.de, Zeit.de, Sueddeutsche.de

- *Booking Systems:* Bahn.de, Lufthansa.de, booking.com, hrs.de

- *Info web pages:* Club web-site, web-site of home town

- Learning platforms: Moodle, openelms

- *Programming tools:* VisualStudio, Eclipse

- Image processing: Photoshop, gimp

- *Online banking:* Online portal of own bank, Starmoney

- *Video portals:* Youtube, Netflix, Amazon Prime

- *Games:* WOW, Minecraft

The survey was conducted by sending an Excel list with the UX factors as rows and the product categories as columns. Each cell could be scored from -3 (totally unimportant) to +3 (very important). Participants could express that the product category and the UX factor did not match, so also had the option of not giving an importance rating. 58 students from a German university took part in the survey.

Figure 14 shows the average importance scores per UX factor and product category. As can be easily seen, the product categories differ largely concerning the importance ratings for the UX aspects. For related categories (e.g., word processing and spreadsheets), very similar patterns emerge. The type of product and thus the usage scenario associated with a product thus determines how important or unimportant certain UX aspects are rated on average.

The study found quite high standard deviations regarding importance judgments. Thus, there are obviously high individual differences regarding what is important.

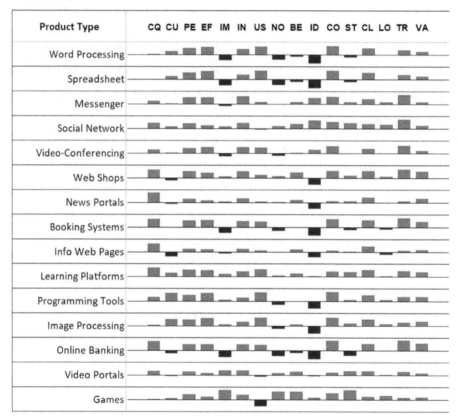

Figure 14: Mean importance rating (range from -3 to +3) for the UX aspects and product categories. The dividing line per category marks the 0 point of the scale, i.e. bars pointing upward represent positive values, bars pointing downward represent negative values.

10.3 Does the importance of UX aspects depend on culture?

A clear limitation of the study described in the previous section is that it was conducted with a special target group, namely German students. As always, this raises the question of whether the results can be generalized. It is currently not possible to answer this question completely, but at least with regards to the questions whether similar results will show in other cultures, some data are available.

In this section, we discuss whether the cultural background of a person has an impact on the importance of UX aspects for the overall satisfaction with a product.

But what is culture or a person's cultural background? Sounds like a self-evident concept, but if you look closer, it is not so easy to define. There are several theoretical attempts to define cultural dimensions that can be used to describe differences between cultural groups (Aparicio, Bacao & Oliveira, 2016; Cronje, 2010; Ertl & Helling, 2014; Tarhini, Hone & Liu, 2013; Zhao, Shen & Collier, 2014; Zhu, Ye & Chang, 2017). Probably the most popular and empirically best investigated theoretical description is the *cultural dimensions* of Hofstede (2001).

The basic idea of Hofstede's model is the assumption that culture is a set of learned traits that cause behaviors or reactions to certain situations to be more likely in some cultures than in others. Thus, differences between cultures result from differences in the core values shared by members of those cultures. This model includes six distinct cultural dimensions, for example *Power distance*, *Individualism/Collectivism* or *Uncertainty avoidance*. Hofstede provides concrete scores for these dimensions for several cultures. Based on these scores, Germany and Indonesia show quite different profiles (see Santoso & Schrepp, 2019 for a detailed discussion of the differences).

The relationship between the Hofstede dimensions and user interface design elements of web sites is discussed in Marcus & Baumgartner (2004) and Marcus & Gould (2001).

The Hofstede model is the best investigated cultural model in term of usability and UX. We used the Hofstede model mainly to provide some evidence that Germany and Indonesia are quite different when it comes to cultural dimensions. Thus, if there is an influence of culture to the importance of different UX aspects for certain product categories, this should become visible when we compare data from these two countries.

A replication for the study of Winter, Hinderks, Schrepp, & Thomaschewski (2017) was set up with a sample of 114 Indonesian students. The design of the study was identical to the design of the study with German students. Of course, the texts for the instructions and the description of the UX aspects were translated. The only other deviation was that some of the examples for the product categories had to be replaced because they were unknown in Indonesia.

Results showed that hedonic UX aspects seem to be of relatively higher importance for Indonesians than for Germans. This result is also in line with some previous research (Santoso, Schrepp, Hinderks, & Thomaschewski, 2017), but the effect size was rather small. The order of importance of UX aspects is similar in both samples. The rank-correlations were quite high. However, the general impression of which qualities are important does not seem to be strongly influenced by culture (see Figure 15).

Furthermore, the data of this study showed that the influence of cultural differences seems to be rather small compared to interindividual differences of persons within a culture or compared to product categories. Thus, personal preferences seem to be more important for the subjective importance of UX quality aspects than the influence of culture.

For designers, this is good news. In cases where design decisions are made based on the importance of UX aspects, it is quite likely that these decisions will be valid for other cultures. It seems unlikely that a completely different design is required for a product's UX to be acceptable in multiple cultures Inevitably, there may be details, such as the icons used in a user interface, that need to be considered because of cultural differences. However, the general impression on the UX qualities that are important seems to be not much influenced.

The same is obviously true for the selection of a UX questionnaire. If a questionnaire covers with its scales the aspects that are most important for the overall impression regarding UX in one culture, this is most likely also the case in another culture. Thus, we do not need to use different questionnaires (of course we need translated versions, but not completely different scales) when evaluating a product in different countries with different cultures.

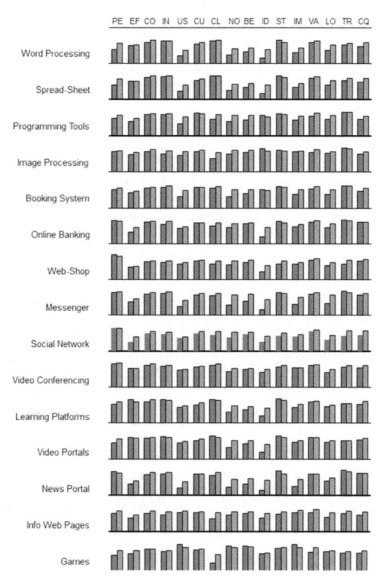

Figure 15: Average importance ratings from the German (dark grey) and Indonesian (light grey) sample.

10.4 Some concrete suggestions

As described above, knowing which UX aspects are important for a product can be quite helpful in making good design decisions. So, if you work as a designer, you will now ask how you can apply these results to your daily work. The same is true if you want to measure UX of a product. Of course, you will try to measure the aspects that are important from the user's point of view. In a practical application, you will of course know the type of your product. Our data from the studies described in this and the previous chapter can thus serve as a first indication concerning the aspects you should consider.

Table 2 shows, per product category, the UX aspects that had an average importance rating greater than 1.5 in both the German and Indonesian study (i.e. the UX aspect was rated as "Important" or "Very Important" on average).

Product category	Important UX Aspects
Word Processing	Perspicuity, Efficiency, Controllability, Intuitive Use, Usefulness, Clarity
Spread-Sheet	Perspicuity, Efficiency, Controllability, Usefulness, Clarity
Programming Tools	Perspicuity, Efficiency, Controllability, Usefulness, Clarity, Customization
Image-Processing	Perspicuity, Efficiency, Controllability, Usefulness, Clarity, Customization
Booking System	Perspicuity, Efficiency, Controllability, Intuitive Use, Usefulness, Clarity, Value, Trust, Content Quality
Online Banking	Perspicuity, Efficiency, Controllability, Intuitive Use, Usefulness, Clarity, Value, Trust, Content Quality
Web-Shop	Perspicuity, Controllability, Intuitive Use, Clarity, Beauty, Value, Trust, Content Quality
Messenger	Perspicuity, Efficiency, Controllability, Intuitive Use, Trust
Social Network	Perspicuity, Controllability, Intuitive Use, Identity, Stimulation, Trust, Content Quality
Video Conferencing	Efficiency, Controllability, Intuitive Use, Usefulness, Trust
Learning Platforms	Perspicuity, Efficiency, Controllability, Intuitive Use, Usefulness, Clarity, Trust, Content Quality
Video Portals	(nothing > 1.5, most important): Intuitive Use, Immersion, Trust, Content Quality
News Portals	Clarity, Content Quality
Info Web Pages	Clarity, Content Quality
Games	Perspicuity, Controllability, Novelty, Beauty, Stimulation, Immersion

Table 2: UX aspects with an importance rating > 1.5 for the different product categories.

The results of the study are helpful when it comes to determining which UX aspects are important for a product in the product categories described.

However, there are also some limitations that should be taken into account.

First, the participants of the study were students, i.e. rather young people with an above-average level of education. With other target groups, there may be deviations in the importance ratings. For example, if you are designing a website for retired people and then want to evaluate it, you should carefully check the relevance of the UX aspects.

Second, of course the list of product categories is not complete. In addition, there may be products that somehow fall between two categories.

In such cases, you can easily find out the relevance of UX aspects by a little study. Since you know the product (e.g. a website) for your evaluation project, it is sufficient to ask some people from your target audience about their importance ratings. This can often be done with a small study with the right target group (e.g. seniors) and requires usually not much effort.

For example, you can print the descriptions of the UX aspects on small cards. This stack of cards can then be ranked by a smaller number of people in the target group (with 10 participants you can already get useful results) in terms of their importance. By calculating the average ranking position (or scaling the data) per UX aspect, you can often get a good impression regarding the UX aspects you should include in the evaluation. If you don't have access to persons from the user group at this point, you can also ask one or more experts who know the product and user group well to do the ranking.

In addition to the user's perspective, there is always the manufacturer's perspective. From the manufacturer's perspective, however, there are often additional UX aspects that are not relevant for the users of the product but play an important role in positioning the product.

Let's look at an example. Suppose you want to evaluate a programming environment. As you can see from Table 2, originality and beauty do not matter from the user's point of view. Let's assume that the programming environment is a new product and will be introduced at large events by presentations and product demos. In such events it is important to get the attention of potential customers. Therefore, originality and beauty of the user interface are very relevant aspects for such product presentations. Thus, you should in this example also evaluate these aspects.

When it comes to deciding which UX aspects to consider for an evaluation, you always need to take two steps. First, determine which UX aspects are important from the perspective of the users of the product. Second, add the UX aspects that are relevant from a marketing perspective.

11 Relation of UX Questionnaires

In the previous chapters we have presented some UX questionnaires and described different UX aspects. Naturally, the question arises how well the different questionnaires cover these aspects. To provide a partial answer to this question, we present a study (see Schrepp, 2020 for the original paper) that compares a larger sample of 40 UX questionnaires.

The following questionnaires were included in the investigation: Attrakdiff2, AttrakWork, CSUQ, DEEP, e4, EUCS, HARUS, HED/UT, INTUI, ISOMETRICS, ISONORM, meCUE, MSPRC, NRL, PSSUQ, PUEU, PUTQ, QUESI, QUIS, SASSI, SUISQ, SUMI, SUPR-Q, SUS, UEQ, UEQ+, UES, UFOS, UMUX, Upscale, USE, UXNFQ, VISAWI, WAMMI, Web-Clic, WEBLEI, WEBQUAL, WEBUSE, WEQ, and WOOS. See Appendix 1 and Appendix 2 for more details on these questionnaires.

Together, these 40 questionnaires contain 1248 individual items. There are major differences concerning the number of scales. For example, SUS or UMUX contain only a single scale representing overall UX quality. Other questionnaires offer many scales, for example WEBQUAL with 9 scales or PUTQ with 8 scales. Some questionnaires even take a modular approach and offer a larger set of scales, for example meCUE with 9 scales or UEQ+ with currently 20 scales, that can be combined to create a concrete questionnaire. These modular questionnaires do not assume that all scales will be used in a single evaluation but allow UX researchers to select the scales they need for a concrete study.

We use the UX aspects described in Chapter 7 to compare the questionnaires: *Content Quality (CQ)*, *Customization (CU)*, *Perspicuity (PE)*, *Efficiency (EF)*, *Immersion (IM)*, *Intuitive Usage (IN)*, *Usefulness (US)*, *Novelty (NO)*, *Beauty (BE)*, *Identity (ID)*, *Controllability (CO)*, *Stimulation (ST)*, *Clarity (CL)*, *Loyalty (LO)*, *Trust (TR)*, and *Value (VA)*.

Some specific UX aspects such as *haptics* or *acoustics* are not considered, since they do only appear in one questionnaire.

For the following analysis, we counted for each questionnaire how many items represent each of the 16 UX aspects. Some items fit two aspects equally well. These are then counted with 0.5 in each of the aspects. All items that correspond to more than three UX aspects or to none of the 16 aspects were assigned to an *Others* category and were ignored in the further analysis. See the table in Appendix 3 for the assignment of items to UX aspects.

Now, for each questionnaire and UX aspect, we divide the number of items representing that aspect by the total number of items in the questionnaire. The resulting number shows how well the UX aspect is represented in a measurement by this questionnaire.

By calculating the Euclidian distance between two questionnaires, we obtain a distance matrix of all 40 questionnaires. We use multi-dimensional scaling (MDS) to visualize these data (Torgerson, 1958). An MDS is based on a set of objects (in the case of this study, the questionnaires) and a matrix showing the similarity or distance for each pair of objects (in our case, the distance matrix described above). The MDS then represents the objects as points in a two-dimensional space such that the Euclidean distance between the points reflects the similarity of the objects as closely as possible. Thus, it is mainly a visualization technique.

The MDS representation in Figure 16 allows for some nice interpretations. In the middle we find with the UEQ+ (20 modular scales with 80 items) and MSPRD (118 attributes used to describe UX), two frameworks that are intended to cover a wide range of UX aspects. In addition, WEBQUAL (9 scales with 36 items) is placed here, which also has a broad distribution of items across many UX aspects.

On the left side in the middle we see a larger group of questionnaires that have a strong focus on the pragmatic quality aspects *Efficiency*, *Perspicuity*, *Intuitive Use*, and *Controllability* and in addition contain many valence items.

The questionnaires on the left side above also have a strong focus on pragmatic aspects, but beyond that also on *Usefulness*.

Below on the left side we see a group of questionnaires that also strongly emphasize on pragmatic quality, but additionally contain many items representing *Content Quality* and *Clarity*. WEQ and WEBLEI also have their focus on pragmatic aspects and content quality, but do not take *Clarity* into account.

Moving to the right, we find questionnaires with a stronger focus on non-task related or hedonic UX aspects. On the bottom left is the VISAWI, which focus purely on beauty (visual aesthetics). A little bit further to the right is the AttrakDiff2 that contains only 7 items concerning pragmatic quality, but 21 concerning *Attractiveness*, *Stimulation,* and *Identity*.

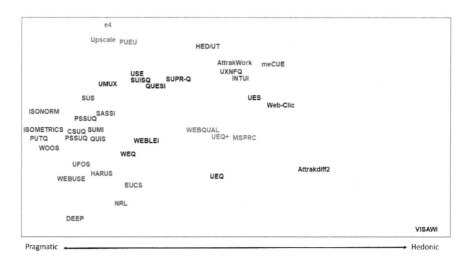

Figure 16: Multi-dimensional scaling of the 40 UX questionnaires.

At the top, there is a group of questionnaires that contain many items that measure non-task related qualities, especially *Stimulation*.

Thus, we can interpret the horizontal axis from left to right as a dimension representing a shift from the measurement of purely pragmatic UX aspects to purely hedonic UX aspects.

Of course, the assignment of the items to UX aspects is done only by the author and others may come to a different classification (for many items it seems to be unambiguous, but of course there are also items where there is room for discussion and different opinions are possible). In addition, other schemes to group the items can be developed and justified. Thus, other images concerning the semantic grouping of the UX questionnaires will be possible and have their justification as well. However, the current result is a first step to get a deeper understanding of how existing UX questionnaires relate to each other and also to show a method to derive such insights.

12 Different methods to measure UX

Questionnaires are a quite popular method to collect user feedback and to measure UX quality. But of course, there are other methods and feedback channels as well. It is important to understand the strengths and weaknesses of all feedback channels in order to make informed decisions based on the data.

We will describe some other popular methods to collect user feedback in this chapter and highlight their advantages and disadvantages compared to UX questionnaires. This will hopefully help to decide how to combine different methods to get a comprehensive picture of the current state of a product and make the best decisions regarding further investments to improve UX quality.

12.1 Customer Feedback

When the first version of a product is available and first customers start using it, feedback from those customers will start coming in immediately. The typical channels are error messages and contacts to the service channel. For products that are used in larger companies, for example larger business software solutions, there are dedicated roles (product owners or people from the development or sales organization) that are contacted directly by customer representatives.

For the long-term success of a product, such customer feedback is very important. You do not want to make your customers unhappy and lose them to the competition. Therefore, you better listen to what they have to say.

Such customer feedback is quite often very specific. Features that are missing or do not work as expected are reported. Concrete change requests are specified.

However, when it comes to UX, this feedback channel has some problematic aspects. First, this is a customer-initiated communication and in most cases the trigger for the customer is that something is not working as expected. Therefore, feedback over this channel is usually biased. Problems and weak points are reported, positive feedback is rare. Customers who are satisfied will not proactively contact you. Thus, if you only look at customer feedback, you will surely underestimate the real UX quality of your products.

For larger enterprise solutions, users at the customer site are usually not allowed to contact the manufacturer of the product directly. This is done either by people from their IT department or by some executives from the business units. Thus, the person giving feedback in such cases is often not the person using the product, and therefore the feedback concerning UX must be interpreted carefully.

12.2 Usability Tests

In a usability test, participants work on a series of prepared tasks with a product. They are observed and problems in the product are inferred from their behavior and comments while working on the tasks or in a final discussion at the end of the test.

Such a test is very well suited to uncover interaction problems. The observed problems usually provide clear indications on how the product can be improved. For example, assume that many participants did not find a functionality because the corresponding menu item was misunderstood. This is a clear result that also directly implies an action (renaming the menu item) to solve the issue.

A usability test creates mainly qualitative data, which makes it difficult to compare versions of a product or different products. Quantitative data can of course also be generated via measured processing times or error rates. However, these are usually based only on data from very few participants, which makes interpretation difficult.

In addition, the tasks in a usability test are often somewhat artificial and do not fully reflect the typical tasks of end users in their normal working environment. Very often, the recruited testers see the product or at least the tested scenario for the first time. This introduces some bias into the results, as problems with terminology and learnability are overestimated. Efficiency problems are often overlooked in such tests, as they often only become apparent when the same task must be done frequently on a typical workday.

Because it is a problem-centric approach, a usability test typically does not provide much information about the strengths of a product. It is possible to obtain qualitative statements concerning strong points of a product in a conversation with the participant after the tasks have been finished. But due to the test situation, even in such a conversation the participants usually focus strongly on the problems found.

Another limitation is that a usability test primarily reveals problems with pragmatic quality, i.e., problems in solving the prepared tasks. The participants and the test administrators are strongly focused on completing the test tasks. Thus, issues with non-task related UX aspects, for example visual aesthetics or stimulation, are usually ignored.

The effort per tested person is very high, i.e. it is usually not possible to test larger groups of persons. Usability tests with >20 participants will therefore be found rather rarely. Tests with 10-15 participants are typical.

What a usability test cannot provide is an indication of how a product evolves over time. It is difficult to compare the problems found in a usability test of a new product version with those of a previous version. Hopefully, the problems found in the last test have been solved. But new problems may have arisen due to new functionalities that were not present in the previous version.

12.3 Expert Reviews

There are several established expert review methods. For example, heuristic evaluation (Nielsen & Molich, 1990) or cognitive walkthrough (Wharton, Rieman, Lewis, & Polson, 1994).

In a heuristic evaluation, a small number of reviewers (experts) test the user interface of a product using some heuristics. In a cognitive walkthrough (Wharton, Rieman, Lewis, & Polson, 1994) several experts jointly go through typical application scenarios of a system from a user's point of view and try to uncover potential problems. Another common type of expert review is to simply check whether an application complies with a given UI guideline.

In all cases, the goal of an expert review is to identify, classify and prioritize the potential problems of a user interface and to make suggestions on how to avoid them. As a result of the review, a list of concrete problems is formulated, and a decision can be made about the severity of the problems and their prioritization for improving product quality.

Expert reviews are a very cost-effective way to evaluate the user experience of a product. All that is needed is a small number of reviewers who should know the usage scenarios of the application being evaluated. There is no need to recruit users. Experts can be experienced UX designers, but with the right guidance they can also be consultants or even end users (Mack & Nielsen, 1994).

A problem with expert reviews is that they focus heavily on classic usability aspects, for example problems with efficiency or learnability. Today, however, a much broader view of UX has prevailed. Aspects such as joy of use, original design, or beauty of the user interface also play a central role in evaluating the overall UX of a product. Classical heuristic evaluation and cognitive walkthrough methods are not designed to cover such aspects.

In Mayer, Schrepp & Held (2018) or Held, Schrepp & Mayalidag (2019) a method for expert review is described that explicitly considers hedonic UX factors and is equally suitable for evaluating the strengths and weaknesses of a product. This method uses the UX aspects described in Chapter 7 as heuristics.

Similar to usability tests, expert reviews focus strongly on existing weaknesses of a product and strengths are often not sufficiently considered. This can be quite problematic, because in eliminating existing problems, one can also unintentionally damage existing strengths of a product.

12.4 Strength and weaknesses of questionnaires

A questionnaire requires a very low effort per participant and is therefore suitable to investigate very large samples, which is important because the UX impression is often highly subjective. If the questionnaire is launched as an online survey directly within a product, it is possible to collect data from a significant part of the user base.

A standard questionnaire provides quantitative data. This makes it easy to compare different versions of a product or different products. Since the scale values range from negative to positive, a questionnaire is equally suitable for finding out the strengths and weaknesses of a product.

However, these scale values can only be used to define weak or strong areas and not concrete features of a product that are perceived as good or bad. If some free text questions are added asking for strong points or possible improvements, this can be compensated to a certain extent.

12.5 Comparison of the methods

The following table shows the strength and weaknesses of the different methods described above. Please note that there are several variations for all of these methods. The classification may not apply equally to all these variations.

Property	Customer Feedback	Usability Test	Expert Review	Quest-ionnaire
Data	Qualitative	Mostly Qualitative	Qualitative	Mostly Quantitative
Ability to produce concrete hints to improve the product	High	High	High	Low, only by special open questions
Ability to provide a balanced view on weak and strong points	Low, problem-centric	Low, problem-centric	Low, problem-centric	High, balanced method
Ability to detect issues concerning task related UX aspects	High	High	High	High
Ability to detect issues concerning non-task related UX aspects	Low	Low	Low	High
Ability to compare versions of a product or different products	Low	Low	Low	High
Effort per participant (study)	Low	High	Low	Low
Ability to detect if the UX of a product is sufficient	Low	Partly	Partly	Yes, if benchmark is available
Ability to determine if investments in UX have paid off	Low	Low	Low	High

Table 4: Comparison of the strength and weaknesses of different UX evaluation methods.

If you compare the strengths and weaknesses of usability tests and questionnaires, you can directly see that these two methods complement each other perfectly. Thus, it is a good practice to collect direct suggestions concerning detailed problems in frequent usability tests and to use questionnaires to measure whether the changes have the intended effects on satisfaction concerning UX. The same applies to a combination of expert reviews and questionnaires.

12.6 The truth lies in the combination of methods

As we have seen, there are several methods to gather information about the UX quality of a product. They all have their specific strength and weaknesses. As a general advice, it is dangerous to base important decisions regarding further developments of a product on only one of these methods. Always try to combine them to get a better overall picture of your products' current UX quality and the best way to improve it.

13 Quality Criteria for UX Questionnaires

The scales of UX questionnaires measure users' perception of their interaction with products. Thus, the questionnaire generates some scores that are then supposed to represent the underlying UX quality, for example efficiency, stimulation, or visual aesthetics.

We all know how to measure physical properties, for example the length of objects. When we use a measuring tape to measure the length of an object, we usually do not ask what property we are measuring and how accurate the result is. Of course, we measure a length and we know very well what that means. Of course, we do not assume that we are measuring with an accuracy to the hundredth of a millimetre. If we need such accuracy, we will use another tool for the measurement.

Things are not so clear with UX questionnaires. They are quite similar to psychological questionnaires or tests because they access subjective impressions of people. For such measurement methods, some additional difficulties have to be taken into account.

The traits measured by psychological tests or UX questionnaires are not so clearly defined. What exactly is meant by introversion as a personality trait or stimulation as a UX quality. In both fields, it must always be questioned whether a questionnaire really measures the qualities it claims to measure and how accurate the results are.

Various quality criteria have been developed to assess the quality of psychological tests. These quality criteria are discussed in this chapter. They also apply to UX questionnaires with some restrictions.

In one important point, UX questionnaires differ from classic psychological questionnaires or tests:

- In typical psychological tests, the test results are used to measure some characteristics of a person, for example intelligence, personality, or interests. Thus, the measurement of characteristics of a single person is the information that is interpreted and should therefore be reliable.

- UX questionnaires measure the impression of a group of users towards the UX of a product. UX researchers are typically not interested in the opinion of individual users. The result that is interpreted is the mean scores of the scales for a sufficiently large target group.

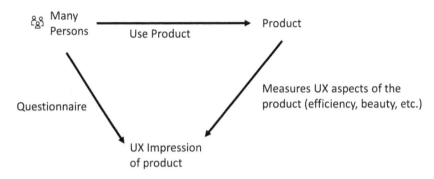

Figure 17: Differences between psychological test (top) and UX questionnaires (bottom).

This pattern is not unique to UX questionnaires. It also occurs, for example, in marketing questionnaires that measure brand impression. Another example are questionnaires in political science that measure people's trust in political institutions or organizations.

We now discuss the quality criteria for psychological tests and show to what extent they also apply to UX questionnaires.

13.1 Objectivity

Objectivity means that the result of the UX questionnaire (the scores for the scales) is independent of the person conducting the study or details in the setup of the study.

When conducting a study with an UX questionnaire, the researcher must of course be careful (as with any empirical method) not to unintentionally influence the participants. Most standard UX questionnaires have some pre-written instructions for the participants explaining how the questionnaire should be completed. Depending on the study and the product being evaluated, some additional instructions are usually necessary. These instructions are the main risk to objectivity. If these instructions are not properly formulated, they can influence the participants answers (more on that in Chapter 15).

However, the evaluation and interpretation of the results is often specified in a manual or handbook for the questionnaire. Sometimes such a handbook is not available, but the basic information is available in a scientific publication describing construction and application of the questionnaire. For the person conducting a study based on a standard UX questionnaire, there is not much room for own interpretations. Objectivity is therefore not really an issue when you use UX questionnaires.

13.2 Reliability

Reliability indicates how accurately a scale of a UX questionnaire measures the corresponding UX aspect. The basic idea is quite simple. If we apply a UX scale twice, we expect to get, with some small random fluctuations, almost the same result for both measurements (Lienert, 1989). If this is not the case, i.e., if the results of two independent measurements differ heavily, we cannot trust the measurement method and it is not wise to base important decisions on such results.

How can this intuitive concept of reliability be formalized to express numerically how reliable a questionnaire is? The basic assumption behind the definition of reliability in classical test theory is that a measured scale value O (average of all items in the scale) results from the true value T in the population under the influence of some random sampling or response errors E, or formally $O = T + E$. Please note that T and E are unknown hypothetical parameters, while O is an empirically observed value. The reliability of a UX scale X is then defined as the product moment correlation between X and the score of a parallel scale Y. A parallel scale is a scale that produces the same *true* value and the same variance of the observed scores (this represents the idea of repeated independent measurement with the same scale).

This is a rather intuitive theoretical formulization of reliability. However, it cannot be used to calculate the reliability of a UX scale in practice because there are no parallel scales. It is clear that any measurement with a questionnaire will have an impact on the participant. The participant will remember some of his or her answers to the items. Or the questions will trigger some reflection on the product, which will be stored in memory. Thus, if you apply a questionnaire once, it will influence a second application of the same or a similar questionnaire. In practice, independent, repeated measurements on the same UX aspects for the same product with the same participants are not possible. Thus, reliability cannot be calculated directly based on the theoretical definition. In addition, reliability in the sense of the definition above cannot be calculated on the basis of a single application of a test scale.

But it is possible to use test results to estimate a lower bound for scale reliability (Sijtsma, 2009). Cronbach's Alpha coefficient α (Cronbach, 1951) is such a lower bound for the, thus Rel(O) >= α. The standardized Cronbach α coefficient is defined as:

$$\alpha = \frac{n * \bar{r}}{(1 + (n - 1) * \bar{r})}$$

In this formula, $\bar{r}$ is the mean correlation of all n items of the scale. Theoretically, α ranges from $-\infty$ to 1, but except for unrealistic cases where the mean correlation between all items of a scale is negative, the value will be between 0 and 1.

Standardized Cronbach's α can be computed easily. It does not require two data collections, such as reliability concepts based on the paradigm of retest-reliability (e.g., Horst, 1966). This and the simple idea behind the coefficient made it quite popular. In applications of a questionnaire, the value is reported to show that a scale has *sufficient reliability* or *internal consistency* for the product being studied and can thus be interpreted.

Although almost all UX questionnaires (this is also true for many questionnaires used in social sciences) use Cronbachs Alpha coefficient, there are some issues with this coefficient. We describe only some of these issues. For a detailed overview and a more in-depth methodological discussion, see Schrepp (2020).

First, if we assume that we have a fixed mean correlation between items, then we can easily see from the definition of α that the coefficient increases with the number of items. This is reasonable, since the influence of response errors on the scale mean decreases with an increasing number of items in the scale. Thus, the reliability of a scale should increase as the number of items increases. On the other hand, considering α alone is not sufficient to judge if a scale in an UX questionnaire is well-designed. A scale with α = 0.83 looks impressive. But if this result comes from 20 items with a mean correlation of 0.2, this does not really speak for a high quality of the scale.

Second, there is no good answer to the obvious question of what a specific value of α means. Is a value of 0.6 an indication of sufficient reliability? Some cookbook like suggestions are repeated over and over in papers. For example, George and Mallery (2003) provide the following rules of thumb: α > 0.9 (Excellent), > 0.8 (Good), > 0.7 (Acceptable), > 0.6 (Questionable), >

0.5 (Poor), and < 0.5 (Unacceptable). Many research papers cite Nunnally (1978) in the sense that an α greater than 0.7 is an indicator of sufficient scale reliability. But the original argumentation in Nunnally (1978) is much more elaborate. He clearly pointed out that the required level of α depends on how critical the decisions are that are made based on the test result and does not argue in the direction of a general acceptable cut point of 0.7 (for details, see Lance, Butts & Michels, 2006). In fact, there is no clear methodological foundation for any statement like α *should exceed x*. All such suggestions are just conventions (Cortina, 1993).

As mentioned above, UX questionnaires measure the impression of a group of users towards some UX-related aspects of a product. Thus, Cronbach's α (this also applies to other methodological concepts of reliability) depends not only on the scale, but also on the product. If we measure several products with the same UX scale, then the observed α values may change. And this change is not just a random change due to some measurement errors, but results from the specific context of the evaluation, that is, the product that is being evaluated. For some specific empirical examples of this dependency, see Schrepp (2020).

For this reason, α can never be interpreted as a quality criterion of a given UX scale or questionnaire. Even if authors report high α values in some initial evaluation studies of a new questionnaire, this does not mean that this will apply to all types of products. In fact, it is only valid for products more or less similar to those being evaluated in the initial studies. Thus, if you use a UX questionnaire, try to check α for the scales used in your study.

But even here, you should be careful. If your sample size is small, then a high value for Alpha should not be interpreted in the sense *reliability of the scale for our data is high and we can trust the results,* nor does a low level of Alpha mean *reliability of the scale is low and we should not interpret the results.* Alpha is quite sensitive to sampling effects, and if your sample size is small, it should be interpreted carefully.

The calculation of α is based on the correlations of the items in a scale and such correlations are quite unstable if the sample size is small. Schönbrodt & Perugini (2013) showed in a simulation study that in typical psychological research situations up to 250 data points are required to get a stable estimate of the true correlation. Of course, α is based on the intercorrelations of all items in a scale and may thus be more stable than a single correlation, but it can be expected that the coefficient will be quite sensitive against sampling effects.

When using UX questionnaires, researchers are not interested in individual opinions concerning UX, but always in the average opinion of a target group. We can get quite stable measurements of a scale mean even if the Alpha value for the scale is quite low. Thus, in UX research, we can accept scales that have only moderate Alpha levels.

We illustrate this with a small simulation study (for details, see Schrepp, 2020). For the simulation, we use a scale from the UEQ (4 items, 7-point answer scale with range 1 to 7) and data from a study with 240 participants. The scale mean is 5.64, the standard deviation is 1.14, and Cronbach's α is 0.81, indicating a high reliability if we follow the cookbook suggestions described above.

Random samples of 20, 30, 40, and 50 participants are drawn from the complete data set. Such sample sizes are not atypical for UX evaluations in practice. For each sample size, 200 such samples were drawn and α and the scale mean were calculated. These values are plotted in Figure 18.

The observed scale means, standard deviations (in parenthesis) and values for α from the sample were as follows:

- *Sample size 20:* 5.62 (0.26) for scale mean, 0.79 (0.12) for α
- *Sample size 30:* 5.61 (0.23) for scale mean, 0.8 (0.09) for α
- *Sample size 40:* 5.62 (0.19) for scale mean, 0.79 (0.08) for α
- *Sample size 50:* 5.63 (0.17) for scale mean, 0.8 (0.08) for α

However, a closer look at the results in the single samples in Figure 18 show a huge variation in the estimated Alpha value. Compared to the huge variation of Alpha, the scale mean is quite stable.

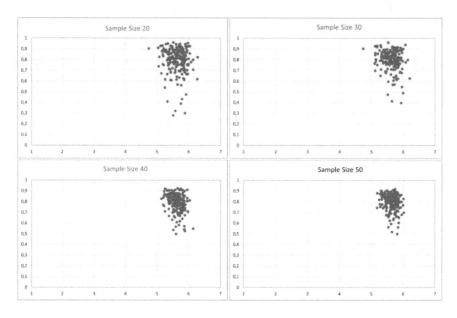

Figure 18: Alpha value and scale mean for 200 simulations with different sample sizes. The horizontal axis represents the scale mean (7-point Likert scale with values from 1 to 7) and the vertical axis the α value.

As the example shows, α is extremely sensitive to sampling. With a sample size of 20, the α values varied between 0.28 and 0.95, that is, nearly the full range of possible α values is observed. In comparison, the computed scale mean is quite stable (it varied between 4.74 and 6.28). Even with a sample size of 50, there is still a relatively huge variation in the α values.

Thus, if the sample size is small and a low α value is observed, there is a high probability that this is due to some sampling effects and not an indicator of a low scale reliability. In these cases, UX researchers should better not pay too much attention to α.

13.3 Validity

A UX scale is valid if it measures what it claims to measure. Of course, that is the most important quality criterion for any measurement method. Assume we have a UX scale that claims to measure users' subjective impression on the efficiency of interaction with a product. If we apply this scale to two products that undoubtedly have different levels of efficiency, and we see no differences in the measured scale values, then obviously this scale is not useful. In this case, it simply cannot be used to distinguish between products with good and poor efficiency.

The bad news is that it is often quite difficult to *prove* that a scale is valid, or to put it in more scientific terminology, to provide evidence of validity.

There are several ways to provide evidence that a UX scale is valid. A quite simple method is to find a set of products that differ concerning the UX aspect measured by the scale. This requires that a reliable external source of information is available, for example expert judgements or data from existing studies concerning these products, that shows these differences. Then the products are evaluated with the UX scale and if the differences in the measured scale values vary accordingly to the expectations, this is considered as an indicator for validity.

If there are already validated scales in other questionnaires available that measure the same UX aspects, this allows a fairly simple investigation of validity. Just measure a couple of products with both scales and the correlation between measurements will somehow indicate if both scales measure the same thing. Since we assume that the old scale is already validated, this can then be interpreted as an indication of the validity of the new scale.

A similar, but less convincing idea is to use correlations to some overall ratings. Thus, to check whether the measured scale value shows a high correlation with overall satisfaction or overall UX impression of a product. This shows that the scale is related to UX but is only a weak indicator of a valid measurement of a particular aspect that is semantically clearly defined, for example, efficiency, controllability, or fun of use.

In my opinion, in UX research the validity of a scale is less critical than in psychological tests. Such tests often attempt to measure latent psychological constructs that are poorly defined and difficult to observe, for example, introversion or neuroticism of a person. The concepts are often intuitively defined and linking the items in the scale to the latent construct is sometimes hard to justify.

UX scales measure the impressions of users towards their interactions with a product. They are typically much easier to understand and define. Thus, there is often a certain face validity and just a look at the items shows a clear connection with the underlying UX aspect.

13.4 Other criteria

Objectivity, reliability and validity are the most important quality criteria for a UX questionnaire. However, they cover more the scientific perspective on a measurement instrument. In practice, UX questionnaires are often used in product development to get an impression concerning of the current state of a product in terms of UX. In such cases, there are often not such high requirements for the accuracy of the measurement, but some practical considerations are definitely important here. We will shortly discuss some quality criteria that influence how easy it is for UX researchers to use a questionnaire in their research projects.

13.4.1 Is the effort for participants acceptable?

Of course, the time required to answer all items in a questionnaire is quite a critical point for practical applications. If the questionnaire is too long, participants may get bored, which decreases the quality of their responses. Or the drop-out rate in an online questionnaire may be too high.

But there is, of course, a trade-off between the length of a questionnaire and the accuracy of the measurement. The more items you use, the lower is the influence of some inaccurate answers to the overall result and the more detailed is the information you get.

Some UX questionnaires contain many items, sometimes up to 100. This gives quite detailed information about a product, but makes them unusable for certain scenarios, for example to be used as an online questionnaire launched directly inside the product. If such questionnaires are used by paid testers at the end of a usability test, the length is not an issue.

Therefore, the absolute length of a questionnaire or a scale is not a good indicator of questionnaire quality. We need to consider the length in relation to the proposed scenario and the requirements concerning the adequacy of the results.

13.4.2 Is the semantic meaning of the scales clearly described?

When we measure the UX of a product with a questionnaire containing different scales, it is important that the meaning of these scales is clearly described. First, we need to communicate results to other people involved in the design or development of a product, for example developers, product owners, or managers. They need to understand what we have measured, and they will potentially base expensive decisions about further developments on these results. Thus, it is mandatory that the meaning of each scale is clearly described in a terminology that can be understood by people outside the UX profession.

There are two potential problems for practical applications. First, scales sometimes contain items with quite different meanings. For example, the scale *System Capabilities* in the QUIS, which contains items related to efficiency or technical performance, controllability and required expertise.

In such cases, it is inherently difficult to communicate the meaning of the scale. Second, sometimes scale names are misleading. This is not so problematic since you always can change them in the internal communications. But you need to be aware to this. Always check the items carefully and derive a meaningful alternative if the original scale name is problematical to communicate the results.

13.4.3 Is the supporting material sufficient?

A UX questionnaire is a tool that UX researchers use to collect data. Of course, the usability of this tool itself is also important. Different questionnaires offer varying levels of support. Sometimes there are only a few (or sometimes only one) scientific papers describing the creation and validation of the questionnaire. Some questionnaires offer a manual or handbook that describes how to use the questionnaire in research and how to analyse and interpret the data. Some of the newer questionnaires additionally offer data analysis tools (often in the form of an Excel-Sheet). You simply load the data into the tool an all required data analysis steps are done by the tool.

For practical use, it can save much effort and avoid many errors if the supporting material is of high quality.

13.4.4 Translations

Especially in multi-national companies it is quite likely that you have to use the same questionnaire in different languages. It is of course important that a participant in a study can fill out the questionnaire in his or her natural language. Even if there is an official company language, this avoids misunderstandings of items and improves data quality.

Let's take a look at an example. A company with locations in different countries offers an intranet to make important information available to employees. This intranet is to be evaluated concerning UX with a questionnaire and the evaluation should take place in all locations.

If you use a standard questionnaire it is helpful if there are already approved translations available. Otherwise, you will have to do the translation yourself (see Chapter 18), which involves a lot of effort.

13.4.5 Costs

Of course, licence fees for a questionnaire can be problematic. The good news is that most UX questionnaires are free to use. Some even offer a website where you can download the supporting material, for example a handbook or a data analysis sheet, for free. Some questionnaires require special materials for the data analysis that must be purchased.

Just a tip. The fact that you have to pay for a questionnaire does not necessarily mean that it is of superior quality. Thus, before you spend money, check if there is a free alternative.

14 How to Develop new Questionnaires

We described a number of standard questionnaires in Chapter 3. In Chapter 5, we have shown how to extend these with some questions that are relevant to the actual study or the product being evaluated. For many research situations, this will already be sufficient. However, there may be situations in which there is no adequate standard questionnaire that allows to measure the intended UX aspects. In such situations, the only chance is to create such a questionnaire yourself. We will describe different methods to do this in this chapter. Which method you should choose depends on your time and resources, and the accuracy of the measurement required for your use case.

If you do not want to measure quantitative data, then a careful design process as described in this chapter is usually not necessary. Simply follow the suggestions in Chapter 5 for formulating good questions, conduct a brief pretest of those questions, and you're done.

If you want to measure UX aspects quantitatively, you should try to follow an established process for constructing the questionnaire. This process should limit the risk that your questionnaire will not meet the quality criteria described in Chapter 13. Please note that careful construction of a questionnaire takes time. If you need the questionnaire in a few days, then the methods described in this chapter will not work!

Some of the methods described in this chapter are scientifically sound ways to construct a questionnaire to measure UX quality. But not all of them! As a UX researcher, you will sometimes face situations where you need to develop a *reasonable but not perfect* instrument (given the specific situation in your project) and do not have the time to go through a lengthy construction process. Practically, the quality required for your newly developed questionnaire depends on the decisions you want to base on the measurement!

14.1 Combine different questionnaires

Sometimes the problem that there is no standard questionnaire that can be used to measure all relevant UX aspects for a product can be solved simply by using several different questionnaires in succession. However, this is not always a good idea. Let us illustrate this with two examples.

As a first example, let's assume that we are conducting a usability test for a product. After the test sessions, we want to collect quantitative data concerning the usability of the product. Since the visual design of the product has changed massively compared to the previous release, we also want to measure the visual aesthetics of the product. In this case, it is appropriate to apply the SUS to measure overall usability and the VISAWI to measure visual aesthetics. Since the questionnaires are handed out after a usability test, the time required to fill out the 10 items of the SUS and the 18 items of the VISAWI is acceptable.

As a second example, let's assume we have a new release of a business application. We have the same intention as described in the last example, i.e. we want to measure overall usability and visual design. But in this example, we want to launch the questionnaire directly in the system. Thus, a few minutes after the user logs in, we automatically start a dialog (triggered by the system). In this dialog we ask the user to give us feedback on the application. If the user agrees (otherwise we simply close the dialog), we open the questionnaire in the browser. Using the SUS and VISAWI in this situation is very problematic. The user would see some demographic questions, 10 items of the SUS and 18 items of the VISAWI, plus maybe some comment fields. The number of users willing to complete this survey will be small or close to zero. Even if we use the short form of the VISAWI with only 4 questions, the questionnaire will be quite long.

If you have access to a sufficient number of users and only need independent assessments (i.e., you do not need an assessment of usability and aesthetics for each participant), it makes sense to conduct two surveys. For example, one can randomly decide per participant whether he or she will only see the VISAWI or the SUS questions. Thus, whether it is advisable to use multiple UX questionnaires depends on the specific context of an evaluation project.

There is an additional problem related to the use of different questionnaires in one study. This can also be explained in the example above, where SUS and VISAWI have to be combined. Both questionnaires use items with statements that participants can agree or disagree with. SUS uses a 5-point answer scale, while VISAWI uses a 7-point answer scale. Both questionnaires offer a benchmark (see Chapter 3), but the types of benchmark are quite different. The SUS benchmark provides a detailed comparison to average products with different categories (see Table 1 in Chapter 3). The VISAWI benchmark supports per sub-scale and for the overall aesthetics value only the decision whether the evaluated product is above or below average. Thus, you can't provide a consistent reporting of the results concerning usability and aesthetics. You have to explain the two ways of representing the results in both questionnaires separately. This makes it difficult to create and present a consistent picture of the results.

14.2 Using modular frameworks

Another option to create a questionnaire that fits your needs is to use a modular framework, for example the UEQ+. This is simply a collection of scales that can be combined by the researcher to create a questionnaire that best fits the needs of specific product evaluations. There is not much to do here. The scales are predefined, which means that you only need to select the scales you need.

Selection of the scales may be based on existing research (see Chapter 10) or on your own understanding of the product being evaluated. Of course, it may happen that the UEQ+ covers most relevant aspects with its scales, but you need to measure in addition an aspect that is not included in the UEQ+. In this case, you can construct your own scales with reasonable effort (see Schrepp & Thomaschewski, 2019). The procedure is similar to the construction of the UEQ (for one scale only) described later in this chapter. It is, of course, much easier than constructing a complete questionnaire.

To illustrate the idea, let's return to the example from the previous section. Our goal is to evaluate usability and visual aesthetics. For usability, we limit ourselves to scales for *Efficiency*, *Dependability*, and *Intuitive Use*. When we select these scales and the scale for *Visual Aesthetics* from the UEQ+ framework, we obtain a questionnaire as shown in Figure 19.

A clear advantage compared to combining different questionnaires is that the resulting questionnaire is quite short (it does not include items that are not needed) and that the format of the different scales is consistent.

Another questionnaire that follows such a modular approach (but has fewer scales available) is the meCUE.

To achieve my goals, I consider the product as

slow ○○○○○○○ fast

inefficient ○○○○○○○ efficient

impractical ○○○○○○○ practical

cluttered ○○○○○○○ organized

In my opinion, the reactions of the product to my input and command are

unpredictable ○○○○○○○ predictable

obstructive ○○○○○○○ supportive

not secure ○○○○○○○ secure

does not meet expectations ○○○○○○○ meets expectations

In my opinion, the visual design of the product is

ugly ○○○○○○○ beautiful

lacking style ○○○○○○○ stylish

unappealing ○○○○○○○ appealing

unpleasant ○○○○○○○ pleasant

In my opinion, using the product is

difficult ○○○○○○○ easy

illogical ○○○○○○○ logical

not plausible ○○○○○○○ plausible

inconclusive ○○○○○○○ conclusive

Figure 19: Items from a questionnaire derived from the UEQ+ with the scales *Efficiency, Dependability, Visual Aesthetics,* and *Intuitive Use.* The optional item concerning the importance of each scale is not used in this example.

14.3 Construct a questionnaire by user centered design

If you use your questionnaire as an online questionnaire, then it is immediately clear that the questionnaire is also a user interface. You place some fields for data entry and some controls for submitting or canceling the responses. However, the intention is somewhat different from a normal input form in an application. However, it is still possible to use methods known from user-centered design to create a UX questionnaire.

Let's go through an example to explain the method. We will first describe the use case for the questionnaire in the example and then the design process.

With many complex products, you cannot assume that a user will be able to use them intuitively. Users have to learn something, even if the user interface of the product is well designed. But to use the product, the user has to acquire some concepts or learn some terminology. Or it must be explained how the concepts in the product map to the real-world problems that the user wants to solve with the help of the product. Typical examples of such products are development environments or complex business software packages.

In such cases, a popular approach is to offer some tutorials through different channels. On the one hand, these tutorials explain how to use the product. But on the other hand, they also arouse interest in the product. Thus, they support marketing to create awareness (especially if you offer a free trial) and help customers to get started quickly. Therefore, it is quite interesting to find out how satisfied users are with such a tutorial. It is unclear which aspects are important for the UX of a tutorial. So, we don't know what to ask in a questionnaire.

We describe in the following the construction of a questionnaire designed to measure the quality of tutorials intended to help users to learn how to use a development environment. Users should be able to provide feedback when they reach the end of a tutorial. To ensure that learners provide feedback and the dropout rate is reasonable, the questionnaire should be short.

The first question that needs to be answered in the construction is what aspects are important for developers when using a tutorial to learn a development tool? To answer this question, a series of short interviews was conducted with 25 software developers. Only such participants were accepted who claimed to have experience with such tutorials and to use them regularly to learn about new development tools.

During the interview, participants were asked concerning good and bad aspects of tutorials for development tools. The specific questions were:

- A good tutorial should …
- A good tutorial should not …

The participant could make verbal comments to complete the sentence, which were noted by the interviewer.

The comments were then clustered in a session with respect to their semantic meaning. Based on the results, it was then decided to use 4 of these clusters (those with the most comments) for the construction of the questionnaire. Semantically these clusters represent:

- *Adequate Length:* A good tutorial should be as short as possible and contain only the most important facts.

- *Structure:* A good tutorial should be clearly structured and presented as a logical sequence of simple steps.

- *Interest:* A good tutorial should be interesting and should motivate the reader to learn more about the topic.

- *Transparency:* The preconditions and the time required to go through the tutorial should be clearly visible before the tutorial is started.

The comments per cluster were used to formulate some items covering aspects of the cluster. Some internal expert rounds were used to select two items per clusters. Since the items should be easy to understand some interviews with a small number of developers were done. Here the items were presented and possible comprehension problems or ambiguities in the wording were identified. Based on the results, some reformulations were made, which were then revisited. Thus, it was an iterative process.

Then an initial questionnaire was created with these 8 items. In addition, a NPS question *How likely is it that you would recommend this tutorial to a friend or colleague?* was added.

In an initial study, 71 computer science students completed this raw questionnaire. Students were asked to rate the last tutorial they had used.

A principal component analysis (this is explained later in this chapter in detail) of the results showed that one component explained the data sufficiently well, i.e., showed that it was sufficient to use a single scale to represent the quality of a tutorial. Items showed quite high correlations. The four items with the highest loading on the component were selected to represent the scale:

- The tutorial contains only relevant information.
- I was satisfied with the duration of the tutorial.
- In my opinion the tutorial was well-structured.
- The tutorial motivates me to learn more about this topic.

A principal component analysis requires a larger data set. If the necessary resources for data collection are not available or you do not want to engage in this procedure, you can also use the method described in the next section to select well-fitting items.

To validate the 4-item scale for tutorial quality, it was used to assess a number of different tutorials. The results showed that scale consistency (measured with the Cronbach Alpha Coefficient, see Chapter 13) was sufficiently high. In addition, the scale was able to distinguish between tutorials of different quality and the scale score correlated highly with NPS scores for the tutorials.

To sum up, the method consists of several steps. First, you conduct a series of qualitative interviews to determine which elements are important for the overall quality you want to measure. Second, you cluster the results of the interviews and formulate items that represent the most important clusters. Third, create a draft version of the questionnaire that includes these items. Forth, ask a larger number of participants to rate several products using the draft version. Fifth, select the best items by some data analytical heuristic, for example based on correlations to an external criterion or through structural data analytic methods, like principal components analysis.

14.4 Determine items that discriminate best

If you have a good understanding of what UX aspects you want to measure and a good list of potential items that describes those UX aspects, then there is a simple method to construct a good questionnaire. As an example, the construction process of the SUS is described here following Brooke (1996). For a detailed description of the SUS, see Chapter 3.

Let's first describe the basic idea underlying the construction process. Suppose you want to construct a scale that measures a UX quality. You have a clear understanding of what this quality means and have used this to construct a larger set of potential items. Now you want to select from this set a subset of items that are best suited to measure the UX aspect.

What is a good item? Of course, the scale should be able to discriminate between different products. An item supports this if the score of the item discriminates between products perceived as good with respect to the intended UX aspects and products perceived as poor with respect to this aspect.

The basis of the construction for SUS (Brooke, 1986) was a list of 50 potential items (statements with a 5-point answer scale) representing usability aspects of a system.

Two systems were identified on the basis of expert judgement regarding their usability. One system was easy to use accordingly to this judgement, the other almost impossible to use. Thus, these two products represent the extreme poles on an assumed usability scale.

For the process to select the best items, a relatively small sample of 20 persons (which included people with a wide range of technical skills) evaluated both systems against all 50 potential items.

The mean rating of each item was then calculated and *The items leading to the most extreme responses from the original pool were then selected* (Brooke, 1996). Thus, the selected items are the items that best discriminate between the highly usable and the highly unusable system in terms of mean item score.

We have focused on the main idea of this construction process because it can be reused for the construction of new questionnaires. Some details specific to the special case of SUS can be found in the original publication by Brooke (1996).

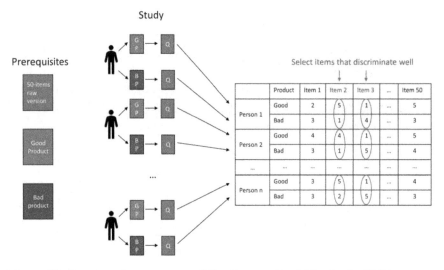

Figure 20: Construction process of the System Usability Scale (SUS).

This construction process is simple and direct. It requires that the item pool used to select the items is already of good quality, i.e., that these items cover what you want to measure. In addition, the products you use to determine which items discriminate best must be representative for the domain in which you intend to apply the questionnaire.

Please note that SUS is still currently the most popular questionnaire for measuring usability! Thus, if these conditions are met, you can get a pretty good result with such a simple method.

14.5 Using Principal Component Analysis

Sometimes it is not entirely clear which combination of UX aspects should be used for a measurement. In such cases, an approach that constructs the scales and items in parallel makes sense. As an example, we show the construction process of the UEQ. Again, we focus on the main process. For details of the creation process, see Laugwitz, Held & Schrepp (2006) or Laugwitz, Schrepp & Held (2008).

When the construction of the UEQ started, the concept of UX was not as well understood as it is today. At that time, interest in new UX aspects (hedonic aspects, such as fun of use or aesthetics) that are not related to classical usability increased strongly. But the nature of these new UX aspects was not well understood. In addition, it was somewhat unclear how these new criteria relate to the classical usability criteria.

The goal of the construction process was to create a questionnaire that could be used for work-related products and thus considers classical usability aspects, but also include the most important hedonic aspects. Which UX aspects should be included was unclear and the scales should therefore result from the construction process.

The questionnaire should measure subjective impressions of users, should be usable as an online questionnaire started directly in the product and as a paper-pencil form after usability tests. Thus, it should be short. Therefore, it was decided to use semantic differentials as item format.

Before we proceed, we need to explain a basic statistical technique underlying such empirical construction processes (quite a few UX questionnaires are constructed this way, so it is useful to understand at least roughly how it works). The technique is called *Principal Component Analysis* (Pearson, 1901 or Hotelling, 1933). We will not go into details of the calculations or the statistics behind the method. We will only explain the basic principle behind it. This is sufficient to apply this method to the practical construction of a UX questionnaire (the analysis itself can be done in any advanced statistical package).

The basic idea of a Principal Component Analysis (short PCA) is to condense the information contained in data sets with many variables (in our case potential items for a UX questionnaire) to a smaller and easier to interpret set of components. The components themselves are calculated as linear combinations of the items.

An analysis with PCA is exploratory in the sense that it suggests an optimal representation of the original complex data set. A PCA suggests how many components should be used and which variables should be selected to represent the components.

In the first step of a PCA, the data matrix (the correlations of the variables in this data matrix) is analyzed. It is calculated how well possible components explain the variance in the data. A scree plot (see the line graph in Figure 21) or scree test (Cattell, 1966) is used to determine how many components should be used to represent the data. The higher the value for a component (they are shown in order from largest to smallest) in the scree plot, the more variance in the data is explained by that component, i.e., the higher is the predictive value of the component. The point beyond which the other components differ only slightly is used to determine an optimal number of components (see the arrow inside the line chart in Figure 21). There are alternative methods for determining the optimal number of factors, such as the Kaiser-Guttman criterion (Guttman, 1954), which selects all components that have a value greater than 1 in the scree plot. In fact, there is no ultimate way to determine the optimal number of components. There are some good heuristics, but to some extent this is also a decision of the researcher.

After the optimal number of components is determined, the items that show high component loadings on one component and low loadings on the other components are selected to represent the component (the researcher decides how many to use). The loadings of an item can be interpreted in terms of how well the item represents the component.

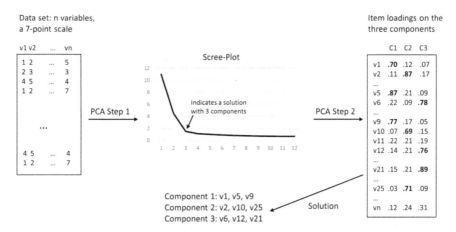

Figure 21: Basic steps of a Principal Component Analysis (PCA).

Of course, this is only a rough description of PCA. It attempts to cover the main ideas so that you can apply the method to questionnaire construction. If you are interested in the mathematical details, most statistical test books contain a detailed description of the method.

Now we can proceed with the description of the construction of the UEQ. In the first step of the process, 15 UX experts were interviewed in two brainstorming sessions. The experts were asked to propose terms related to user experience. The list of suggested terms was then consolidated by a smaller team. This list contained 221 adjectives.

In a second round, 7 UX experts were asked to select the 25 terms they thought were most relevant from the list. They could also mark an unlimited number of terms as not appropriate with a veto. Adjectives that appeared less than twice in the top 25 lists or received more than one veto were removed. For the remaining 80 attributes, the best matching antonym was determined (items should take the form of semantic differentials). The order of the adjective pairs and the polarity of each pair was then randomized. This procedure resulted in an initial 80-item draft version of the questionnaire.

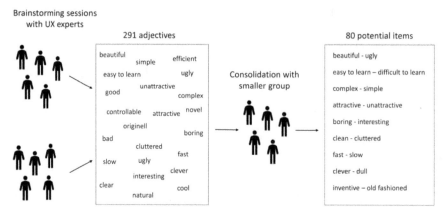

Figure 22: Construction of a first draft version by UX experts.

This 80-item draft version of the questionnaire was used in six investigations with different products (for details see Laugwitz, Schrepp & Held, 2008). In total, 153 participants provided complete data sets.

The item set contained items measuring general attractiveness or valence toward a product. These items naturally show high correlations with all other items. Therefore, the item set was divided into two subsets. The first subset contains 14 items that represent judgement on a pure acceptance/rejection dimension. These valence items do not provide information about the reason for accepting or rejecting a product. Examples of items from the first subset are *good/bad* or *pleasant/unpleasant*. The second subset contains the remaining 66 items from the item pool.

A PCA of the first subset of items suggests a solution with one component. This component explained 60% of the observed variance in the data. The corresponding scale is called *Attractiveness*. The six items with the highest loading on the component were selected to represent this scale.

The PCA of the second subset of items suggests a solution with five components. These five components explain 53% of the observed variance in the data. The scales corresponding to the components are named according to the items that showed the highest loading on the component as *Perspicuity* (examples for items: *easy to learn / difficult to learn, complicated / easy*), *Dependability* (*unpredictable / predictable, secure / not secure*), *Efficiency* (*fast / slow, inefficient / efficient*), *Novelty* (*inventive / conventional, conservative / innovative*) and *Stimulation* (*boring / exciting, not interesting / interesting*).

Four items with high loadings on the scale and low loadings on all other scales were selected to represent each scale.

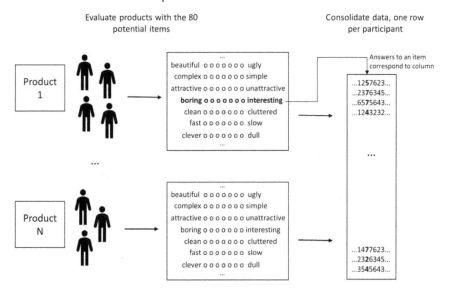

Figure 23: Evaluation of different product with the 80 potential items.

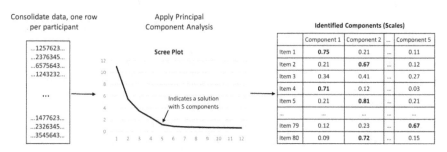

Figure 24: Construction of the scales using Principal Component Analysis.

This method requires some effort. First, you must construct a set of candidate items through a careful process. Second, you need to collect data for a set of products using this draft item set. Since items are always interpreted in the context of the product being evaluated, the correlations between two items may vary between different products. Since these correlations are the basis for the construction of components in PCA, it is important not to base the item selection process on a single product. You must have a sample of products that somehow represent the products for which you will later use the questionnaire. Then the scales and the items are extracted by a PCA and the result is validated in some studies.

This approach has the clear advantage that it constructs the most relevant scales and the items that best represent these scales empirically. Thus, if you are unsure which aspects you should measure for a particular product area, this method has the clear advantage that the constructed scales have empirical relevance. The disadvantage of the method is of course the high effort for construction.

This method of constructing questionnaires is quite similar to the typical approach to construct psychological test (which are actually questionnaires with a different intention). Several popular UX questionnaires are constructed accordingly to this method. For example, the AttrakDiff2, the UEQ or the VISAWI.

14.6 Quality control

After you have created your questionnaire, you should check whether it meets the quality criteria described in Chapter 13. Suitable methods for this have already been described in this chapter.

It depends on the questionnaire and your planned application scenario which measures for quality control of the questionnaire make sense and how far you should go. If you only want to use the questionnaire internally in your company for a clearly specified type of products, then you do not need to expend much effort here. Depending on the decisions you want to draw from the results, it is a good idea to simply use the new questionnaire for your products and check reliability and validity on the basis of these initial applications.

If you want to make the questionnaire available to others as well, and if it is to be used for many different product types, more effort is of course required. In this case, you should conduct some studies to check reliability and validity for different product types before publishing the questionnaire.

15 Collecting Data

Once you have determined which UX aspects you should evaluate and found one or more UX questionnaires that can cover the spectrum of those UX aspects, all you need is data. That is, you need to find persons who are willing and able to answer questions about the product's user experience. In this chapter, we describe some points you should consider when planning your data collection.

15.1 Acceptable length of a questionnaire

Depending on the setup of your user research different length of questionnaires are acceptable. Thus, before you decide to use a concrete questionnaire you have to answer the question if the participants of your study are willing to spend enough time to answer all items.

For studies with payed participants the length of a questionnaire is not as crucial as for studies with voluntary participants. If you place a questionnaire at the end of a usability test and the testers are paid for their time, they will accept even very long questionnaires, like the ISOMETRICS. However, there is also a risk that test participants get bored and the quality of their responses will decrease over time.

If you place a link to a questionnaire in a product to get your users' opinion on certain UX aspects, a questionnaire that is too long will fail completely. The dropout rate will be high, and you will get only feedback from a small fraction of users. If you have a huge user base, this number may still be high enough to do some solid statistical data analysis. But in such cases the group of users providing feedback is certainly not representative of your user base. You will only receive feedback from users who have a particular motivation to do so. In many cases, these will be users who are either very dissatisfied or angry about the product or users who are quite happy with the product. Thus, there is a risk that the feedback is heavily biased, and it is dangerous to draw conclusions about further product development from such data.

Of course, it is not possible to provide clear guidance on the maximal length of a questionnaire for a particular research setup. But let's look on two examples.

As a first example, let's assume an online questionnaire that is triggered by an action in a web shop. After customers submitted their order, the questionnaire is displayed in a dialog. In such cases, the questionnaire must be very short. A single rating scale plus a field for textual comments is acceptable. It is important that the user gets the immediate impression that it will not require much time to provide feedback. Avoid a scrollbar or any navigation elements in the dialog. The full content and the submit button should be visible immediately.

As a second example, let's assume that a customer has purchased an expensive technical product. After some time, a link to an online questionnaire concerning satisfaction and first experience with the product is emailed to the customer. It is acceptable if the questionnaire takes several minutes to complete in such situations. This may even create a positive impression. It was an expensive product and sending the questionnaire shows that you care about your customers. Make sure that the customer can enter suggestions or remarks in some comment fields in such scenarios.

15.2 Collect data after a usability test

As we have already seen, a classic usability test and a UX questionnaire complement each other very well. In such a usability test, the participant works through several prepared tasks with the product. This phase is usually followed by a group discussion including the moderator, the participant and other people who observed the test session.

Always hand out a UX questionnaire directly between the end of the task processing and the discussion (an exception is the ASE, which should be conducted after each scenario)! The feedback collected by the questionnaire should reflect the participant's immediate impression of the product. Of course, the impression of the participants will be influenced by the discussion. For example, some points that massively disturbed the participant will be perceived as less problematic after the moderator has provided an explanation for the system behavior.

Some of the recruited users may not have much experience with questionnaires in general. In particular, questionnaires with unusual item formats, for example semantic differentials, should be introduced properly. The item format should be explained to the participants.

Imagine that you have never filled out a UX questionnaire before and that you have just spent one hour testing a business software. Then you will be asked to fill a questionnaire (for example the UEQ) without further comment. You will see items like:

good O O O O O O O bad

If you have never seen a questionnaire of this kind, it will probably look strange. And if something seems strange and incomprehensible at first glance, people will not spend much effort to answer carefully!

The problem certainly occurs more with modern item formats, e.g. semantic differentials. It is not so critical for items in the form of statements (relating to specific product characteristics), with an agree/disagree scale. However, it is definitely a good idea to explain to the participant why the questionnaire should be filled out. For example, by using a sentence such as *It would be nice if you could fill out a questionnaire that captures your personal impression of the product*. It also helps to point out that this is an established questionnaire for measuring user-friendliness. This emphasizes that the information is relevant and motivates the participant to put some effort in answering the questions carefully.

If the usability test takes place in a usability lab, i.e. if the moderator and the participant are in the same room, it is a good idea to hand out the questionnaire in a paper and pencil form. The participant has already worked with a user interface for some time. Participants often feel quite comfortable with such a media break. This helps many participants to concentrate on the items.

15.3 Using online questionnaires

Online questionnaires are a very convenient way to collect user feedback. It is possible to send a questionnaire to a large number of people without much effort or to make it available directly in the product to be evaluated (e.g. in a web store).

However, online questionnaires also have some disadvantages. In most cases, the researcher does not have much control over who participates in such a questionnaire, especially if it is started directly in a website or tool. In addition, the data quality is usually much lower than in paper-pencil questionnaires. Thus, it is quite important to control the data quality and remove responses that look suspicious before data analysis (how to do that is described in the following chapter).

Motivating people to participate in an online questionnaire by offering them a reward can cause some undesirable side effects concerning data quality. A typical reward offered in such cases is participation in a lottery, where there are a few but quite attractive prizes to be won. In such cases, there is always a certain number of participants who click through the questionnaire as quickly as possible without really thinking about their answers. I have seen data from such scenarios where more than 25% of the answers were quite suspicious. Of course, this can have a big impact on the results.

The alternative of simply not offering rewards for participation and hoping that enough participants with intrinsic motivation will take part is not always possible. Because online surveys are so easy and inexpensive to conduct, we are all exposed to a flood of such surveys. Thus, the general willingness to provide feedback voluntarily is declining.

In scenarios where purely intrinsic motivation is sufficient, no further incentives should be used. One example is a questionnaire in which members of a club (or society or any other closed group of people) are asked to rate their club's web presence. Another example are situations where employees of a company are asked to evaluate the company's intranet or tools they must use during their daily work. In these examples, the people addressed (or at least hopefully a sufficiently large number of them) have some intrinsic motivation (attachment to the club, interest in improving the intranet in the future) to participate.

15.4 Collect data directly in the product

The easiest way to recruit users to fill out a questionnaire is to place a link or button that launches the questionnaire directly in the product. It is also possible to trigger the display of the questionnaire by user actions, for example, to display it when the user submits an order or logs out of an application.

An obvious advantage of these methods is that you can access users when they are in the context of use. The user has a direct impression of the product in such situations and the feedback is typically much more accurate than in situations where the last interaction with the product was some time ago and the user has to rely on memory to answer the questions.

However, there are also some points that can be problematic. If the prompt for feedback is triggered by the product based on user actions, this can be annoying. For example, assume the logout button triggers the display of a dialog that asks *We would like to know your impression about our application. Would you please fill out a short survey?*.

Not many users will participate! It is simply the wrong point in time. The user is just about to log out and most likely already has an idea in mind what to do next. The dialog just causes an extra click to get rid of it, and this won't make users happy.

It is less disruptive to use a passive mechanism. Place a clearly visible link or button in the user interface that politely asks for feedback.

If you want to use an active trigger to ask for feedback, you should choose the mechanism carefully to avoid negative reactions from your users. As mentioned earlier, it is not a good idea to ask for feedback after the user has clicked the logout button. It is also not a good idea to ask immediately after the user logs in. First, users log in usually with a specific intention, they have something to do in your product or on your website. Thus, asking for feedback right after the user logs in is annoying to the user. Second, after users have interacted with your product for some time, their impression regarding the UX is based on an actual experience and this makes the feedback much more accurate as if they just logged in and give feedback based on past experiences. Thus, in such situations it seems to be a good idea to trigger the questionnaire after a certain delay, for example after the user has spent 5 minutes in the system.

In addition, if the user is actively asked for feedback, make sure that this does not happen too often. If such a request comes in every session and the user has to click it away every time, this is very annoying. We use questionnaires to ask the users about their impression concerning the UX of our products, not to destroy that impression! Ask once and then plan a quite long delay before asking the same user again.

15.5 Response Bias

If you are collecting data on the UX of a product via questionnaires and want to use this data as a basis for decision-making for the further development of the product, then you should clarify how representative your data is.

In fact, in many situations, the data will not be representative for your user base. We illustrate this with a few examples.

Suppose you are collecting feedback directly in an enterprise software product. Users must use this product as part of their daily work. You place a feedback button in the user interface and if the user clicks on that button, the following dialog opens.

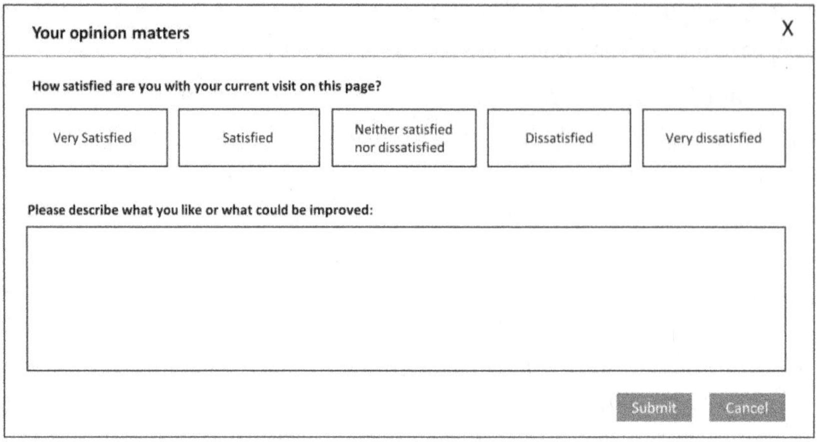

Figure 25: A simple feedback form in a product.

The dialog allows a simple satisfaction rating and a comment. Of course, in such a scenario, the comments themselves give important hints for improvements. Their interpretation is not biased.

But the rating is most likely skewed. Assume you code the response from 1 (very dissatisfied) to 5 (very satisfied) and you get an average rating of 3.7. Is that a representative rating of overall user satisfaction? Or asked another way, if you send a similar one-item questionnaire to your entire user base by email, would you expect the same result?

Why is this feedback most likely biased? Users must actively click on such a feedback button to participate in the questionnaire. And, of course, they can give feedback more than once. It wouldn't make sense to allow them to click the button only once. You want their comments to improve the product, and whenever a user has something to share, you should listen.

But when does a user click on the feedback button? When he or she has something to comment on! In most cases, this will be a situation where the user encounters a problem (this will have a negative impact on the satisfaction rating). However, it can also be the case (typically less often) when the user is positively surprised about a product feature (this will have a positive impact on the satisfaction rating). If everything works as expected, it is unlikely that a user will give feedback. Thus, extreme negative and extreme positive ratings will be overrepresented and in general there will be a negative bias in the average satisfaction rating.

Sounds pretty unpleasant, but in fact it depends on how you interpret the data whether this is really a problem. If you use the data to see a trend in user satisfaction, then it is not an issue. For example, if you calculate the average rating per month and check if this increases of decreases over time. The bias will be almost the same in each month and you can ignore it. However, if you compare the rating with a satisfaction rating obtained by another method (for example, by data obtained from an email campaign), you should be quite careful.

As a second example, let's assume a larger non-profit organization that operates a website to roll out information to members. To gather information about member satisfaction with the website's UX, an online questionnaire is emailed to all members of the organization. The results highlight some issues and a new version of the site is created. To measure whether the changes had the intended effect, the same UX questionnaire is emailed again to all members. However, since the participation rate in the first round was quite low, every member who completes the questionnaire is entered into a lottery with some quite interesting prizes.

Of course, it is problematic to compare the result of the two questionnaires. The more the member feels connected to the organization, the more likely he or she is to fill out the questionnaire in the first round. For the second round, it is quite different. Here, members are additionally motivated by the lottery. Since the affiliation of the members has most likely an influence on the UX rating, the method used to collect the data will have an impact.

15.6 Design of online forms for the questionnaire

If you are using an online questionnaire, it is of course important to design the online forms that display the items in such a way that they are easy to use for the participants.

We won't go into details of general form design here, since such a questionnaire is not much different from any other interactive tool, so the usual UI design principles apply. But there are some specific points we want to discuss here.

Let's assume again as an example that a UX questionnaire can be opened directly in a product, either by clicking a button or triggered by the system, e.g. 5 minutes after the user has logged in. The questionnaire contains the two items of the UMUX-LITE and a comment field.

Figure 26 shows a possible layout of the online form. The dialog shows the two items of the UMUX-LITE. When the users click on the *Next* button, the comment field is displayed, and the user can then (optionally) enter a comment.

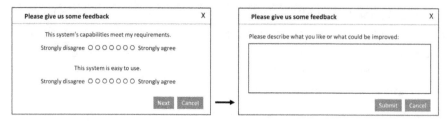

Figure 26: Potential design of the online form for the UMUX-LITE.

However, this simple looking design has a problem. The user cannot see at first glance how many questions will be included. This leaves it unclear how much effort will be required to complete the questionnaire. This will cause many users to simply close the dialog and leave the questionnaire.

A much better solution can be seen in Figure 27. It is immediately clear that it is only a very short questionnaire. All items are immediately visible. It is also clear that the comment field is not required and if there is no specific comment only two selections have to be made.

Figure 27: Alternative design for the online form.

If possible, always display an online questionnaire on a single page. It is more convenient for participants to scroll than to take multiple navigation steps between pages. In addition, the length of the scroll bar is already a good indicator of the length of the questionnaire. If parts of the questionnaire are hidden behind the navigation to other pages, this is not transparent for the participant and often leads to a higher dropout rate.

Sometimes a questionnaire needs to be split into several pages. For example, because it is simply extremely long or because some questions should be displayed or hidden depending on the answers the participant has given to other questions. In such cases, you should include a progress indicator on each page to give participants an indication of how far they have come in answering the questions.

If the individual pages require different effort, you should not only use the number of processed pages as an indicator! For example, suppose you have divided a longer questionnaire into 5 pages. The first page contains the instructions, the second page contains 30 statements about the product's UX with a 7-point agree/disagree scale, the third page contains 10 demographic questions, the fourth page contains 2 fields to enter comments, and the fifth page contains just text thanking the participant for taking the time to complete the questionnaire. Now assume you are a participant. You read the instructions and click *Next* to move to the second page. The progress bar indicates that you have completed 1 of 5 steps. Then you will see the 30 items. You fill them in and click *Next*. The indicator shows that you have completed 2 of 5 steps and now you see 10 questions again. Quite likely, either at step 2 or here, you get the impression that this is too much effort and you decide to abort.

Always show the actual time already spent in such a progress indicator. So do a quick pre-test and roughly estimate how much time is needed to work on each page (including the time needed to read the instruction). Then add up those times and show per page the relative time required for that page. In the example above, let's assume that the pretest shows that it takes approximately 100 seconds to read the instruction on page 1, 300 seconds to answer the 30 items on page 2, 100 seconds to answer the demographic questions, and 100 seconds to enter some comments. Then the progress indicator should show 0% on page 1, 17% on page 2, 67% on page 3, 83% on page 4, and 100% on page 5. This helps the participant to realistically estimate the time needed to finish and avoids some dropouts due to overestimation.

If you want to display a longer questionnaire directly in a product and this is triggered by the product (i.e. the product decides to ask the current user for feedback based on some logic), you should not display the questionnaire directly. Put a dialog box that politely asks the user for feedback, clearly states how much time is needed to complete the questionnaire and allows the user to simply decline to give feedback.

15.7 Formulating instructions

We have already described that a questionnaire used in a usability test should be filled out before a detailed discussion with the participant. This avoids influencing the participant by the contents of this discussion.

Similar effects have to be considered when formulating the instruction of a questionnaire. Of course, some instruction or motivation of participants is always necessary. You need to explain why people should participate, how you will handle the data, and what your general intention is.

If the questionnaire is sent to an email distribution list, such a general instruction is typically included in the invitation email. If the questionnaire is triggered directly in the product, it is either on a separate invitation page or on a dialog containing a link to the online questionnaire, or it is placed at the top of the page containing the questionnaire.

Be careful not to influence the participants with this instruction. Let's look at an example. Suppose we have a university's website and a list of students' email addresses. We randomly draw a large target group from the list of all students and send a questionnaire to measure the UX of the website via email. The email contains a general instruction and a link to the online questionnaire.

Which of the following phrases should you choose?

- We are always striving to improve the quality of our services for our students. Therefore, we would like to ask you to complete the following questionnaire regarding the quality of our website.

- You have certainly visited the website of our university in the last few months. We are naturally interested in how satisfied or dissatisfied you are with this website and therefore ask you to fill out the following questionnaire.

- In recent months, many students have complained about our university's website. In order to get a better picture of where the most urgent need for improvement is, we would like to ask you to fill out the following questionnaire.

Well, I think it is quite clear that the third alternative is extremely problematic. It already suggests that the website has a problem. That creates an expectation among the participants. They will certainly remember more negative than positive impressions of the website when answering the questions. The result will be more negative than with a neutral instruction.

The first alternative also creates a problem, although it is much smaller. The wording ("improve quality") suggests that there is something to improve. The effect here is certainly not as massive as with the third alternative.

The second alternative is completely neutral in terms of the quality of the page. There is no indication of good or bad quality, and this type of instruction is unproblematic.

15.8 Fit to target group

Before you start an evaluation project with a questionnaire, you should clarify whether this questionnaire fits to your intended target group. Otherwise, you run the risk of spending a lot of effort to generate data that cannot be interpreted properly and is thus useless. Let us explain this with some examples.

In a project, the UEQ was to be used to evaluate a website designed for children. The items of the UEQ are semantic differentials (pairs of terms with opposite meanings). The UEQ is used in quite many application scenarios, thus the researchers did not expect any problems. In this specific project, however, there were massive comprehension problems with some of the items. These problems were caused by the fact that the interviewed children were too young.

A detailed analysis revealed that the problems fell into two categories:

- The item contained foreign words whose exact meaning was not known to the children. An example is the item conservative/innovative.

- The opposite terms were understood but transferring their meaning to the context of evaluating an interactive product required a high degree of abstraction and caused misinterpretations. One example was the item valuable/inferior.

The observed problems ultimately led to the construction of a special UEQ version for children (only available in German), in which an attempt was made to replace the critical items with pairs of terms more in line with children's language comprehension (see Hinderks, Schrepp, Rauschenberger, Olschner, Thomaschewski, 2012).

Problems can also arise if the target group surveyed has little experience with questionnaires and the questions contradict the expectations and self-image of the users surveyed.

Let's imagine you evaluate a new version of a financial software. The participants are employees of financial institutions (usually quite conservative people) who are contacted through an email campaign that contains a link to an online questionnaire. If you use a questionnaire like the AttrakDiff2, meCUE or the UEQ, participants will be confronted with items like:

- stylish / silent (AttraktDiff2).
- The product is like a friend to me. (meCUE)
- boring / exciting (UEQ)

If participants are not prepared for what it is all about, such questions can easily trigger reactance (*Are they kidding? Why should my financial accounting be exciting? It's not a thriller, is it?*) and this will have a negative impact on data quality.

Of course, this does not mean that semantic differentials or questionnaires with a more modern item format cannot be used in such cases. However, you must carefully instruct the participants, e.g., as already described above, by mentioning in the cover letter or in the instructions that the questionnaire is an established UX standard questionnaire that is intended to measure the immediate emotional experience of software use.

In order to avoid problems of this kind, it is advisable to conduct a small pre-test when you first approach a special group of users and if you are unsure how they will react. Here you can first test with a few participants whether there are any problems in using the questionnaire before you distribute it to a large group of people.

16 Data analysis

Once the data has been successfully collected, the next step is to carefully analyze it to derive some insights. The details of data analysis depend on the questionnaire. Some standard questionnaires offer data analysis tools (often as Excel files) where you simply enter the data and get some standard analysis automatically.

In this chapter I will try to explain some important procedures that are applicable to many questionnaires. These should help the researcher to interpret the data correctly and to get the most out of the results.

16.1 Some statistical basics

Working with questionnaires requires some basic statistical knowledge. I will in this section not try to introduce basic statistical concepts. There are a lot of good textbooks for that. I assume that the reader knows what means, standard deviations or significance tests are. I will discuss how to apply these basic concepts when interpreting results of a questionnaire and how to avoid basic mistakes.

16.1.1 Scale means and confidence

Most UX questionnaires offer several scales. The most important result of a product evaluation with a UX questionnaire are clearly the scale mean values, i.e., the average score over all over all the participants' answers and all the items assigned to the scale.

The following two figures show an example of such an evaluation from the UEQ (taken from the UEQ data analysis tool available on www.ueq-online.org).

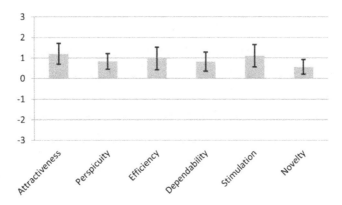

Figure 28: Example of an UEQ evaluation with low confidence.

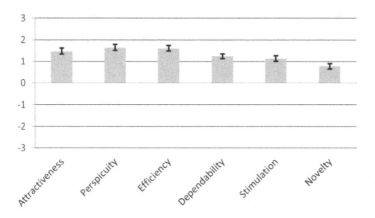

Figure 29: Example of an UEQ evaluation with high confidence.

In addition to the pure scale means, the confidence interval (visualized by the line at the top of the bars) is also of high importance for the interpretation of the results. The width of the confidence interval provides information about how accurately the mean of the scale was measured. The smaller the interval, the more likely it is that the measured scale value represents the true value in the population of all users. Thus, in the example above, the scale values from the second study are much more reliable than the scale values from the first study. Let us explain this in a bit more detail.

Suppose we measure the UX of a web store with the UEQ. A group of 50 randomly selected users fills out the questionnaire. Of course, not all 50 users will have the same impression regarding the UX of the store. If we select a second sample of 50 users and compare the scale means from both samples, they will differ. Thus, sampling effects in the selection of participants lead to different results.

Let us now imagine that we could repeat the measurement with a scale as often as we like. The confidence interval for a given probability of error (usually $\alpha = 0.05$, i.e. a probability of error of 5%) is then the range in which the measured scale values of the repetitions lie with a probability of $1-\alpha$. At $\alpha = 0.05$, 95% of these hypothetical replicates lie within the confidence interval and 5% lie outside.

This effect can be illustrated by a small simulation study. The basis for the study is a larger data set with several hundred individual responses from a product evaluation with the UEQ. From this data set, we now draw 1000 samples of 30 randomly selected participants. Figure 30 shows the distribution of the 1000 calculated scale scores for the UEQ scale *Perspicuity* (4 items).

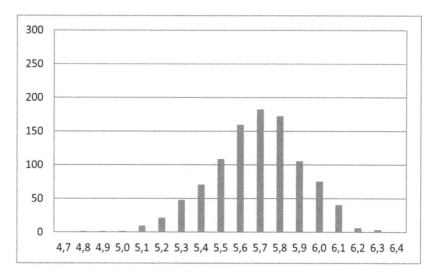

Figure 30: Distribution of scale mean for 1000 randomly drawn samples with size 30.

Of course, it is not possible to repeat a measurement with a UX questionnaire as often as desired, i.e. to calculate the confidence interval by many repetitions. But if you know the scale mean and its standard deviation, it is possible to estimate the confidence interval from the data of a study (under an assumption about the distribution of the mean, typically a normal distribution is assumed).

Which factors influence the width of a confidence interval? There are two relevant influencing variables (in addition to the error probability, which must of course be specified). If all respondents more or less agree in their assessment of the UX aspect (i.e., the standard deviation is small), the random selection of the participants has less influence than if different people give a very different assessment. Therefore, the smaller the standard deviation, the narrower the confidence interval.

The sample size also has an influence. The larger the sample, the more accurate is the estimation of the overall population mean. Thus, the larger the sample, the narrower the confidence interval.

This can be illustrated with a second simulation. If we draw samples of 50 participants instead of 30 in the simulation described above, the width of the distribution of the scale means is much smaller.

151

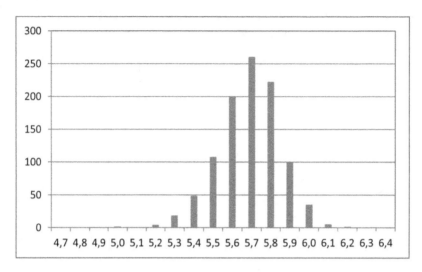

Figure 31: Distribution of scale mean for 1000 randomly drawn samples with size 50.

A look at the confidence intervals helps to avoid overinterpretation of the results of a UX questionnaire. If only a small sample was surveyed or there is great disagreement among the respondents about the evaluation of the product, the confidence intervals of the scales are usually large. In such cases, the measured scale value is obviously very inaccurate and should therefore be interpreted with caution. Important decisions for the future of a product or a new product version should never be derived from such data.

16.2 Apply and interpret significance tests

When we compare two products (for example, a new version with the previous version or a product with a competing product) in terms of their scale values, we need to distinguish real from random effects.

As an example, let's assume that we measure a value of 1.8 on the *Efficiency* scale of the UEQ for our new product version. For the old version, we measured 1.5 on the same scale some time ago. Of course, not all our users share the same opinion regarding the efficiency of the product. That is, such a difference can be caused either by a real improvement or by some luck in randomly selecting the respective respondents.

How can we clarify whether the effect is real or just random? To decide this question, we have to compare both results via a significance test. This can easily be done with a statistical software (Excel also offers such functions for data analysis).

152

There are always misunderstandings about the term significance. Significance of a result is often confused with importance or magnitude of the difference. This is certainly due to the way the term is used in everyday language (*a significant improvement* is often used in the sense of a large improvement). Statistically, the significance of a difference for a given error rate simply means that the difference is not due to random influences. A probability that the statement is wrong is explicitly stated. If a difference in scale values is significant at a 5% error rate, the difference is not due to random effects with 95% confidence.

Statistical significance has nothing to do with the importance of a difference. Let's assume that on a scale with values from 1 to 7, we have determined a scale value 5.12 for a product A and a scale value 5.17 for a product B. This is not a very large difference. If our sample contains only 30 participants, it is probably not significant statistically, i.e., it cannot be ruled out with sufficient certainty that it is a purely random effect. On the other hand, if we have 10,000 data, even such a small difference can be classified as non-random, i.e., statistically significant. However, that does not make it more important, i.e. we will certainly not want to make any important decisions regarding the UX quality of the two products based on such a minimal difference in scale value.

If we have two scales and their confidence intervals (for the specified confidence level) do not overlap, then the scale values are also significantly different with this confidence level (error probability). However, the reverse is not true! Even if the confidence intervals overlap, there may be a significant difference. The detailed explanation of this point would lead here too far, there I refer again to statistical textbooks. But even if the confidence intervals overlap slightly, it is worthwhile to perform a significance test.

16.3 Data quality

Not every participant will carefully fill out a UX questionnaire. In any data set, there are usually some answers that are somewhat problematic or questionable.

Especially if you are working with an online questionnaire, you should keep this aspect in mind. With an online questionnaire, you have little or no control over how participants complete the questionnaire. The data quality in such online questionnaires depends heavily on the motivation of the participants.

When people participate on a voluntary basis, data quality is usually a less serious issue. If you motivate participants with a reward, for example participation in a lottery, things are different. In this case, there will be some participants who answer the questions quickly and without thinking much, in order to get the reward with as little effort as possible. Such random answers contain no substantial information about the UX of the product and thus can have a negative impact on the conclusions you draw from the results.

The proportion of questionable answers varies greatly between studies, as it depends on several factors. In my own experience of using the UEQ in online questionnaires, I have seen cases where up to 25% of the answers were suspect. It is therefore important to detect and remove suspicious answers before analyzing the data. There are three main techniques for this, which we will describe below.

The first technique searches for typical patterns in the data that indicate that the participant has not answered carefully. Participants who quickly click through a questionnaire without actually answering the items often produce easy recognizable patterns in their answers, e.g., by ticking the same answer category for all items. These can be recognized relatively easily, and the corresponding answers can be excluded.

The second technique is based on the assumption that all items in a scale measure a similar property. Unless the questionnaire had a fundamental problem in its construction, it is reasonable to assume that this assumption is true. Thus, if a participant carefully completes the questionnaire, responses to items in a scale should be reasonably consistent. However, if a participant answers without thinking much about the questions, there is a fairly high probability that some items on the scale will be rated very positively and others very negatively. If many such inconsistencies are found in a person's data, that is at least a good indication of sloppy completion.

The third technique is based on the fact that careful answers take time. If you click quickly through a questionnaire without reading the items properly and without thinking much about your answer, you will be much faster than if you answer seriously. Thus, suspicious answers can be identified via unusually short response times.

16.3.1 Detect suspicious answer patterns

When participants click through a questionnaire as quickly as possible, they often use simple strategies when ticking off answer options. In many cases, these can be recognized directly without deeper analysis.

Let's look at a small example. Figure 32 shows 3 completed UEQ questionnaires (they are displayed in the middle next to each other). Which of these answers are suspicious?

The answer to this question is quite simple. In the case of the first (from left to right) questionnaire in Figure 32 (labeled as Pattern 1), we see a geometrically appealing zigzag pattern. How likely is it that something like this would occur in a serious response? In the case of the second questionnaire in Figure 32 (labeled as Pattern 2), we see a participant who started seriously but apparently lost the desire to continue after 8 items (this is a very typical pattern). The third questionnaire (labelled as Pattern 3) shows no abnormalities, i.e., it does not appear suspicious at this level of analysis.

16.3.2 Find inconsistent answers

In most UX questionnaires, the items are grouped into several scales (some questionnaires have only one scale). The items of a scale measure similar aspects of the user experience with a product. If the items of a scale are answered very differently by one person, this may indicate that the items are not answered seriously.

As an example, consider a person's responses to the items on the *Perspicuity* scale of the UEQ:

not understandable	O O O O O X O	understandable
easy to learn	O O O O O O X	difficult to learn
complicated	O O O O O X O	easy
clear	O O O O O X O	confusing

Quite obviously, this response is inconsistent. The product is rated as very understandable, difficult to learn, very easy and very confusing.

Putting all items in the order negative (1) to positive (7), we see that the ratings range from 1 (difficult to learn/easy to learn) to 6 (not understandable/understandable), i.e., the distance between the best and the worst rating is 5. This distance between the best and the worst rating of an item within a scale can easily be used as an indicator of inconsistencies (Schrepp, 2016).

	Pattern 1	Pattern 2	Pattern 3	
annoying	●○○○○○○	○○○○○●○	○○○○○●○	enjoyable
not understandable	○●○○○○○	○○○○○●○	○○○○○●○	understandable
creative	○○●○○○○	○○●○○○○	○○●○○○○	dull
easy to learn	○○○●○○○	○●○○○○○	○○●○○○○	difficult to learn
valuable	○○○○●○○	○○●○○○○	○○●○○○○	inferior
boring	○○○○○●○	○○○○○●○	○○○○●○○	exciting
not interesting	○○○○○○●	○○○○○●○	○○○○○●○	interesting
unpredictable	○○○○○●○	○○○○○●○	○○○○○●○	predictable
fast	○○○○●○○	○○○●○○○	○●○○○○○	slow
inventive	○○○●○○○	○○○●○○○	○○●○○○○	conventional
obstructive	○○●○○○○	○○○●○○○	○○○○○●○	supportive
good	○●○○○○○	○○○●○○○	○●○○○○○	bad
complicated	●○○○○○○	○○○●○○○	○○○○○●○	easy
unlikable	○●○○○○○	○○○●○○○	○○○○○●○	pleasing
usual	○○●○○○○	○○○●○○○	○○○○●○○	leading edge
unpleasant	○○○●○○○	○○○●○○○	○○○○○●○	pleasant
secure	○○○○●○○	○○○●○○○	○○●○○○○	not secure
motivating	○○○○○●○	○○○●○○○	○●○○○○○	demotivating
meets expectations	○○○○○○●	○○○●○○○	○○○○○●○	does not meet expectations
inefficient	○○○○○●○	○○○●○○○	○○○○○○●	efficient
clear	○○○○●○○	○○○●○○○	○●○○○○○	confusing
impractical	○○○●○○○	○○○●○○○	○○○○○○●	practical
organized	○○●○○○○	○○○●○○○	○●○○○○○	cluttered
attractive	○●○○○○○	○○○●○○○	○●○○○○○	unattractive
friendly	●○○○○○○	○○○●○○○	○●○○○○○	unfriendly
conservative	○●○○○○○	○○○●○○○	○○○○○●○	innovative

Figure 32: Some answer patterns in a UEQ questionnaire.

Assuming that all items of a scale measure similar properties, a participant should not give too different ratings for the items of a scale. That is, the distance between the best and the worst rating of an item on the scale should not be too large. Of course, it is always possible that a participant misinterprets a term, accidentally marks the wrong category, or that the special experiences of the participant during product usage cause an unexpected rating for one item in a scale. If there is a single deviation of this type, one will not want to discard the entire response. However, if such a deviation is observed on several scales, this is a clear indication that the participant did not answer the items carefully.

How one defines such a heuristic for excluding responses in detail is to a certain extent a matter of taste. For the UEQ, a record is discarded if for at least 3 of the 6 scales a distance > 3 is found between the best and the worst value of an item of the scale. This heuristic was evaluated with existing data and showed good results (Schrepp, 2016).

Of course, it is necessary to adapt this kind of heuristic to each questionnaire, since different questionnaires have a different number of scales and a different number of response options per item. A good heuristic must, on the one hand, recognize random response patterns with a high degree of certainty and, on the other hand, not classify a response as random in case of only a few inconsistencies.

As general advice, it is not a bad idea to exclude a record only if it has inconsistencies for about half of the scales. As a cutoff for inconsistent responses, it is advisable to take half of the answer scale. For an even number, exactly half (i.e. 4 for an 8-point answer scale) and for an odd number, half minus 1 (i.e., 3 for a 7-point answer scale).

Of course, these are only rough heuristics that help to establish a procedure for cleaning the data. If you have already collected some data with the questionnaire, you can of course use these data sets to further adapt and improve the heuristics (see Schrepp, 2016).

16.3.3 Use response times to detect problematic response

If a participant fills out a questionnaire without really thinking about the items, his or her response time will be much lower than the response time of a participant who fills out the questionnaire carefully. Therefore, measuring response time in online questionnaires provides an easy way to identify cheaters.

The basic idea of this method is to define a lower limit MT (in seconds) for the response. This limit is chosen under the assumption that a carefully responding participant cannot complete the questionnaire in less than MT seconds. Once MT is defined, all responses from participants with shorter response times are simply deleted.

But how to define MT? There is a precise theoretical approach and a very simple practical approach. Let's start with the theoretical approach.

The lower limit MT can be estimated using cognitive modeling. Cognitive modeling methods, for example GOMS (Card, Moran & Newell, 1983) or CogTool (John, Prevas, Salvucci & Koedinger, 2004), use models of human information processing to estimate the time required to complete a task in an interactive system (in our case, answering all items in the questionnaire) from the cognitive and physical steps required for navigation or data entry.

In GOMS analysis (Card, Moran & Newell, 1983), user interaction in processing a task is decomposed into elementary operators. The task processing time is then estimated from the known times (such average times are determined in experiments, e.g., John & Kieras 1996; Olson & Olson, 1990; Schrepp & Fischer, 2007) of these elementary operators. Operators are basic physical (for example, pressing a key or clicking with the mouse) or cognitive processes (for example, retrieving information from memory or mentally preparing for the next step in an action sequence) that the user must perform when processing a task with the product.

Different persons require different times for physical or cognitive operations. The GOMS analysis abstracts from the times of concrete persons by using typical average values. For example, keystroke when typing a string 0.23 seconds, positioning the mouse pointer 0.44 seconds, mental preparation 1.2 seconds, and so on. Using these times for the elementary operations, one can estimate an average processing time for a given task. The trick is simply to break the task into a sequence of such elementary operations and then sum up the values of the operator times.

CogTool is freely available software that enables cognitive modeling of computer-based tasks (see, John, Prevas, Salvucci & Koedinger, 2004 or John & Salvucci, 2005). CogTool implements the GOMS method with some additional operators and limited consideration of parallel information processing. Cogtool's predictions are more accurate than a simple GOMS analysis with standard parameters, since some details are considered (for example, the detailed length of a mouse movement). For our purpose, a simple GOMS analysis (this can be easily done in an Excel spreadsheet or even with a calculator) is accurate enough.

The method is quite simple to perform. As an example, let's look at the UEQ. The items of the UEQ are semantic differentials with a 7-point response scale:

Good O O O O O O O Bad

To answer such an item, it is required (see Schrepp, 2016) to:

- focus the visual attention on the left term (Look at)
- understand the meaning of this term (Think)
- focus the visual attention on the right term (Look at)
- understand the meaning of this term (Think)
- decide which term fits better (Think)
- move the mouse to the corresponding radio button, assuming that the hand is already on the mouse (Position Mouse Pointer)
- perform a mouse click (Mouse click)
- mentally prepare for the next item (Think)

The terms in parentheses denote the corresponding operators in Cogtool. An estimate of the necessary processing time with CogTool results in a total time of 5.6 seconds per item.

If we use a plain GOMS analysis with the operator times 1.2 second for *Think*, 0.44 seconds for *cursor placement*, 0.2 seconds for a *Mouse Click* and 0.36 seconds for a *Look at* we would arrive at $4*1.2 + 0.4 + 0.2 + 2*0.36 = 6.14$. As usual the GOMS estimate is a bit longer than the Cogtool estimate. Since it is more accurate, we continue with the Cogtool estimation in the example.

If this is taken as a basis for the entire questionnaire, the total processing time for the 26 items is approximately 146 seconds. This is the minimum time to be expected. In real applications of the UEQ, higher response times are generally observed. Participants need higher decision times for some items because they have to think about their exact interpretation. On average, a UEQ takes around 3 minutes to be completed.

If the participant only clicks quickly through the questionnaire, at least 3 think operators are not necessary (mental preparation for processing the next items is still required). The time per item should then be closer to 2 seconds per item. Thus, in such cases, we assume that one answer category per item is randomly selected (think) and clicked (mouse move and clicked).

With a purely random click through, a total time of 52 seconds is to be expected.

The method is of course applicable to all question formats. For questions consisting of longer statements, it is necessary to consider the time for reading the statement, i.e. how exactly the cognitive modeling is to be performed depends strongly on the questionnaire and item type. However, the general idea is always to measure in the online questionnaire how long it takes the participant to process the questions and to determine the total processing time from this. If this is significantly shorter for several questions than the value determined by cognitive modeling, this is a clear indication that items were not processed carefully.

If you work with cognitive modeling, it is easy to determine MT. Suppose you have estimated the time to complete the questionnaire. In our example, this time is 145 seconds. We call this time OT. In addition, there is an estimation for the time required if the participant does not answer seriously by removing some of the think operators. In our example, this time is 52 seconds. We call this time CT. We now define MT = (OT + CT) / 2. Thus, we exclude all responses that were closer to CT than to OT. In our example we would then use MT = 97 seconds.

We have simplified the modelling in our example to work out the idea. In a practical example, you need to consider all the elements on the online questionnaire in the cognitive modelling. Thus, if you have added some demographic questions, they need to be taken into account and also the click on the button to submit the questionnaire. You can ignore comment fields, since someone who just clicks through the questionnaire as fast as possible will ignore them.

If you feel that a cognitive modelling approach is too difficult or time consuming for your project, there is a simple alternative that works well in practice.

Recruit one person (a friend or you can do it yourself). This person should rate the product with your questionnaire. Instruct the person to repeat this rating process for the same product several times, without thinking about the answers again each time. From the first repetition, the same answers should simply be entered again as quickly as possible.

You will observe that the times for filling out the questionnaire quickly become shorter at first and then settle around a constant after a certain point (usually after 3-5 runs). That is, the times converge to a time that is quite close to the time that can also be determined from cognitive modeling. This time corresponds to the time needed to complete the questionnaire purely physically, without thinking about the meaning of the items.

In Figure 33, I repeated this myself 9 times for the 26 items of the UEQ and one product. Shown are the times between the first click on a UEQ item and the final click on the *Submit* button in the online questionnaire.

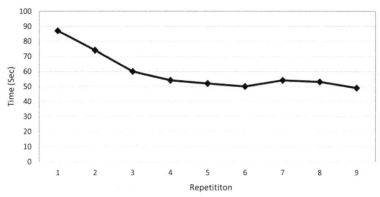

Figure 33: Observed times to fill an UEQ with 9 repetitions.

This means that a participant who seriously fills out the questionnaire for this product can't actually answer any faster by human standards (unless it's an alien or Superman, but those are rather rare to find as participants in online surveys). Participants who just click through randomly end up in this range. The MT can now be calculated as the average of the first processing time (corresponding to OT in cognitive modeling) and the constant against which the processing times converge (corresponding to CT in cognitive modeling). This is of course only a rough estimation, but with this simple method one already arrives at a useful lower limit for the acceptable processing time.

16.4 Check if the items were interpreted correctly

In addition to random response errors and participants who simply click through the items as quickly as possible and do not give serious answers, there are also systematic errors. Such errors result from a wrong understanding of items. Depending on the context of the survey, participants of a study may interpret an item differently than intended by the creator of the questionnaire.

What causes such misinterpretations? Items in a questionnaire are always interpreted in the context of the study. In the case of a UX questionnaire, this context is of course defined by the product being evaluated. The environment in which the evaluation takes place can also play a role. If a

161

questionnaire is used in the context of a usability test, the specific tasks in the test can influence the interpretation of an item. If a questionnaire is displayed directly in the product, e.g., when a buyer logs out of a web store, then the user's previous actions in the product can play a role.

Let's take a look at examples I have seen in practical studies with the UEQ. There is a special version of the UEQ in simplified language (only available in German) for children and adolescents. This version contains an item *time-saving/time-consuming*. This is intended to measure the efficiency of user interaction. However, in a study of a social network, this item was apparently interpreted by many users as *the social network robs me of my time*. It is clear that *time-consuming* in this case is actually not negative in the sense of product quality (on the contrary, the social network is apparently so attractive that it tempts the user to spend too much time in it). It is also clear that in this interpretation does not cover efficiency.

Another example is the item *not secure/secure* from the UEQ. It is intended as an indicator of controllability, i.e. do users feel that they can safely control their interactions with the system. For business applications or other products where the concept of data security does not play a major role for the user (because the user assumes that this is simply a given or that he or she personally does not have to worry about it), the item also always shows very high correlations with the other items of the *Dependability* scale of the UEQ. However, in applications such as social networks or online banking (where people are personally concerned about their own data), the item is often interpreted as *my data is safe*.

It is usually difficult to detect such possible misinterpretations before the study. The only chance is to validate the questionnaire in a larger pretest (here you always need a relatively large amount of data, since usually only a part of the participants choose the alternative interpretation, i.e. with few data sets it is difficult to detect such an effect). However, there is often neither time nor budget for such a pretest. It is also questionable what is the point of such a preliminary investigation. Do we change to another questionnaire? Do we cancel the survey in such a case?

Such a misinterpretation of a single item has only a limited influence on the overall result (in the example above, one of 26 UEQ items is affected). Thus, practically you can simply start, collect data, and then check whether there is a corresponding effect during data analysis. In such a case, one can then remove the item in question from the evaluation or at least point out that it is a problematic item when interpreting the data.

Fortunately, finding such potentially problematic items is quite easy. The items of a questionnaire are grouped into several scales. The items of a scale measure a UX aspect, i.e. all items of a scale measure related semantic aspects. Therefore, all items of a scale should have similar mean values and should also correlate reasonably with each other.

To find potentially misinterpreted items, look at the item means per scale. If there is an item that deviates massively from the other items, this could be an indication of misinterpretation. Then examine the correlations of the items per scale. If all items except one are highly correlated, this could also be an indication of misinterpretation.

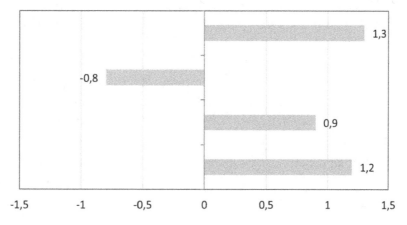

Figure 34: Mean values of the 4 items of a scale. Which one is maybe misinterpreted?

Another method to detect misinterpreted items is to check Cronbach's Alpha Coefficient (see Chapter 13) or the correlations between the items in a scale.

As an example, consider at the following correlation matrix of 4 items in a scale:

	Item 1	Item 2	Item 3	Item 4
Item 1	1			
Item 2	0.54	1		
Item 3	0.45	0.61	1	
Item 4	0.21	0.11	0.09	1

Items 1, 2, and 3 show relatively high correlations with each other. Item 4 shows only very low correlations with the other items of the scale. Thus, there is possibly a misinterpretation.

But caution is needed here if your data set is small. Correlations are very sensitive to sampling errors. With small sample sizes, such patterns can occur simply by bad luck.

16.5 Distribution of answers per item

Some products are polarizing. There are users who love the product, but also users who hate it. This can refer to the entire product, or only to certain UX aspects or single items. Especially UX aspects, which are very subjective and where you find strong personal preferences between people, can trigger very different perceptions among users.

A good example is the visual design of an application. If you ask about the aesthetics of the design, you will often find strong disapproval in one larger group of users and strong approval in another equally large group. The same is true for originality or stimulation.

The fact that a product is polarizing in terms of a UX aspect is of course a very important information for further improvement of the product. Therefore, UX researchers want to find such information in the data. Such effects are clearly visible in the data, but not in the scale scores.

Let's look at an example that explains the phenomenon. Suppose we have a questionnaire with a 7-item response scale. For an item A, we observe the following distribution of values.

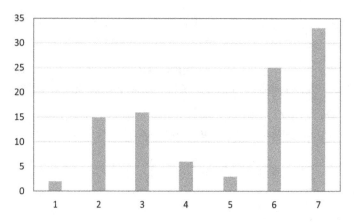

Figure 35: Distribution of responses with two peaks to a hypothetical item.

For another item B, the following distribution is observed.

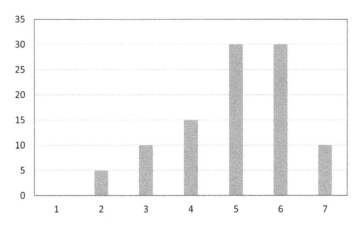

Figure 36: Single-peaked distribution of responses to a hypothetical item.

The item mean values are 5.0 in both cases, only the standard deviation is naturally higher for item B. However, the distribution of the answers is very interesting for the interpretation of the results.

For item A, there are obviously two groups with very different views regarding the UX quality represented by this item. A larger group of participants apparently reacts rather enthusiastically, while another group of about 30% of the participants is not really satisfied. Let's assume that item A is the question about the beauty of the user interface. The mean value is positive. However, this results from the fact that half of the users are enthusiastic, while a large group does not really find the design beautiful. If the product is a web store, for example, the operator will not be particularly satisfied because the design does not really appeal to a third of potential customers. There will probably be a need for action here in order to arrive at a generally accepted design.

For item B, on the other hand, there is no indication that the measured UX quality is polarizing. There are a larger number of people who gave the item a quite positive rating of 5 or 6, and a smaller number of people with neutral to reserved ratings (but you always have those). If this item is the question about the beauty of a web store's design, there would certainly be no reason to fear that the perception of the design would differ greatly among different user groups.

So, as the example shows, it may well be worth looking at the distribution of responses for the individual items to get information beyond the scale mean. These can be more valuable for the conclusions derived from the data than the mean values themselves!

In the examples above, we used the distribution of the individual items. However, the same argument applies to the distribution of the complete scale values (mean of all items of a scale) per participant.

17 Presenting the Results

When the data collection and analysis is finished, it is time to present and share the results. In most cases, the target audience for such a presentation of UX questionnaire results consists of persons who are responsible for the development or marketing of the product.

Of course, everyone has his or her own and very personal presentation style. Personally, I feel often quite uncomfortable presenting results slides that I did not create myself. Therefore, you will find here only a small collection of concrete tips and tricks for the presentation of questionnaire results, which come from my own experience.

I will not go into detail about the best methods for communicating questionnaire results using charts. There are a number of good books on this subject, for example Kosslyn (1993) and there is no point in repeating such general principles in this chapter.

17.1 Create trust in the method

Typical participants in a presentation of the results of a UX questionnaire are product owners, managers, or members of the development team. These people usually have little or no experience with the application and interpretation of UX questionnaires. In addition, they have a certain idea of the UX quality of the product they are developing and define the value of their work by this. Negative results of an assessment with a questionnaire can therefore easily be interpreted by these people as criticism of their work. Especially in the case of poor results, product managers or developers tend to feel attacked in their self-image. A typical defensive reaction in such cases is to cast doubt on the results of the questionnaire in general.

It is therefore very important to create confidence in the method. For example, mention at the beginning of the presentation that you have used an established scientifically based questionnaire (if you use a standard questionnaire) and possibly cite the relevant publications. If you or colleagues in your company have already used the same questionnaire for other studies, it is usually a good idea to mention this as well.

This helps your audience understand that your results are not simply based on a series of arbitrary questions but follow a sound approach. In any case, it prevents the simplest defensive reaction, which is to doubt that the questionnaire measures anything reasonable at all.

17.2 Explain the meaning of the scales

A central part of the results presentation are the mean values of the scales. Here it is important that the participants understand the semantic meaning of these scales. The pure scale names can easily be misunderstood by people without the appropriate background. As we have seen in a previous chapter, the scale names are not always easy to interpret without a concrete look at the items of a scale.

For example, what does the originality scale in the UEQ mean? Why should accounting software be original? Is this another weird idea from the UX colleagues? Here you can explain, for example, that it is of course important for the positioning of the product, e.g. at trade fairs or on marketing pages on the internet, to attract the attention of potential customers. And original design, i.e. a design that stands out from competing products, is a good way to attract attention.

This means that for each scale it should be explained briefly what the scale means and why it makes sense to measure the underlying UX aspect. You can adapt the scale names to the terminology commonly used in your company. The scale name itself is only a summary of the meaning of all items in a scale, i.e. arbitrary within certain limits. As long as the data is only presented in your own company, you can easily change it to make it more understandable. For example, you can rename the UEQ scale name *Originality* to *Interest*, if that fits your company's terminology better.

A clear understanding of the meaning of the scales is necessary to derive recommendations from the results. Meaningful recommendations for improvements can only be discussed if the persons involved are able to relate the scales to product features and design elements.

17.3 Simplify if possible

Results from a questionnaire are often quite detailed. Details help to analyze the data and to draw valid conclusions from it. However, in a presentation too much details can be a problem. You have to present complicated things in a short period of time and too much details may hinder the participants to get the main message. Thus, try to present only the most important points.

Let's look at an example. Figure 37 shows the distribution of the answers of 4 items with a 7-point scale. The top visualization shows the detailed distribution of the answers per item in a staked bar chart. For the bottom chart answer alternatives 1 to 3 (negative) respectively 5 to 7 (positive) are shown in the same color. This obviously loses some detail information, but

168

makes the chart much easier to read, transfers still the main message and helps to visually identify the items with less positive rating simply by comparing the width of the dark grey area.

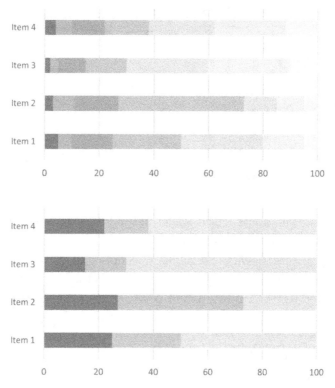

Figure 37: Simplified graphics often transfer the main message much better.

17.4 Relate results to problems in usability tests

If the questionnaire is used after a usability test, it is useful to relate the problems found in the test to the values of the scales (e.g. many problems with the terminology and a low value of a scale measuring comprehensibility). An example is shown in Figure 38.

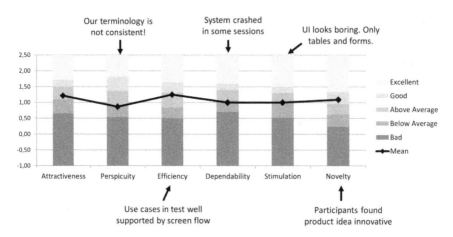

Figure 38: Relating questionnaire results to a benchmark and some concrete findings in a usability test.

It is also important not to let the values of the scales stand alone. Compare them to results from a previous version or to results for other products that have been assessed with the same questionnaire in the past. If the questionnaire provides a benchmark, explain the benchmark to the audience and relate your results to the values in the benchmark data set. Scale values alone are usually not easy to interpret.

17.5 How to present comments

A typical extension of standard questionnaires is to add some fields where the user can enter some comments about the product. Of course, these comments contain a lot of detailed information about the product. Sometimes suggestions for improvements can be derived directly from such comments.

For a presentation of the results, such comments are problematic. They are simply too detailed to fit into such a format. However, there are some typical mechanisms for including them.

One way to give an overview of the contents of such a large collection of comments is to transform them into a word cloud. Simply copy all comments into a large text file and import it into one of the available world cloud generators. These generators will remove typical fill word like "and" or "is" from the text basis. However, this is usually not sufficient, and some manual clean-up is required to produce a meaningful representation.

Another technique to reduce the complexity of such data is a sentiment analysis. Here, comments are automatically classified into positive, neutral, and negative comments and the number of comments in each category gives a (limited) insight into the general impression.

Often some specific comments are selected and included in the result presentation. This can be helpful if these selected comments point out specific problems and suggest measures to fix them. Such statements represent *real authentic feedback from users* and therefore typically make some impression on the audience. The problem is that these selected statements are the information that participants may remember (this is real user feedback and is more easily remembered than any numerical results) and therefore they often determine the overall impression that the results leave on the audience.

If you have one hundred comments and carefully pick out a handful to present these explicitly, then you can massively influence (or maybe we better call it manipulate) the impression of the audience. For example, if you have data showing that your users are quite satisfied with the product, but then pick out 5 quite negative comments and present those at the end of the results presentation, it will influence the overall impression heavily.

Thus, be careful with picking and presenting individual user comments. Intentionally or unintentionally, this can have a big impact on how the audience remembers the results.

17.6 Use creative presentations

Some standard questionnaires also provide materials for data analysis and elementary presentation of results. These are usually neutral and scientific. However, presentations can often be spiced up with some alternative representations of the results with little effort. Sometimes this can also provide additional insights into the data.

Of course, there are no limits to creativity and imagination here. Finally, I would like to present an example of a special visualization of UEQ results, which I have used several times in presentations.

The example shown in Figure 39 uses a word cloud to show how the items of the UEQ are rated. For this purpose, the mean ratings of the items across all participants were mapped to font sizes. The better the rating, the bigger the font size.

Figure 39: Results of an evaluation with the UEQ visualized as a world cloud. Font sizes correspond to mean rating of the items.

Such a graphic can be used to catch the attention of the participants during a result presentation. Word clouds are widely used these days, so you don't have to explain the graphic at length. It also provides a certain qualitative view on the results, which is immediately accessible to participants who are not so familiar with statistics. And a certain tendency of the results can already be deduced from it. How the relationship between the rating on the answer scale and the font size is calculated is of secondary importance. One possible way to do this is, for example, described in Rummel & Schrepp (2019). However, such kinds of visualizations should be used with caution. They can also be misleading. Use them only to catch interest. The true value of your results lies in the measured scale values.

Creating word clouds from semantic differentials is quite natural, as the item format fits very well to this kind of presentation. However, the same technique can be applied to questionnaires where the items consists of statements. It makes no sense to display the complete statements in the cloud. But you can simply summarize each statement in a short phrase and use these reduced representations of the items in the cloud. Below is an example of a word cloud generated from results of an evaluation with the VISAWI. Again, the average scale value is mapped to the font size.

Figure 39: Word cloud generated from the results of a product evaluation with the VISAWI.

18 Create translations

To avoid misinterpretations of items, it is of course beneficial if participants can fill out the questionnaire in their natural language. Thus, if you are conducting research for a global company, you may face the challenge of creating translations of a UX questionnaire. This can happen for a standard questionnaire for which no language version exists in the desired language, or for a UX questionnaire that you have created yourself.

Creating translations sounds trivial, but there are a few theoretical and practical issues that make this task quite challenging.

The first problem is that natural languages have different ways to express semantic meaning. A UX aspect may be easy to describe in one language, but the corresponding concept or terms may not exist in another language. Thus, a creative solution may be required to express the original meaning, and it is always questionable whether this will not also create a small shift in the meaning of the item. Moreover, there are always several ways to translate an item into another language. Which one is the best? Which of these translations most adequately covers the meaning of the original item?

Thus, it seems necessary to check whether the translation behaves in the same way as the original questionnaire. In principle, it is possible to validate a translation through an empirical study. Simply test the same product with a similar target group in two countries. If items change in meaning, this becomes visible when looking at the pattern of all correlations between all items in the questionnaire.

In practice, there are some problems with this simple idea. First, correlations are not very robust to sampling effects (Schönbrodt & Perugini, 2013). You really need large samples in both countries. Second, if you test a product in two countries, the product will naturally be translated. The two country versions will therefore not be identical. For example, if you see differences in learnability or understandability scores in the results of the two language versions of your questionnaire, it may be due to problems in the translation of your questionnaire, or it may be due to the translation of the product itself. However, other UX aspects may also be affected. For example, since languages also differ in the average length of terms, the translation of a user interface can also have a negative impact on the layout. Third, it is difficult to justify how similar two target groups in two different countries are. For example, suppose you are testing a product in two countries with two groups of students. Depending on the educational systems, the average age of the students in the two countries may be different. The level of education required to attend a university may be different. Depending on the country, proficiency in the native language may differ (in multi-lingual countries the language used in the questionnaire may be one of several languages participants speak, and perhaps not their native language). All these factors, of course, have an impact on the outcome, and they are quite difficult to control for. Fourth, there may be cultural differences that cause different evaluations of a product, i.e., the items are well translated and have the same meaning as in the original version, but the participants perceive the UX qualities differently in the two countries. Therefore, it is practically difficult to guarantee in advance that a translation of a UX questionnaire will in some sense be of good quality or produce results similar to the original.

Therefore, it is very difficult to create truly bulletproof translations. I have been working on the development of the UEQ for several years. Over the years, more than 30 translations have been created for this questionnaire. The translations are triggered by UX researchers who want to use the questionnaire in a language for which no translation exists yet. To enable UX researchers to produce good translations, we have developed a process that usually guarantees adequate quality for new language versions. Our experience with this process has been very good, so I will describe it briefly.

To describe the process, we need to define some terms. The language into which the questionnaire is to be translated is called the *target language*. The language of the questionnaire, which is used as a basis for translation, is called the *source language*.

In the first step, a native speaker of the target language translates the questionnaire from the source language (this is the optimal case) or an already approved translation (in the case of the UEQ, the English version typically serves as the basis for the translation process) to the target language.

In the second step, a second person (ideally a native speaker of the source language) translates the new version back into the source language. This second person should not be involved in the first translation step and should be not familiar with the source language version.

In the third step, the two translators go through the translation together. Cases where the back translation of the item into the source language deviates massively from the original item in terms of semantic meaning

175

indicate potential problems. At the end of this discussion, a first translated version in the target language is created.

In the fourth step, the translated version is made available (in the case of UEQ, there is a central website that contains all materials including translations) to all interested persons. Feedback from UX researchers using the translated version is collected and, if possible, raw data are analyzed to identify problems. If there is evidence that the meaning of a translated item deviates from the original, steps are taken to address this.

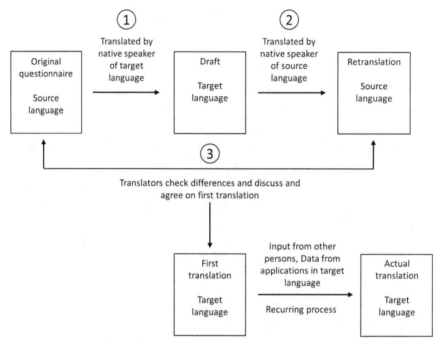

Figure 41: Sketch of the main steps of the described translation process.

We use this process to create translations for the UEQ since several years. My personal experiences with this process are quite positive. It does, of course, not guarantee that there is always a perfect translation available. But the impact of inaccuracies is limited, and in the long run, possible inaccuracies are detected and corrected.

To guarantee a good translation it is important that the translator has some UX background knowledge. The items of a UX questionnaire have a certain intention, and if this is not properly understood by the translator, this can lead to misinterpretations and subsequently to a poor result. At least the translator should understand that the items are intended to uncover the users' impressions towards products and should understand the scale structure of the questionnaire, i.e. which items are intended to measure which UX aspects.

Even if there are problems with the translation of some items, the impact on the measured scale means is usually small. If one of four items in a scale has a small shift in meaning (and it is extremely unlikely that drastic changes in meaning will occur when translators work along the process described) this will have only a small impact on the scale mean. Thus, the translation may not behave perfectly like the original, but still produce reasonable results.

As soon as others start to reuse such translated versions, problematic items become visible. The UX researcher using such a translation often asks directly about some phrases. In addition, problematic items show lower correlations than expected to the other items in the same scale. Thus, if you check the Cronbach Alpha coefficient for the translated scales, such problems will become visible immediately. But do not overreact! Items are always interpreted in the context of the evaluated product. Thus, the evaluated product itself can induce some changes in meaning. If you have only one study available in which an item shows unexpected correlations with the other items in the scale, it is advisable not to change the item. If this occurs in several studies with different products, this is a clear indication that something went wrong during translation.

A point that must be discussed is for which questions the quality of a translation is important. If you are using a translated questionnaire to compare products or to track the development of a product over time, this question is clearly not highly relevant. Even if the translation has minor deviations from the original, these will always influence the measurement in the same direction. If you only use this questionnaire for comparisons, the differences will still be meaningful.

If you are trying to compare results achieved in different countries with different language versions, the quality of the translation is obviously a relevant point. The same applies when you refer to the benchmark data to decide how good or bad your results are compared to the other products in the benchmark dataset.

Bibliography

Aparicio, M., Bacao, F.& Oliveira, T. (2016). Cultural impacts on e-learning systems' success. Internet High Education, 31, pp. 58–70.

Aufderhaar, K., Schrepp, M. & Thomaschewski, J. (2019). Do Women and Men Perceive User Experience Differently? International Journal of Interactive Multimedia and Artificial Intelligence, 5, pp. 63-67.

Bargas-Avila, J. A., & Brühlmann, F. (2016). Measuring user rated language quality: Development and validation of the user interface Language Quality Survey (LQS). International Journal of Human-Computer Studies, 86, pp. 1-10.

Benedek, J. & Miner, T. (2002). Measuring Desirability: New methods for evaluating desirability in a usability lab setting. Usability Professionals Association, 2002 Conference Proceedings.

Birkhoff, G.D. (1933). Aesthetic Measure, Cambridge, USA: Harvard University Press.

Bonsiepe, G. A. (1968). A method of quantifying order in typographic design. Journal of Typographic Research, 2, pp. 203-220.

Boos, B. & Brau, H. (2017). Erweiterung des UEQ um die Dimensionen Akustik und Haptik. In: Hess, S. & Fischer, H. (Eds.), Mensch und Computer 2017 - Usability Professionals, Regensburg: Gesellschaft für Informatik e.V., pp. 321 – 327.

Bradley, M.M. & Lang P. J. (1994): Measuring emotion: The self-assessment manikin and the semantic differential. Journal of Behavior Therapy and Experimental Psychiatry, 25(1), pp. 49–59.

Brockmyer, J. H., Fox, C. M., Curtiss, K. A., McBroom, E., Burkhart, K. M. & Pidruzny, J. N. (2009). The development of the Game Engagement Questionnaire: A measure of engagement in video game-playing. Journal of Experimental Social Psychology, 45(4), pp. 624-634.

Brooke, J. (1996). SUS-A quick and dirty usability scale. Usability Evaluation in Industry, 189(194), pp. 4-7.

Brooke, J. (2013). SUS A Retrospective. Journal of Usability Studies, 8(2), pp. 29-40.

Card, S., Moran, T.P. & Newel A. (1983). The Psychology of Human Computer Interaction. Mahwah: Lawrence Erlbaum Associates.

Cattell, R.B. (1966). The Scree Test for the Number of Factors. Multivariate Behavioral Research. 1 (2), pp. 245–276.

Chang, V. (1999). Evaluating the effectiveness of online learning using a new web based learning instrument. Proceedings Western Australian Institute for Educational Research Forum 1999.

Chiew, T. K. & Salim, S. S. (2003). Webuse: Website usability evaluation tool. Malaysian Journal of Computer Science, 16(1), pp. 47-57.

Chin, J. P., Diehl, V. A. & Norman, K. L. (1988). Development of an instrument measuring user satisfaction of the human-computer interface. In Proceedings of the SIGCHI conference on Human factors in computing systems, New York: ACM, pp. 213-218.

Cortina, J.M. (1993). What is coefficient Alpha? An examination of theory and applications? Journal of Applied Psychology, 78(1), pp. 98-104.

Cronbach, L.J. (1951). Coefficient alpha and the internal structure of tests. Psychometrika, 16, pp. 297-334.

Cronje, J.C. (2010). Using Hofstede's cultural dimensions to interpret cross-cultural blended teaching and learning. Computers & Education, 56, pp. 596–603.

Davis, F.D. (1989). Perceived Usefulness, Perceived Ease of Use, and User Acceptance of Information Technology. MIS Quarterly, 13(3), pp. 319-340.

Davis, F. (1986). A technology acceptance model for empirically testing new end-user information systems - Theory and results, PhD Thesis, Massachusetts Inst. of Technology.

Davis, F., Bagozzi, P. & Warshaw, P. (1989). User acceptance of computer technology - A comparison of two theoretical models. Management Science, 35(8), pp. 982–1003.

Deci, E. L. & Ryan, R. M. (2000). The 'what' and 'why' of goal pursuits: Human needs and the self-determination of behavior. Psychological Inquiry, 11, pp. 227-268.

Deng, L. & Poole, M.S. (2012). Aesthetic design of e-commerce web pages – Webpage Complexity, Order and preference. In Electronic Commerce Research and Applications, 11(4), pp. 420-440.

Dick, A., Dipankar, C. & Gabriel, B. (1990). Memory-Based Inference During Consumer Choice. Journal of Consumer Research, 17, pp. 82–93.

Dion, K.K., Berscheid, E. & Walster, E. (1972). What is beautiful is good. Journal of Personality and Social Psychology, 24, pp. 285–290.

Doll, W. J. & Torkzadeh, G. (1988). The measurement of end-user computing satisfaction. MIS Quarterly, pp. 259–274.

Doney, P. & Cannon, J. (1997). An examination of the nature of trust in buyer-seller relationships. Journal of Marketing, 51(2), pp. 11-27.

Elling, S., Lentz, L. & De Jong, M. (2007). Website Evaluation Questionnaire: Development of a research-based tool for evaluating informational websites. Lecture Notes in Computer Science, 4656, pp. 293–304.

Ertl, B.& Helling, K. (2014). Individual and Socio-Cultural Framing of e-Learning. IGI Global.

Everard, A. & Galletta, D.F. (2003). Effect of Presentation Flaws on Users Perception of Quality of On-Line Stores Web Sites: Is it Perception that Really Counts? Proceedings of the Second Annual Workshop on HCI Research in MIS, Seattle, WA, December 12-13, pp. 60-65.

Finstadt, K. (2010). The Usability Metric for User Experience. Interacting with Computers, 22(5), pp. 323-327.

Ford, G.T. & Smith, R.A. (1987): Inferential Beliefs in Consumer Evaluations: An Assessment of Alternative Processing Strategies. Journal of Consumer Research, 14, pp. 363-371.

George, D. & Mallery, P. (2003). SPSS for Windows step by step: A simple guide and reference. 11.0 update (4th ed.). Allyn & Bacon.

Guttman, L. (1954): Some necessary conditions for common factor analysis. Psychometrika, 19, pp. 149–161.

Harbich, S., Hassenzahl, M. & Kinzel, K. (2007). e4-Ein neuer Ansatz zur Messung der Qualität interaktiver Produkte für den Arbeitskontext. Oldenbourg Verlag.

Hassenzahl, M. (2001). The effect of perceived hedonic quality on product appealingness. International Journal of Human-Computer Interaction, 13(4), pp. 481–499.

Hassenzahl, M., Burmester, M. & Koller, F. (2003). AttrakDiff: Ein Fragebogen zur Messung wahrgenommener hedonischer und pragmatischer Qualität. In: J.Ziegler; G. Szwillus (Hrsg.), Mensch & Computer 2003. Interaktion in Bewegung, Stuttgart, Leipzig: B.G. Teubner, pp. 187-196.

Hart, S. G. & Staveland, L. E. (1988). Development of NASA-TLX (Task Load Index): Results of Empirical and Theoretical Research. In Hancock, P. A.; Meshkati, N. (Eds.). Human Mental Workload. Advances in Psychology, 52, pp. 139–183. Amsterdam: North Holland.

Held, T., Schrepp, M. & Mayalidag, R. (2019). User Experience Review - Ein einfaches und flexibles Verfahren zur Beurteilung der User Experience durch Experten. Mensch und Computer 2019-Usability Professionals.

Hekkert, P., Smelders, D. & van Wieringen, P. (2003). Most advanced, yet acceptable: Typicality and novelty as joint predictors of aesthetic preference in industrial design. British Journal of Psychology, 94, pp. 111-124.

Hinderks, A., Schrepp, M., Rauschenberger, M., Olschner, S. & Thomaschewski, J. (2012). Konstruktion eines Fragebogens für jugendliche

Personen zur Messung der User Experience. In: Brau, H.; Lehmann, A.; Petrovic, K.; Schroeder, M. (Hrsg.); Usability Professionals 2012, pp. 78 – 83.

Hinderks, A., Schrepp, M., Domínguez Mayo, F.J., Escalona, M.J. & Thomaschewski, J. (2019). Developing a UX KPI based on the User Experience Questionnaire. Computer Standards & Interfaces, 65, pp. 38-44.

Hofstede, G. (2001). Culture's Consequences – Comparing Values, Behaviors, Institutions and Organizations Across Nations, 2. Edition, Thousand Oaks: London, Neu Delhi.

Hone, K. S. & Graham, R. (2000). Towards a tool for the subjective assessment of speech system interfaces (SASSI). Natural Language Engineering, 6(3-4), pp. 287–303.

Horst, P. (1971). Messung und Vorhersage – Eine Einführung in die psychologische Testtheorie. Beltz-Verlag: Weinheim, Berlin, Basel.

Hotelling, H. (1933). Analysis of a complex of statistical variables into principal components. Journal of Educational Psychology. 24 (6), pp. 417–441.

Hulsmeier, D., Schell-Majoor, L., Rennies, J., & van de Par, S. (2014). Perception of sound quality of product sounds: A subjective study using a semantic differential. In: INTER-NOISE and NOISE-CON Congress and Conference Proceedings, 249(7), pp. 843-851. Institute of Noise Control Engineering.

Hurtienne, J. & Naumann, A. (2010). QUESI—A questionnaire for measuring the subjective consequences of intuitive use. Interdisciplinary College, pp. 536.

Ilmberger, W., Schrepp, M. & Held, T. (2009). Was verursacht den Zusammenhang zwischen Ästhetik und Usability. In: H. Wandke; S. Kain & D. Struve (Hrsg.): Mensch & Computer 2009. Oldenbourg Verlag, pp. 383-392.

ISO 9241-110: Ergonomic requirements for office work with visual display terminals (VDTs) - Part 110: Guidance on usability. International Organization for Standardization.

ISO 9241-210: Ergonomics of human-system interaction -- Part 210: Human-centred design for interactive systems. International Organization for Standardization.

Isen, A. M. (2000). Positive affect and decision making. In Lewis, M., Haviland, J.M. (Eds.): Handbook of emotions (2nd edtion), New York: Guilford Press, pp. 417–435.

Ijsselsteijn, W. A., de Kort, Y. A. W. & Poels, K. (2013). The Game Experience Questionnaire. Eindhoven: Technische Universiteit Eindhoven.

Jennett, C., Cox A.L., Cairns, P., Dhoparee, S., Epps, A., Tijs, T. & Walton, A. (2008). Measuring and Defining the Experience of the Immersion in Games. International Journal of Human-Computer Studies, 66(9), pp. 641-661.

John, B.E. & Kieras, D.E. (1996): The GOMS family of user interface analysis techniques: Comparison and Contrast. ACM Transactions on Computer-Human Interaction, 3(4), pp. 320-351.

John, B., Prevas, K., Salvucci, D. & Koedinger, K. (2004) Predictive Human Performance Modeling Made Easy. In: Dykstra-Erickson, E. & Tscheligi, M. (Eds.), Proceedings of CHI Conference on Human Factors in Computing Systems, pp. 455 – 462. New York: ACM Press.

John, B. E. & Salvucci, D. D. (2005). Multi-Purpose Prototypes for Assessing User Interfaces in Pervasive Computing Systems. IEEE Pervasive Computing, 4(4), pp. 27-34.

Karlin, B. & Ford, R. (2013). The Usability Perception Scale (UPscale): A measure for evaluating feedback displays. In: Proceedings of the 2013 Human Computer Interaction (HCII) Conference. Las Vegas, NV: ACM.

Keiningham, T.L., Aksoy, L., Cooil, B. & Andreassen, T.W. (2008). Linking Customer Loyalty to Growth. Sloan Management Review, pp. 50–57.

Kim, J. & Moon, J.K. (1998). Designing towards emotional usability in customer interfaces – trustworthiness of cyber-banking system interfaces. Interacting with Computers, 10, pp. 1-29.

Kirakowski, J. & Corbett, M. (1993). SUMI: The software usability measurement inventory. British Journal of Educational Technology, 24(3), pp. 210-212.

Kirakowski, J. & Cierlik, B. (1998). Measuring the usability of web sites. In Proceedings of the Human Factors and Ergonomics Society annual meeting, 42(4), pp. 424-428. Sage CA: Los Angeles.

Klein, A., Hinderks, A., Schrepp, M. & Thomaschewski, J. (2020). Construction of UEQ+ Scales for Voice Quality - Measuring User Experience Quality of Voice Interaction. In: Proceedings of the Conference on Mensch und Computer (MuC '20). Association for Computing Machinery, New York, NY, USA, pp. 1–5.

Konradt, U., Wandke, H., Balazs, B. & Christophersen, T. (2003). Usability in online shops: scale construction, validation and the influence on the buyers' intention and decision. Behaviour & Information Technology, 22(3), pp. 165-174.

Kosslyn, S.M. (1993). Elements of Graph Design. W.H. Freeman and Company, New York.

Kurosu, M. & Kashimura, K. (1995). Apparent usability vs. inherent usability: experimental analysis of the determinants of the apparent usability. Denver, Colorado: Conference Companion of human factors in computing systems, pp. 292–293.

Kurosu, M. (2015). Usability, quality in use and the model of quality characteristics. In: International Conference on Human-Computer Interaction, pp. 227-237. Springer, Cham.

Lallemand, C., Koenig, V. & Gronier, G. (2014). How relevant is an expert evaluation of user experience based on a psychological needs-driven approach? In Proceedings of the 8th Nordic conference on human-computer interaction: Fun, fast, foundational, pp. 11-20.

Lance, C. E., LaPointe, J. A. & Stewart, A. M. (1994). A test of the context dependency of three causal models of halo rater error. Journal of Applied Psychology, 79(3), pp. 332

Lance, C. E., Butts, M. M. & Michels, L. C. (2006). The source of four commonly reported cutoff criteria. Organizational Research Methods, 9(2), pp. 202–220.

Laugwitz, B.; Schrepp, M. & Held, T. (2006). Konstruktion eines Fragebogens zur Messung der User Experience von Softwareprodukten. In: A.M. Heinecke & H. Paul (Eds.): Mensch & Computer 2006 – Mensch und Computer im Strukturwandel. Oldenbourg Verlag, pp. 125 – 134.

Laugwitz, B., Schrepp, M. & Held, T. (2008). Construction and evaluation of a user experience questionnaire. In: Holzinger, A. (Ed.): USAB 2008, LNCS 5298, pp. 63-76.

Lavie, T. & Tractinsky, N. (2004). Assessing dimensions of perceived visual aesthetics of web sites. International Journal of Human-Computer-Studies, 60, pp. 269-298.

Lewis, J. R. (1991). Psychometric evaluation of an after-scenario questionnaire for computer usability studies: The ASQ. ACM Sigchi Bulletin, 23(1), pp. 78-81.

Lewis, J. R. (1992). Psychometric evaluation of the post-study system usability questionnaire: The PSSUQ. In Proceedings of the Human Factors and Ergonomics Society Annual Meeting, 36(16), Sage CA: Los Angeles, pp. 1259-1260.

Lewis, J. R., Utesch, B. S. & Maher, D. E. (2013). UMUX-LITE: when there's no time for the SUS. In Proceedings of the SIGCHI Conference on Human Factors in Computing Systems, pp. 2099-2102.

Lewis, J.R. & Erdinc, O. (2017). User Experience Rating Scales with 7, 11, or 101 Points: Does it matter? Journal of Usability Studies, 12(2), pp. 73-91.

Lewis, J.R. & Sauro, J. (2018). Item benchmarks for the System Usability Scale. Journal of Usability Studies, 13(3), pp. 158–167.

Lienert, G. A. (1989). Testaufbau und Testanalyse. Psychologie Verlags Union.

Lin, H., Choong, Y. & Salvendy, G. (1997) A Proposed Index of Usability: A Method for Comparing the Relative Usability of Different Software Systems. Behaviour & Information Technology, 16(4/5), pp. 267-278.

Loewy, R. (1951). Never leave well enough alone. New York: Simon and Schuster.

Loiacono, E.T., Watson, R.T. & Goodhue, D.L. (2007). WebQual: An Instrument for Consumer Evaluation of Web Sites. International Journal of Electronic Commerce, 11(3), pp. 51-87.

Lund, A. M. (2001). Measuring usability with the USE questionnaire. Usability Interface, 8(2), pp. 3-6.

Mack, R. L. & Nielsen, J. (1995). Usability inspection methods: Executive summary. In Readings in Human–Computer Interaction, pp. 170-181. Morgan Kaufmann.

Marcus, A. & Gould, E.W. (2001). Cultural dimensions and global web design: what? So What? Now what?. In: Proceedings of the 6th Conference on Human Factors in the Web, Austin Texas.

Marcus, A. & Baumgartner, V.J. (2004). Mapping user-interface design components vs. culture dimensions in corporate websites. Visible Lang. J. MIT Press, 38(1), pp. 1–65.

Mayer, D., Schrepp, M. & Held, T. (2018). Beurteilung der UX Qualität durch Experten. Mensch und Computer 2018 - Usability Professionals.

Miller, R. B. (1968). Response time in man-computer conversational transactions. In: Proceedings of the December 9-11. Fall joint computer conference, Part I, pp. 267-277. ACM.

Minge, M. & Riedel, L. (2013). meCUE – Ein modularer Fragebogen zur Erfassung des Nutzungserlebens. In: S. Boll, S. Maaß & R. Malaka (Eds.): Mensch und Computer 2013: Interaktive Vielfalt, München: Oldenbourg Verlag, pp. 89-98.

Mohs, C., Hurtienne, J., Kindsmüller, M.C., Israel, J.H. & Meyer, H.A (2006). IUUI – Intuitive Use of User Interfaces: Auf dem Weg zu einer wissenschaftlichen Basis für das Schlagwort "Intuitivität". MMI Interaktiv, 11, pp. 75-84.

Moshagen, M. & Thielsch, M. T. (2010). Facets of visual aesthetics. International Journal of Human-Computer Studies, 68(10), pp. 689-709.

Moshagen, M. & Thielsch, M. T. (2013). A short version of the visual aesthetics of websites inventory. Behaviour & Information Technology, 32(12), pp. 1305-1311.

Müller, K. & Schrepp, M. (2013). Visuelle Komplexität, Ästhetik und Usability von Benutzerschnittstellen. In: Boll, S.; Maaß, S. & Malaka, R. (Eds.), Mensch & Computer 2013, München: Oldenbourg Verlag, pp. 211 - 220.

Nakamura, J. & Csikszentmihalyi, M. (2009). Flow Theory and Research. In: Lopez, S. & C. Snyder (Eds.), The Oxford Handbook of positive Psychology, Ch. 18, pp. 195- 206.

Nielsen, J. (1993). Usability Engineering, Academic Press, San Diego, CA.

Nielsen, J. (1999) Trust or Bust: Communicating Trustworthiness in Web Design (Nielsen Norman Group). Available online: https://www.nngroup.com/articles/communicating-trustworthiness/.

Nielsen, J., & Molich, R. (1990). Heuristic evaluation of user interfaces. In Proceedings of the SIGCHI conference on Human factors in computing systems, pp. 249-256.

Ngo, D.C., Teo, L.S. & Byrne, J.S. (2000). Formalizing guidelines for the design of screen layouts. Displays, 21, pp. 3-15.

Nordlight Research, 2008. NLR web scan Instrumentenentwicklung [NRL web scan development]. Hilden, Germany: Rafael Jaron.

Norman, D. (2003). Emotional Design: Why We Love (Or Hate) Everyday Things. Boulder Colorado: Basic Books.

Nunnally, J. C. (1978). Psychometric theory (2nd ed.). McGraw-Hill.

Okamoto, S., Nagano, H. & Ho, H.-N. (2016). Psychophysical Dimensions of Material Perception and Methods to Specify Textural Space. In H. Kajimoto, Saga, S. & Konyo, M. (Eds.), Pervasive Haptics: Science, Design, and Application, pp. 3-20. Springer, Tokyo.

Olson, J.R. & Olson, G.M. (1990): The growth of cognitive modelling in human-computer interactions since GOMS. Human-Computer Interaction, 5, pp. 221-265.

O'Brien, H. L., Cairns, P. & Hall, M. (2018). A practical approach to measuring user engagement with the refined user engagement scale (UES) and new UES short form. International Journal of Human-Computer Studies, 112, pp. 28-39.

Pearson, K. (1901). On Lines and Planes of Closest Fit to Systems of Points in Space. Philosophical Magazine. 2 (11), pp. 559–572.

Polkosky, M. D. (2008). Machines as mediators: The challenge of technology for interpersonal communication theory and research. In E. Konjin (Ed.), Mediated Interpersonal Communication, pp. 34–57. New York, NY: Routledge.

Polkosky, M. D. & Lewis, J. R. (2003). Expanding the MOS: Development and psychometric evaluation of the MOS-R and MOS-X. International Journal of Speech Technology, 6(2), pp. 161-182.

Preece, J., Rogers, Y. & Sharpe, H. (2002). Interaction design: Beyond human-computer interaction. Wiley, New York.

Prümper, J. (1997). Der Benutzungsfragebogen ISONORM 9241/10: Ergebnisse zur Reliabilität und Validität. In: Software-Ergonomie'97, pp. 253-262. Vieweg+ Teubner Verlag.

Rafaeli, A. & Vilnai-Yavetz, I. (2004). Instrumentality, aesthetics and symbolism of physical artefacts as triggers of emotion. Theoretical Issues in Ergonomics Science, 5, pp. 91-112.

Reber, R., Schwarz, N. & Winkielman, P. (2004). Processing Fluency and Aesthetic Pleasure: Is Beauty in the Perceiver's Processing Experience? Personality and Social Psychology Review, 8(4), pp. 364-382.

Reichheld, F. F. (2003). The one number you need to grow. Harvard business review, 81(12), pp. 46-55.

Roberts, M. N. (2007). Complexity and aesthetic preference for diverse visual stimuli. Unpublished Doctoral Dissertation. Universitat de les Illes Balears.

Rummel, B. & Schrepp, M., (2018). UX-Fragebögen: Was steckt in der Varianz?. In: Dachselt, R. & Weber, G. (Eds.), Mensch und Computer 2018 - Workshopband. Bonn: Gesellschaft für Informatik e.V.

Rummel, B. & Schrepp, M. (2019). UX Fragebögen und Wortwolken. Mensch und Computer 2019 - Workshopband. Bonn: Gesellschaft für Informatik e.V.

Ryan, R. M. (1995). Psychological needs and the facilitation of integrative processes. Journal of Personality, 63, pp. 397-427.

Santos, M. E. C., Polvi, J., Taketomi, T., Yamamoto, G., Sandor, C. & Kato, H. (2015). Toward standard usability questionnaires for handheld augmented reality. IEEE computer graphics and applications, 35(5), pp. 66-75.

Santoso, H. B. & Schrepp, M. (2019). The impact of culture and product on the subjective importance of user experience aspects. Heliyon, 5(9).

Santoso, H., Schrepp, M., Hinderks, A. & Thomaschewski, J. (2017). Cultural Differences in the Perception of User Experience. In: Burghardt, M., Wimmer, R., Wolff, C. & Womser-Hacker, C. (Eds.), Mensch und Computer

2017 - Tagungsband. Regensburg: Gesellschaft für Informatik e.V., pp. 267-272.

Sauro, J. (2015). SUPR-Q: A Comprehensive Measure of the Quality of the Website User Experience. Journal of Usability Studies, 10(2), pp. 68-86.

Schönbrodt, F. D. & Perugini, M. (2013). At what sample size do correlations stabilize? Journal of Research in Personality, 47(5), pp. 609–612.

Schrepp, M. & Fischer, P. (2007). GOMS models to evaluate the efficiency of keyboard navigation in web units. Eminds – International Journal of Human Computer Interaction 1(2), pp. 33-46.

Schrepp, M., Olschner, S. & Schubert, U. (2013). User Experience Questionnaire Benchmark - Praxiserfahrungen zum Einsatz im Business-Umfeld. In: Brau, H.; Lehmann, A.; Petrovic, K.; Schroeder, M. (Eds.), Usability Professionals 2013, pp. 348 – 353.

Schrepp, M., Hinderks, A. & Thomaschewski, J. (2014). Applying the User Experience Questionnaire (UEQ) in Different Evaluation Scenarios. In: Marcus, A. (Ed.): Design, User Experience, and Usability. Theories, Methods, and Tools for Designing the User Experience. Lecture Notes in Computer Science, Volume 8517, Springer International Publishing, pp. 383-392.

Schrepp, M. & Müller, K (2015). Übersichtlichkeit als Mediator zwischen Ästhetik und Usability? In: Diefenbach, S., Henze, N. & Pielot, M. (Eds.), Mensch & Computer 2015 – Tagungsband, DE GRUYTER, pp. 73-82.

Schrepp, M. (2016). Datenqualität bei Online-Fragebögen sicherstellen. S. Hess & H. Fischer (Eds.): Mensch und Computer 2016 – Usability Professionals.

Schrepp, M., Hinderks, A. & Thomaschewski, J. (2017). Construction of a benchmark for the User Experience Questionnaire (UEQ). International Journal of Interactive Multimedia and Artificial Intelligence, 4(4), pp. 40-44.

Schrepp, Martin; Hinderks, Andreas; Thomaschewski, Jörg (2017). Design and Evaluation of a Short Version of the User Experience Questionnaire (UEQ-S). IJIMAI 4 (6), pp. 103–108.

Schrepp, M. & Thomaschewski, J. (2019). Design and Validation of a Framework for the Creation of User Experience Questionnaires. International Journal of Interactive Multimedia and Artificial Intelligence, 5(7).

Schrepp, M. (2020). A Comparison of UX Questionnaires - What is their underlying concept of user experience? In: Hansen, C., Nürnberger, A. & Preim, B. (Eds.), Mensch und Computer 2020 - Workshopband. Bonn: Gesellschaft für Informatik e.V.

Schrepp, M., Otten, R., Blum, K. & Thomaschewski, J. (2021). What causes the dependency between perceived aesthetics and perceived usability? International Journal of Interactive Multimedia and Artificial Intelligence.

Schrepp, M. (2020). On the usage of Cronbach's Alpha to measure reliability of UX scales. Journal of Usability Studies, 15(4).

Schwarz, N. (2002). Situated cognition and the wisdom of feelings. In Feldman-Barrett, L., Salovey, P. (Eds.): The wisdom of feeling: Psychological processes in emotional intelligence, New York: Guilford Press, pp. 144–166.

Sheldon, K. M., Elliot, A. J., Kim, Y. & Kasser, T. (2001). What is satisfying about satisfying events? Testing 10 candidate psychological needs. Journal of Personality and Social Psychology, 89, pp. 325-339.

Sijtsma, K. (2009). On the use, misuse, and the very limited usefulness of Cronbach's Alpha. Psychometrika, 74, pp. 107-120.

Spangenberg, E. R., Voss, K. E. & Crowley, A. E. (1997). Measuring the hedonic and utilitarian dimensions of attitude: a generally applicable scale. Advances in Consumer Research, 24, pp. 235-241.

Tarhini, A., Hone, K. & Liu, X. (2013). User acceptance towards web-based learning systems: investigating the role of social, organizational and individual factors in European higher education. In: The 2013 International Conference on Information Technology and Quantitative Management. Elsevier, pp. 189–197.

Thielsch, M. T. & Jaron, R. (2012). Das Zusammenspiel von Website-Inhalten, Usability und Ästhetik. In H. Reiterer & O. Deussen (Eds.): Mensch & Computer 2012, München: Oldenbourg, pp. 123-132.

Thielsch, M. & Hischfeld, G. (2019): Facets of Web-Site Content. Human-Computer Interaction, Vol. 34(4), pp. 279-327.

Thüring, M. & Mahlke, S. (2007). Usability, aesthetics and emotions in human–technology interaction. International Journal of Psychology, 42(4), pp. 253-264.

Torgerson, W. S. (1958). Theory & Methods of Scaling. New York: Wiley.

Tractinsky, N. (1997). Aesthetics and Apparent Usability: Empirical Assessing Cultural and Methodological Issues. CHI'97 (http://www.acm.org/sigchi/ chi97/proceedings/paper/nt.htm).

Tractinsky, N., Katz, A.S. & Ikar, D. (2000). What is beautiful is usable. Interacting with Computers, 13, pp. 127–145.

Ullrich, D. & Diefenbach, S. (2010). INTUI. Exploring the Facets of Intuitive Interaction. In J. Ziegler & A. Schmidt (Eds.) Mensch & Computer 2010, pp. 251-260. München: Oldenbourg.

Väätäjä, H., Koponen, T. & Roto, V. (2009). Developing practical tools for user experience evaluation: A case from mobile news journalism. In European Conference on Cognitive Ergonomics: Designing beyond the Product---Understanding Activity and User Experience in Ubiquitous Environments. VTT Technical Research Centre of Finland.

Venkatesh, V. & Davis, F. (2000). A theoretical extension of the technology acceptance model: Four longitudinal field studies. Management Science, 46(2), pp. 186–204.

Watson, D., Clark, L. A. & Tellegen, A. (1988). Development and validation of brief measures of positive and negative affect: the PANAS scales. Journal of personality and social psychology, 54(6), pp. 1063-1070.

Wharton, C., Rieman, J., Lewis, C. & Polson, P. (1994). The cognitive walkthrough method: A practitioner's guide. In: Usability inspection methods, pp. 105-140.

Whitefield, T. W. A. (2000). Beyond prototypicality: Toward a categorical-motivation model of aesthetics. Empirical Studies of the Arts, 18, pp. 1–11.

Willumeit, H., Gediga, G. & Hamborg, K. (1996). IsoMetrics(L): Ein Verfahren zur formativen Evaluation von Software nach ISO 9241/10. Ergonomie und Informatik, 27, pp. 5-12.

Winter, D., Hinderks, A., Schrepp, M. & Thomaschewski, J. (2017). Welche UX Faktoren sind für mein Produkt wichtig? In: Hess, S. & Fischer, H. (Eds.), Mensch und Computer 2017 - Usability Professionals. Regensburg: Gesellschaft für Informatik e.V., pp. 191 – 200.

Yang, T., Linder, J. & Bolchini, D. (2012). DEEP: Design-Oriented Evaluation of Perceived Usability. International Journal of Human-Computer Interaction, 28(5), pp. 308–346.

Yom, M. & Wilhelm, T. (2004). WOOS – Ein Messinstrument für die wahrgenommene Orientierung in Online-Shops. In: R. Keil-Slawik, H. Selke, G. Szwillus (Hrsg.): Mensch & Computer 2004: Allgegenwärtige Interaktion, pp. 43–53. München: Oldenbourg Verlag.

Zhao, F., Shen, K.N. & Collier, A. (2014). Effects of national culture on e-government diffusion—a global study of 55 countries. Information & Management, 51, pp. 1005–1016.

Zhu, D.H., Ye, Z.Q. & Chang, Y.P. (2017). Understanding the textual content of online customer reviews in B2C websites: a cross-cultural comparison between the U.S. and China. Computers in Human Behavior, 76, pp. 483–493.

Appendix 1: List of UX Questionnaires

Abbreviation	Full name	Main Reference
ASQ	After Scenario Questionnaire	Lewis (1991)
AttrakDiff2		Hassenzahl, Burmester & Koller (2003)
AttrakWork		Väätäjä, Koponen, & Roto (2009)
CSAT	Customer Satisfaction	*Often used marketing metric, no main reference*
CSUQ	Computer System Usability Questionnaire	Lewis (1992)
DEEP	Design-Oriented Evaluation of Perceived Usability	Yang, Linder & Bolchini (2012)
e4	Erledigen, Engagieren, Entdecken, Erfinden	Harbich, Hassenzahl & Kinzel (2007)
EUCS	End User Computing Satisfaction	Doll & Torkzadeh (1988)
HARUS	Handheld Augmented Reality Usability	Santos, Polvi, Taketomi, Yamamoto, Sandor & Kato (2015)
HED/UT	Hedonic/Utilitarian	Spangenberg, Voss & Crowley (1997)
INTUI	Intuitive Interaction	Ullrich & Diefenbach (2010)
ISOMETRICS		Willumeit, Gediga & Hamborg (1996)
ISONORM		Prümper (1997)
meCUE	Modular Evaluation of key Components of User Experience	Minge & Riedel (2013)
MSPRC	Microsoft Product Reaction Cards	Benedek & Miner (2002)

NPS	Net Promotor Score	Reichheld (2003)
NRL	NRL Web Scan	Nordlight Research, 2008
PSSUQ	Post-Study System Usability Survey	Lewis (1992)
PUEU	Perceived Usefulness and Ease of Use	Davis (1989)
PUTQ	Purdue Usability Testing Questionnaire	Lin, Choong & Salvendy (1997)
QUESI	Questionnaire for the subjective consequences of intuitive use	Hurtienne & Naumann (2010)
QUIS	Questionnaire for User Interaction Satisfaction	Chin, Diehl & Norman (1988)
SASSI	Subjective Assessment of Speech System Interfaces	Hone & Graham (2000)
SUISQ	Speech User Interface Service Quality	Polkosky (2008)
SUMI	Software Usability Measurement Inventory	Kirakowski & Corbett (1993)
SUPR-Q	Standardized User Experience Percentile Rank Questionnaire	Sauro (2015)
SUS	System Usability Scale	Brooke (1996)
UEQ	User Experience Questionnaire	Laugwitz, Schrepp & Held (2008)
UEQ-S	User Experience Questionnaire – Short form	Schrepp, Hinderks & Thomaschewski (2017)
UEQ+	Modular User Experience Questionnaire	Schrepp & Thomaschewski (2019)
UES	Usefulness Satisfaction and Ease of Use	Lund (2001)
UFOS	Usability Fragebogen für Online-Shops	Konradt, Wandke, Balazs & Christophersen (2003)

UMUX	Usability Metric for User Experience	Finstad (2010)
Upscale	Usability Perception Scale	Karlin & Ford (2013)
USE	User Engagement Scale	O'Brien, Cairns & Hall (2018)
UXNFQ	UX Needs Fulfillement Questionnaire	Sheldon, Elliot, Kim & Kasser (2001)
VISAWI	Visual Aesthetics of Website Inventory	Mooshagen & Thielsch (2010)
VISAWI-S	Visual Aesthetics of Website Inventory – Short form	Mooshagen & Thielsch (2013)
WAMMI	Website Analysis and Measurement Inventory	Kirakowski & Cierlik (1998)
Web-Clic	Website-Clarity, Likeability, Informativeness, Credibility	Thielsch & Hischfeld (2019)
WEBLEI	Web-based Learning Environment Instrument	Chang (1999)
WEBQUAL	Website Quality	Loiacono, Watson & Goodhue (2007)
WEBUSE	Website Usability Evaluation	Chiew & Salim (2003)
WEQ	Website Evaluation Questionnaire	Elling, Lentz & De Jong (2007)
WOOS	Wahrgenommene Orientierung in Online Shops	Yom & Wilhelm (2004)

Appendix 2: Find Relevant Questionnaires

In this appendix you will find 50 very brief descriptions of established UX questionnaires. These descriptions are intended to help UX practitioners to find questionnaires that best fit their research questions.

For each questionnaire, we give short information about the scope (i.e. if the questionnaire is only to be used for certain product categories or in certain research contexts), the number of items and their format. This should help determine whether it fits the type of product being studied and the practical constraints on the time it will take participants to answer the questions.

In addition, we provide a short semantic interpretation of the scales. This interpretation is based on the items in the scales. It is of course a bit difficult to capture in one or two sentences the meaning of complex scales containing several items. Thus, do not take these descriptions too serious. Use them to get a first overview about the UX qualities measured by the questionnaire. If you think the questionnaire fits to your needs, then you should always verify the interpretation yourself before you use the questionnaire. Don't forget, the true meaning of a scale is in the items! To make access to this detail information easy, we provide a reference to a research paper describing the questionnaire.

For many practical applications, you may need a translated version of a questionnaire. Such translations are available for many questionnaires. But it is almost impossible to get a clear picture of the available languages, and of course that picture is constantly changing. Thus, we decided not to include this information. In most cases, a quick search of your country's UX communities will help to find out if a published translation is available.

Some questionnaires offer a website containing detailed information and additional materials to download. These websites were active when this book is published (June 2021).

ASQ - After Scenario Questionnaire

Application area: Short questionnaire that should be used as part of usability testing sessions. Can be applied several times during a test session.

Length: 3 items on 1 scale, *Item format:* Statements with a 7-point answer scale.

Interpretation of the scale: Overall impression concerning usability of a scenario.

Reference: Lewis, J. R. (1991). Psychometric evaluation of an after-scenario questionnaire for computer usability studies: The ASQ. ACM Sigchi Bulletin, 23(1), pp. 78-81.

AttrakDiff2

Application area: Not restricted to special product types or application scenarios.

Length: 28 items on 4 scales, *Item format:* Semantic differential with a 7-point answer scale.

Interpretation of the scales:

- *Attractiveness:* Overall impression of the product. Do users like it or dislike it?
- *Pragmatic Quality:* Measures usability related aspects of the interaction.
- *Stimulation:* Is the product exciting? Is the design original and novel?
- *Identity:* Is the product of high quality or high value? Does owning or using the product improve prestige?

Remarks: Strong focus on non-task related (hedonic) UX aspects. Only 7 of the 28 items represent classical usability criteria. Thus, not so well-suited to evaluate products that are mainly used to in a working context.

Main Reference: Hassenzahl, M., Burmester, M. & Koller, F. (2004). AttrakDiff: Ein Fragebogen zur Messung wahrgenommener hedonischer und pragmatischer Qualität In J. Ziegler & G. Szwillus (Eds.), Mensch & Computer 2003. Interaktion in Bewegung, pp. 187-196. Stuttgart, Leipzig: BG Teubner.

Website: http://www.attrakdiff.de/

AttrakWork

Application area: Adaption of the AttrakDiff2 to work related products (systems for mobile news journalism).

Length: 36 items on 5 scales, *Item format:* Semantic differential with a 7-point answer scale.

Scales and their interpretation: Contain the same scales as the Attrakdiff2 plus an additional scale called *Task and goal achievement*. This scale covers the impression that the product supports own work goals and saves effort.

Remarks: This is an adaption of the AttrakDiff2 to work related contexts (UX of mobile news journalism systems). The wording of some items in the AttrakDiff2 scales are therefore adapted to this new context. However, the semantic interpretation of the 4 scales taken from AttrakDiff2 stays the same. The wording of the items is specific to systems used for mobile news journalism. It is unclear if the questionnaire can be used for work related products in other domains.

Main Reference: Väätäjä, H., Koponen, T. & Roto, V. (2009). Developing practical tools for user experience evaluation: A case from mobile news journalism. In European Conference on Cognitive Ergonomics: Designing beyond the Product---Understanding Activity and User Experience in Ubiquitous Environments. VTT Technical Research Centre of Finland.

CSAT - Customer Satisfaction

Application area: Single item questionnaire that measures customer satisfaction. Not restricted to specific product categories.

Length: 1 Item, *Item format:* Statement with a 5-point answer scale.

Scale interpretation: Overall satisfaction of a customer or user with a product.

Main Reference: Commonly used marketing metric, a clear main reference could not be identified.

DEEP - Design-Oriented Evaluation of Perceived Usability

Application area: Measures usability of websites.

Length: 19 items on 6 scales, *Item format:* Statements with a 5-point answer scale.

Scales and their interpretation:

- *Perceived Cognitive Effort:* Is it easy and effortless to learn how to use the website?
- *Perceived Content:* Are the texts on the website easy to understand and useful?
- *Perceived Layout Consistency:* Is the layout of different pages consistent?
- *Perceived Navigation:* Is it easy to find relevant information?

- *Perceived Structure and Information Architecture:* Is the structure of the website clear and well organized?
- *Perceived Visual Guidance:* Are colors or visual highlighting helpful for orientation on the website?

Main Reference: Yang, T., Linder, J. & Bolchini, D. (2012). DEEP: Design-Oriented Evaluation of Perceived Usability. International Journal of Human-Computer Interaction, 28(5), pp. 308–346.

EUCS - End User Computing Satisfaction

Application area: Measures usability of work-related products or systems.

Length: 12 Items on 5 scales, *Item format:* Statements with a 5-point answer scale.

Scales and their interpretation:

- *Accuracy:* Items concerning accuracy of the system.
- *Content:* Items concerning quality and usefulness of provided content.
- *Ease of use:* Abstract items concerning ease of use or usability.
- *Format:* Items concerning clarity and format of system output.
- *Timeliness:* Items concerning actuality of content and the time required to get content.

Remarks: The scales are a bit hard to interpret. Sometimes semantics of different items on one scale are quite different.

Main Reference: Doll, W. J. & Torkzadeh, G. (1988). The measurement of end-user computing satisfaction. MIS Quarterly, June, pp. 259–274.

E4

Application area: Not restricted to special product types or application scenarios.

Length: 18 items on 4 scales, *Item format:* Statements with a 7-point answer scale.

Scales and their interpretation (German scale names in parenthesis):

- *Engage (Engagieren):* Do I forget time when I work with the product? Do I play around with the product even after I have finished my tasks?
- *Invent (Erfinden):* Can I use the product for new and unusual use cases for which it was not actually intended?

- *Discover (Entdecken):* Is the product useful, does it contain functions that will be potentially useful for me in the future?

- *Finish (Erledigen):* Can I complete my tasks with the product fast and efficient?

Main Reference: Harbich, S., Hassenzahl, M. & Kinzel, K. (2007). e4-Ein neuer Ansatz zur Messung der Qualität interaktiver Produkte für den Arbeitskontext. Oldenbourg Verlag.

GEQ - Game Engagement Questionnaire

Application area: Computer games.

Length: 19 items on a single scale, *Item format:* Statements with a 5-point answer scale.

Interpretation of the scale: Level of engagement (immersion) in a computer game.

Reference: Brockmyer, J. H., Fox, C. M., Curtiss, K. A., McBroom, E., Burkhart, K. M. & Pidruzny, J. N. (2009). The development of the Game Engagement Questionnaire: A measure of engagement in video game-playing. Journal of Experimental Social Psychology, 45(4), pp. 624-634.

HARUS - Handheld Augmented Reality Usability

Application area: Augmented reality applications on handheld devices.

Length: 16 items on 2 scales, *Item format:* Statements with a 7-point answer scale

Scales and their interpretation:

- *Comprehensibility:* Is the display of information easy to scan and understand? Does the display react fast enough?

- *Manipulability:* Is it easy to control the application? Does the interaction require a lot of muscle strength?

Remarks: The scales are not so easy to interpret. Both contain many different aspects related to cognitive effort and muscular effort.

Main Reference: Santos, M. E. C., Polvi, J., Taketomi, T., Yamamoto, G., Sandor, C. & Kato, H. (2015). Toward standard usability questionnaires for handheld augmented reality. IEEE computer graphics and applications, 35(5), pp. 66-75.

HEDUT – Hedonic / Utilitatian

Application area: Measuring the hedonic and utilitarian (HED-UT) elements of a product. Not restricted to interactive products. The questionnaire was developed inside general consumer research.

Length: 24 items on 2 scales, *Item format:* Semantic differential with a 7-point answer scale.

Scales and their interpretation:

- *Hedonic:* Is the product funny, enjoyable, delightful, amusing?
- *Utilitarian:* Is the product useful, practical, efficient, effective?

Main Reference: Spangenberg, E. R., Voss, K. E. & Crowley, A. E. (1997). Measuring the hedonic and utilitarian dimensions of attitude: a generally applicable scale. Advances in Consumer Research, 24, pp. 235-241.

INTUI - Intuitive Interaction

Application area: Measures intuitive interaction with a product. Not restricted to special products or application scenarios.

Length: 17 items on 4 scales, *Item format:* Semantic differential with a 7-point answer scale

Scales and their interpretation:

- *Effortlessness:* Can the product be used naturally, easily and effortlessly?
- *Gut feeling:* Can the product be used without thinking, just guided by feelings?
- *Magical Experience:* Is the interaction inspiring, fascinating or like a magical experience?
- *Verbalizability:* Is it hard to explain in retrospect how I did things?

Main Reference: Ullrich, D. & Diefenbach, S. (2010). INTUI. Exploring the Facets of Intuitive Interaction. In J. Ziegler & A. Schmidt (Eds.) Mensch & Computer 2010, pp. 251-260. München: Oldenbourg.

Website: http://www.intuitiveinteraction.net/

ISOMETRICS

Application area: Not restricted to special product types or application scenarios.

Length: 75 items on 7 scales, *Item format:* Statements with a 5-point answer scale.

Scales and their interpretation:

- *Suitability for the task:* Does the product offer all functionality that is required for the user to reach his or her goals? Can the user work efficiently?

- *Self-descriptiveness:* Does the product offer all required information to the user? Does it give suitable feedback on the current system status?

- *Controllability:* Does the user feel in control of the interaction? Does the product react as expected to user input or user actions?

- *Conformity with user expectations:* Does the displayed information and the design of the user interface correspond to the expectations of the user? Is the product design consistent?

- *Error tolerance:* Does the product support the user to avoid or to recover fast from errors?

- *Suitability for individualization:* Can the user adapt the product to his or her personal working style or to personal preferences?

- *Suitability for learning:* Is It easy for the user to learn how to use the product?

Remarks: The scales correspond to the ISO dialog principles.

Main Reference: Gediga, G., Hamborg, K. C. & Düntsch, I. (1999). The IsoMetrics usability inventory: An operationalization of ISO 9241-10 supporting summative and formative evaluation of software systems. Behaviour & Information Technology, 18(3), pp. 151-164.

Website: http://www.isometrics.uni-osnabrueck.de/

ISONORM

Application area: Not restricted to special product types or application scenarios.

Length: 35 items on 7 scales, *Item Format:* Statements with a 7-point answer scale.

Scales and their interpretation:

- *Suitability for the task:* Does the product offer all functionality that is required for the user to reach his or her goals? Can the user work efficiently?

- *Self-descriptiveness:* Does the product offer all required information to the user? Does it give suitable feedback on the current system status?

- *Controllability:* Does the user feel in control of the interaction? Does the product react as expected to user input or user actions?

- *Conformity with user expectations:* Does the displayed information and the design of the user interface correspond to the expectations of the user? Is the product design consistent?

- *Error tolerance:* Does the product support the user to avoid or to recover fast from errors?

- *Suitability for individualization:* Can the user adapt the product to his or her personal working style or to personal preferences?

- *Suitability for learning:* Is It easy for the user to learn how to use the product?

Remarks: Oriented on the 7 ISO dialog principles. Similar to ISOMETRICS, but shorter.

Main Reference: Prümper, J. (1997). Der Benutzungsfragebogen ISONORM 9241/10: Ergebnisse zur Reliabilität und Validität. In Software-Ergonomie'97, pp. 253-262. Vieweg + Teubner Verlag.

LQS - Language Quality Survey

Application area: Language quality in texts displayed in websites and user interfaces.

Length: 10 items, *Item format:* Statements with a 5-point answer scale.

Interpretation of the scale: Overall language quality of the texts.

Remarks: The paper cited below reports an exploratory factor analysis of the items which extracts two factors that can be used as sub-scales. These sub-scales can be interpreted as *Linguistic correctness of the text* and *Readability of the text.*

Reference: Bargas-Avila, J. A. & Brühlmann, F. (2016). Measuring user rated language quality: Development and validation of the user interface Language Quality Survey (LQS). International Journal of Human-Computer Studies, 86, pp. 1-10.

meCUE – Modular Evaluation of key Components of User Experience

Application area: Not restricted to special product types or application scenarios.

Length: 33 items on 9 scales (Modular), *Item Format:* Statements with a 7-point answer scale.

Scales and their interpretation:

- *Usability:* Is the product easy to use? Is it easy to learn how to use it?

- *Usefulness:* Is the product useful? Can I reach my goals with the product?

- *Visual aesthetics:* Is the product attractive, stylish and creatively designed?

- *Commitment:* Would it be a huge problem to lose the product? Does the product feel like a friend?

- *Status:* Does the product improve my prestige? Do others perceive me differently because I own the product?

- *Loyalty:* Would I buy the product again? Is the product superior to other products?

- *Intention to use:* Do I want to use the product as often as possible?

- *Negative Emotions:* Is the product frustrating? Does it make me angry?

- *Positive Emotions:* Is the product relaxing? Does it make me happy?

Main Reference: Minge, M. & Riedel, L. (2013). meCUE-Ein modularer Fragebogen zur Erfassung des Nutzungserlebens. Mensch & Computer 2013: Interaktive Vielfalt.

Website: http://mecue.de/home/start.html

MOS-X – Mean opinion scale

Application area: Measures users' subjective assessments of synthetic speech output.

Length: 15 items on 4 scales, *Item format:* Statements with a 7-point answer scale.

Interpretation of the scales:

- *Intelligibility:* Is the voice easy to understand? Is the articulation precise?

- *Naturalness:* Does the voice sound pleasant, natural, human?

- *Prosody:* Does the rhythm and intonation sound natural.

- *Social Impression:* Does the voice sound trustworthy, enthusiastic, confident?

Main Reference: Polkosky, M. D. & Lewis, J. R. (2003). Expanding the MOS: Development and psychometric evaluation of the MOS-R and MOS-X. International Journal of Speech Technology, 6(2), pp. 161-182.

MSPRC - Product Reaction Cards

Application area: No special application domain. Can be applied for all types of interactive products.

Length: 118 attributes, no scales.

Scales: No scales, purely qualitative result. Items cover a wide range of UX aspects.

Remarks: Does not provide a quantitative measurement.

Main Reference: Benedek, J. & Miner, T. (2002). Measuring Desirability: New methods for evaluating desirability in a usability lab setting. Proceedings of Usability Professionals Association.

NASA-TLX – NASA Task Load Index

Application area: Measures perceived workload during task processing. Not restricted to special application types.

Length: 6 items on 6 sub-scales and an overall scale for perceived workload, *Item format:* Statements with a 21-point answer scale.

Scales (Items): Mental demand, Physical demand, Temporal demand, Overall performance, Effort, Frustration level.

Reference: Hart, S. G. & Staveland, L. E. (1988). Development of NASA-TLX (Task Load Index): Results of Empirical and Theoretical Research. In Hancock, P. A.; Meshkati, N. (Eds.). Human Mental Workload. Advances in Psychology, pp. 139–183. 52. Amsterdam: North Holland.

NPS - Net Promoter Score

Application area: Single item questionnaire that measures customer loyalty or satisfaction.

Length: 1 Item, *Item format:* Statement with a 11-point answer scale.

Scale interpretation: One scale for customer loyalty.

Remarks: Due to the scoring logic a huge sample is required to get stable results.

Main Reference: Reichheld, F. F. (2003). The one number you need to grow, Harvard Business Review, 81(12), pp. 46–54.

NRL Web Scan

Application area: User Impression of websites.

Length: 23 items on 3 scales, *Item format:* Statements with a 4-point answer scale.

Scales and their interpretation:

- *Usability:* Detailed items concerning the general usability, e.g. placement of elements, search capabilities, visibility of navigation elements.

- *Content:* Detailed items concerning the quality of the information on the website, e.g. usefulness of text, ease of understanding, length of texts.

- *Design:* Detailed items concerning visual design aspects, e.g. fonts, contrasts, professional appearance.

Main Reference: Nordlight Research, 2008. NLR web scan Instrumentenentwicklung [NRL web scan development]. Hilden, Germany: Rafael Jaron.

Website: https://www.nordlight-research.com/de/loesungen/ kommunikationsforschung/website-umfrage.html

PANAS – Positive and negative affect scales

Application area: Can be used to measure the mood of a user. General psychological questionnaire, not restricted to UX measurement.

Length: 20 items on 2 scales, *Item format:* Single words that describe emotions, 5-point answer scale.

Interpretation of the scales:

- *Positive Affect:* Positive emotions (excited, enthusiastic, proud, interested, etc.).

- *Negative Affect:* Negative emotions (nervous, afraid, upset, scared, etc.).

Main Reference: Watson, D., Clark, L. A. & Tellegen, A. (1988). Development and validation of brief measures of positive and negative affect: the PANAS scales. Journal of personality and social psychology, 54(6), pp. 1063-1070.

PSSUQ - Post-Study System Usability Questionnaire

Application area: To be used at the end of a usability test. Not restricted to special types of products.

Length: 16 items on 3 scales, *Item format:* Statements with a 7-point answer scale.

Scales and their interpretation:

- *System Usefulness:* Covers ease of learning, ease of use, and the impression that tasks can be done quickly with the product.

- *Information Quality:* Covers aspects related to recovery from errors, how easy it is to find the required information in the screens and how useful this information is.

- *Interface Quality:* Overall impression of the interaction with the product. Do users like the interface, are they satisfied, is the interaction pleasant?

Remarks: There is also a version available (called CSUQ) that can be used as a questionnaire for end users. Items differ slightly in their formulation.

Main Reference: Lewis, J. R. (1992). Psychometric evaluation of the post-study system usability questionnaire: The PSSUQ. In Proceedings of the Human Factors and Ergonomics Society Annual Meeting, 36(16), pp. 1259-1260. Sage CA: Los Angeles.

PUEU - Perceived Usefulness and Ease of Use

Application area: Products used in a professional context.

Length: 12 items on 2 scales, *Item format:* Statements with a 7-point answer scale.

Scales and their interpretation:

- *Perceived Ease of Use:* Is it easy to learn how to use the system? Is the system flexible? Is the system clear and understandable?

- *Perceived Usefulness:* Does the system increase my productivity and effectiveness on the job? Is it useful in my job?

Remarks: Measures the two main prerequisites for the acceptance of a new technology. Oriented on the Technology Acceptance Model.

Main Reference: Davis, F.D. (1989). Perceived Usefulness, Percevied Ease of Use, and User Acceptance of Information Technology, MIS Quarterly, 13, pp.319-340.

PUTQ - Purdue Usability Testing Questionnaire

Application area: To be used at the end of a usability test. Strong focus on classical usability criteria.

Length: 100 items on 8 scales, *Item format:* Statements with a 7-point answer scale.

Scales and their interpretation:

- *Consistency:* Is the design of important elements (labels, wording, display of information) consistent in all screen of the product?

- *Minimal Memory Load:* Does the user need to remember a lot of things? Does the product support the user by highlighting, defaulting and easy to remember commands?

- *User Guidance:* Are error messages helpful? Does it provide easy ways to cancel or undo actions? Does the user have full control?

- *Learnability:* It the design of the product logical? Is it easy to learn?

- *Compatibility:* Is the product compatible with typical conventions? Does it conform to user expectations?

- *Flexibility:* Is it flexible to use? Can the user adapt it to own preferences?

- *Minimal Action:* Can tasks be completed with minimal effort?

- *Perceptual Limitation:* Is it easy to orient in the product? Are design elements clearly visible and easy to recognize?

Main Reference: Lin, H. X., Choong, Y. Y. & Salvendy, G. (1997). A proposed index of usability: a method for comparing the relative usability of different software systems. Behaviour & Information Technology, 16(4-5), pp. 267-277.

QUESI - Questionnaire for the subjective consequences of intuitive use

Application area: No special application area. Can be applied for all types of interactive products.

Length: 14 items on 5 scales, *Item format:* Statements with a 5-point answer scale.

Scales and their interpretation:

- *Subjective mental workload:* Is it possible to use the product without thinking or the need to concentrate?

- *Perceived achievement of goals:* Is it possible for the user to reach all of his or her goals?

- *Perceived effort of learning:* Is the usage of the product clear and easy from the start?

- *Familiarity:* Was the interaction with the product clear and familiar?

- *Perceived error rate:* Did any problems or errors came up during use?

Main Reference: Hurtienne, J. & Naumann, A. (2010). QUESI—A questionnaire for measuring the subjective consequences of intuitive use. Interdisciplinary College, pp. 536.

QUIS - Questionnaire of User Interaction Satisfaction

Application area: No special application area. Can be applied for all types of interactive products.

Length: 27 items on 5 scales, *Item format:* Statements with a 10-point answer scale.

Scales and their interpretation:

- *Overall reaction:* A valence dimension, measures if a user has a bad or good impression towards the product.

- *Learning:* Measures how easy it is to learn how to use the system and if this is possible by pure exploration.

- *Terminology & System Information:* Is the terminology easy to understand and fits to the tasks? Is the system feedback concerning user actions adequate?

- *Screen:* Measures the impression concerning the overall information architecture and navigation.

- *System Capabilities:* Contains items concerning efficiency or system speed, controllability and required expertise to use the system.

Main Reference: Chin, J.P, Diehl, V.A. & Norman, K.L. (1988). Development of an instrument measuring user satisfaction of the human–computer interface. In: Proceedings of CHI 1988, ACM, Washington, DC, pp. 213-218.

SAM – Self Assessment Mannequin

Application area: Language-free method to measure emotions (pleasure, arousal, dominance). General psychological instrument, not restricted to UX.

Length: 3 rows with 5 pictograms, *Item format:* Each dimension is represented by 5 pictograms.

Remarks: Easy to perform method to measure affective reactions to a system. Language-free method. Participants just have to select the pictogram which describes best their actual affective state.

Reference: Bradley, M.M. & Lang P. J. (1994): Measuring emotion: The self-assessment manikin and the semantic differential. Journal of Behavior Therapy and Experimental Psychiatry, 25(1), pp. 49–59.

SASSI - Subjective Assessment of Speech System Interfaces

Application area: Systems that use voice interaction.

Length: 33 items on 6 scales, *Item format:* Statements with a 7-point answer scale.

Scales and their interpretation:

- *Annoyance:* Is the interaction boring, frustrating, or inflexible?
- *Cognitive Demand:* Is it cognitively demanding to use the system?
- *Habitability:* Do I always know where I am and what to say?
- *Likeability:* Is the system pleasant and friendly? Do I enjoy using it?
- *Speed:* Does the system respond fast?
- *System Response Accuracy:* Is the system reliable, dependable, and accurate?

Main Reference: Hone, K. S. & Graham, R. (2000). Towards a tool for the subjective assessment of speech system interfaces (SASSI). Natural Language Engineering, 6(3-4), pp. 287–303.

SUISQ - Speech User Interface Service Quality

Application area: Interactive voice response applications used in customer service scenarios.

Length: 25 Items on 4 scales, *Item format:* Statements with a 7-point answer scale.

Scales and their interpretation:

- *User Goal Orientation:* Do I feel in control and confident when I use the system? Do I want to use it again?
- *Customer Service Behavior:* Is the system polite and friendly? Does it use everyday language?
- *Speech Characteristics:* Does the system's voice sounds natural and pleasant?
- *Verbosity:* Is the interaction efficient? Is the system to talkative?

Main Reference: Polkosky, M. D. (2008). Machines as mediators: The challenge of technology for interpersonal communication theory and research. In E. Konjin (Ed.), Mediated Interpersonal Communication, pp. 34–57. New York, NY: Routledge.

SUMI - Software Usability Measurement Inventory

Application area: Clear focus on classical usability criteria. Somehow restricted to evaluate products used in a working environment.

Length: 50 items in 5 scales, *Item format:* Statements with a 3-point answer scale.

Scales and their interpretation:

- *Efficiency:* Items cover aspects of technical response time and the impression that the product does not cause unnecessary effort to perform the typical tasks.

- *Learnability:* Items focus on the effort and difficulty to learn how to use the product. It also covers if the user has the impression that he or she can use the product intuitively or at least acquire the required skills without help by others.

- *Control:* Items describe if the user feels that he or she can adequately control and predict the behavior of the product.

- *Helpfulness:* Items describe if the supporting information material or documentation is adequate or if the product provides helpful hints during interaction.

- *Affect:* Quite heterogenous scale that covers aspects like fun of use, visual design, emotional responses, and loyalty.

Remarks: The assignment of the items to the scales and the scoring procedure are not published. You need to buy a license to get this information.

Main Reference: Kirakowski, J. & Corbett, M. (1993). SUMI: The software usability measurement inventory. British Journal of Educational Technology, 24(3), pp. 210-212.

Website: http://sumi.uxp.ie/

SUPR-Q - Standardized User Experience Percentile Rank Questionnaire

Application area: User experience of commercial websites or web shops.

Length: 8 items on 4 scales, *Item format:* Statements with a 5-point answer scale.

Scales and their interpretation:

- *Appearance:* Is the website clean, simple, and attractive?

- *Loyalty:* Is it likely that I recommend the website to others? Will I use the website again?

- *Trust:* Do I feel confident and comfortable conducting business on the website?

- *Usability:* It the website easy to use and easy to navigate?

Remarks: A license is required for the benchmark and the tools required to interpret the results (see website).

Main Reference: Sauro, J. (2015). SUPR-Q: a comprehensive measure of the quality of the website user experience. Journal of usability studies, 10(2), pp. 68-86.

Website: https://measuringu.com/product/suprq/

SUS - System Usability Scale

Application area: No special application domain. Fits quite well to evaluate products that are mainly used for work or to achieve clearly defined tasks. Short enough to be used as online questionnaire or at the end of usability tests.

Length: 10 items on 1 scale, *Item format:* Statements with a 5-point answer scale

Scale interpretation: Overall impression on usability. Items cover mainly ease of use and usefulness, perceived complexity, consistency, and ease of learning.

Remarks: A benchmark is available.

Main Reference: Brooke, J. (1996). SUS-A quick and dirty usability scale. Usability evaluation in industry, 189(194), pp. 4-7.

UEQ, - User Experience Questionnaire

Application area: No special application domain. Can be applied for all types of interactive products.

Length: 26 items in 6 scales, *Item format:* Semantic differential with a 7-point answer scale.

Scales and their interpretation:

- *Attractiveness:* Overall impression of the product. Do users like or dislike it?

- *Efficiency:* Can users solve their tasks without unnecessary effort? Does the product react fast on inputs?

- *Perspicuity:* Is it easy to get familiar with the product and to learn how to use it?

- *Dependability:* Does the user feel in control of the interaction with the product? Is it secure and predictable?
- *Stimulation:* Is it exciting and motivating to use the product? Is it fun to use the product?
- *Novelty:* Is the design of the product creative? Does it attract the interest of users?

Remarks: The UEQ does not have an overall value, just the 6 scale means are offered. But there exists an extension that allows to calculate an overall UX KPI.

Main Reference: Laugwitz, B., Held, T. & Schrepp, M. (2008). Construction and evaluation of a user experience questionnaire. In Symposium of the Austrian HCI and Usability Engineering Group, pp. 63-76. Springer, Berlin, Heidelberg.

Website: www.ueq-online.org

UEQ-S - User Experience Questionnaire – Short version

Application area: Same as UEQ.

Length: 8 items in 2 scales, *Item format:* Semantic differential with 7-point answer scale.

Scales and their interpretation:

- *Hedonic Quality:* Covers aspects of fun of use or stimulation and creative design.
- *Pragmatic Quality:* Covers aspects of efficiency, learnability, and controllability.

Main Reference: Schrepp, M.; Hinderks, A. & Thomaschewski, J. (2017): Design and Evaluation of a Short Version of the User Experience Questionnaire (UEQ-S). IJIMAI 4 (6), pp. 103–108.

Website: www.ueq-online.org

UEQ+ - Modular Extension of the User Experience Questionnaire

Application area: No special application domain. Can be applied for all types of interactive products. Due to the modular approach and the 20 available scales it is possible to use it also for quite special product types and application scenarios.

Length: Modular Approach, select from 20 scales, each scale consists of 5 items

Scales and their interpretation: Due to the many scales and the fact that new scales will be added over time, we do not explain the scales in detail here. Scales and their semantical meaning are described on the website ueqplus.ueq-research.org.

Main Reference: Schrepp, M. & Thomaschewski, J. (2019). Design and Validation of a Framework for the Creation of User Experience Questionnaires. International Journal of Interactive Multimedia and Artificial Intelligence, 5(7).

Website: ueqplus.ueq-research.org

UES - User Engagement Scale

Application area: No special application domain. Can be applied for all types of interactive products. Measures user engagement with a product.

Length: 12 items on 4 scales (short version) & 30 items on 4 scales (long version), *Item Format:* Statements with a 5-point answer scale.

Scales and their interpretation:

- *Focused attention:* Is the user absorbed in the interaction? Does the user lose track of time? This is in fact the UX aspect of immersion, described in Chapter 7.

- *Perceived usability:* Mixture of valence items (annoyed, discouraged, frustrated) and usability related items (confusing, feel in control).

- *Aesthetic appeal:* Is the application attractive and aesthetically pleasing. This corresponds the UX aspect of visual aesthetics described in Chapter 7.

- *Felt involvement:* Mixture of items related to stimulation (fun), loyalty (recommend to friends) and usefulness (rewarding, usage was a success, using it was worthwhile).

Remarks: The scales *Perceived usability* and *Felt involvement* are not so easy to interpret. Semantically the items in these scales relate to different aspects of UX.

Main Reference: O'Brien, H. L., Cairns, P. & Hall, M. (2018). A practical approach to measuring user engagement with the refined user engagement scale (UES) and new UES short form. International Journal of Human-Computer Studies, 112, pp. 28-39.

UFOS - Usability Fragebogen für Online-Shops [Usability Questionnaire for online shops]

Application area: Restricted to online shops.

Length: 80 items on 7 scales, *Item format:* Statements 5-point answer scale

Scales and their interpretation:

- *General usability:* Is it easy and fast to shop? Is the structure of the shop clear and logical? Is important information available and easy to find?

- *Accessibility of general conditions:* Are additional costs clearly stated? Are conditions concerning delivery and return of products transparent?

- *Product search:* Is it easy to search for products? Can I find products fast?

- *Shopping basket and ordering:* Is it easy to handle (add or remove products) the shopping basket? Is it easy to see what products are already contained in the basket?

- *Product overview:* Is the categorization of products easy to understand? Are the product lists clear and easy to scan?

- *Self-descriptiveness:* Is it easy to learn how to use the shop? Does the target of links conform to the expectations?

- *Product characteristics:* Are the products clearly described? Are the illustrations and pictures of the products helpful?

Remarks: There is a second version with just 47 items. See Christophersen, T. (2006). Usability im Online-Shopping. Dissertation, Christian-Albrechts-Universität Kiel.

Main Reference: Konradt, U., Wandke, H., Balazs, B. & Christophersen, T. (2003). Usability in online shops: Scale construction, validation and the influence on the buyers' intention and decision. Behaviour & Information Technology, 22(3), pp. 165-174.

UMUX - Usability Metric for User Experience

Application area: No special application domain. Can be applied for all types of interactive products.

Length: 4 items on 1 scale, *Item format:* Statements with a 7-point answer scale.

Scale interpretation: Overall impression concerning the usability of the product.

Remarks: There is a short version just containing 2 items called UMUX-LITE.

Main Reference: Finstad, K. (2010). The usability metric for user experience. Interacting with Computers, 22(5), pp. 323-327.

Website: https://measuringu.com/umux-lite/

UPSCALE - Usability Perception Scale

Application area: Restricted to measure UX of the visualization of feedback graphs.

Length: 8 items on 2 scales, *Item format:* Statements with a 5-point answer scale.

Scales and their interpretation:

- *Ease of use:* Is the image easy to understand and does it contain useful information?

- *Engagement:* Do I like to use the visualization frequently? Do I feel confident about the correct interpretation of the image?

Remarks: Restricted to the evaluation of interactive feedback graphs, thus a very special use case.

Main Reference: Karlin, B. & Ford, R. (2013). The Usability Perception Scale (UPscale): A measure for evaluating feedback displays. In: Proceedings of the 2013 Human Computer Interaction (HCII) Conference. Las Vegas, NV: ACM.

USE - Usefulness Satisfaction and Ease of Use

Application area: Not restricted to special product types or application scenarios.

Length: 30 items on 4 scales, *Item Format:* Statements with a 7-point answer scale.

Scales and their interpretation:

- *Usefulness:* Does the product help me to be more productive or efficient? Does the product help me to save time and effort?

- *Ease of use:* Is the product flexible, error tolerant, easy to use, consistent? Can it be used without instructions?

- *Ease of learning:* Is it easy and fast to learn how to use the product?

- *Satisfaction:* Is the product pleasant and fun to use? Would I recommend it to others?

Remarks: The ease of use scale covers a couple of different classical aspects of usability. The aspect of intuitive use is part of this scale and not part of learnability.

Main Reference: Lund, A. (2001). Measuring usability with the USE questionnaire. Usability and User Experience Newsletter, STC Usability SIG, 8(2), pp.1–4.

UXNFQ - UX Needs Fulfillement Questionnaire

Application area: No special application domain. Can be applied for all types of interactive products.

Length: 30 items on 7 scales, *Item format:* Statements with a 5-point answer scale.

Scales and their interpretation: The scales (*Autonomy, Competence, Influence, Pleasure, Relatedness, Security, Self-Actualizing*) correspond to the psychological needs described in Chapter 2 of this book.

Remarks: This entry refers to two research instruments to measure the fulfillment of psychological needs. In Sheldon, Elliot, Kim & Kasser (2001) a questionnaire to measure 10 general psychological needs is described. In Lallemand & Koenig (2017) an adaption of this approach to measure UX Needs fulfillment in interactive products is described.

Main References: Sheldon, K. M., Elliot, A. J., Kim, Y. & Kasser, T. (2001). What is satisfying about satisfying events? Testing 10 candidate psychological needs. Journal of Personality and Social Psychology, 89, pp. 325–339.

Lallemand, C. & Koenig, V. (2017). Lab testing beyond usability: challenges and recommendations for assessing user experiences. Journal of Usability Studies, 12(3), pp. 133-154.

VISAWI - Visual Aesthetic of Website Inventory

Application area: Designed to measure the visual aesthetics of websites. But it can be used for all types of products with a graphical user interface.

Length: 18 items on 4 scales, *Item format:* Statements with a 7-point rating scale.

Scales and their interpretation:

- *Simplicity:* Is the user interface well-structured, and easy to scan?
- *Diversity:* Does the user interface look interesting, inventive, and inspired?

- *Colorfulness:* Are the chosen colors attractive and is the color composition harmonic?
- *Craftmanship:* Does the design look up-to-date and professional?

Main Reference: Moshagen, M. & Thielsch, M. T. (2010). Facets of visual aesthetics. International Journal of Human-Computer Studies, 68(10), pp. 689-709.

Website: https://visawi.uid.com

VISAWI-S - Short version of the Visual Aesthetic of Website Inventory

Application area: Same as VISAWI.

Length: 4 items on 1 scale, *Item format:* Statements with a 7-point answer scale.

Scale interpretation: Overall impression concerning the visual aesthetic of the interface.

Main Reference: Moshagen, M. & Thielsch, M. T. (2013). A short version of the visual aesthetics of websites inventory. Behaviour & Information Technology, 32(12), pp. 1305-1311.

Website: https://visawi.uid.com

WAMMI - Website Analysis and Measurement Inventory

Application area: Measures the user experience of websites.

Length: 20 items on 5 scales, *Item format:* Statements with a 5-point answer scale.

Scales and their interpretation:

- *Attractiveness:* Do I like to use the website? Is it attractive?
- *Controllability:* Do I have full control over the interaction when I use the website? Does it react predictably?
- *Efficiency:* Does the website load fast? Can I find content efficiently?
- *Helpfulness:* The design of the website supports me to find the information I need?
- *Learnability:* Is the website logical and intuitive to use?

Main Reference: Kirakowski, J. & Cierlik, B. (1998). Measuring the usability of web sites. In Proceedings of the Human Factors and Ergonomics Society annual meeting (Vol. 42, No. 4, pp. 424-428). Sage CA: Los Angeles.

Website: www.wammi.com

Web-Clic - Website-Clarity, Likeability, Informativeness, Credibility

Application area: Measures the subjective perception of users towards the content of websites.

Length: 12 items on 4 scales, *Item format:* Statements with a 7-point answer scale.

Scales and their interpretation:

- *Clarity:* Is the content of the website easy to understand and clearly presented?
- *Likeability:* Is the website interesting? Does the user enjoy reading the content?
- *Informativeness:* Is the information on the website useful and of high quality?
- *Credibility:* Is the information on the website trustworthy.

Main Reference: Thielsch, M. & Hischfeld, G. (2019): Facets of Web-Site Content. Human-Computer Interaction, Vol. 34(4), pp. 279-327.

Website: https://www.meinald.de/forschung/web-clic/

WEBLEI - Web-based Learning Environment Instrument

Application area: Evaluation of online learning platforms or environments.

Length: 57 items on 4 scales, *Item format:* Statements with a 5-point answer scale.

Scales and their interpretation:

- *Co-participatory activities:* Is the interaction with tutors and other students satisfactory?
- *Emancipatory activities:* Can I access learning material and activities at times suitable for me and in my own pace?
- *Information structure and design activities:* Is the quality of the learning material sufficient?
- *Qualia:* Is it easy to use the system? Do I enjoy learning in this environment?

Remarks: The scales contain many items with semantically quite different content. It is for some of the items not immediately clear from their formulation why they are assigned to the corresponding scales. Thus, it is hard to describe the scale meaning in some short sentences.

Main Reference: Chang, V. (1999). Evaluating the effectiveness of online learning using a new web-based learning instrument. Proceedings Western Australian Institute for Educational Research Forum 1999.

WEBQUAL - Website Quality

Application area: Evaluation of websites used to interact with companies or organizations.

Length: 36 items on 12 scales, *Item format:* Statements with a 7-point answer scale

Scales and their interpretation:

- *Ease of use - Intuitive operations:* Is it easy to use and operate?
- *Ease of use - Understanding:* Are the texts on the website easy to understand?
- *Entertainment - Flow, Emotional Appeal:* Do I feel happy and cheerful when I use the website?
- *Entertainment - Inovativeness:* Is the website creative and innovative?
- *Entertainment - Visual Appeal:* Is the visual design of the website appealing?
- *Relationship - Better than alternatives:* Does it save me time and effort to use the website instead of other ways to contact the organization?
- *Relationship - Completeness:* Can I complete all relevant contacts with the website?
- *Relationship - Consistent Image:* Does the website fit to the marketing image of the company?
- *Usefulness - Informational Fit-to-Task:* Does the information on the website meet my information needs?
- *Usefulness - Interactivity:* Does the website support me to get information tailored to my personal needs?
- *Usefulness - Response Time:* Does the website react fast?
- *Usefulness - Trust:* Is the data that I enter in save hands?

Main Reference: Loiacono, E.T., Watson, R.T. & Goodhue, D.L. (2007). WebQual: An Instrument for Consumer Evaluation of Web Sites. International Journal of Electronic Commerce, 11(3), pp. 51-87.

WEBUSE - Website Usability Evaluation

Application area: Evaluation of websites.

Length: 30 items on 4 scales, *Item Format:* Statements with a 5-point answer scale

Scales and their interpretation:

- *Content & Organization:* Is the content of the website easy to access, understand and relevant?

- *Navigation & Links:* Is the navigation in the website easy to understand?

- *Performance & Effectiveness:* Does the website respond fast? Is the website available most of the time? Can it be used efficiently? Does it provide clear messages?

- *User Interface Design:* Is the design of the website attractive, consistent, and easy to understand?

Remarks: Some of the scales contain items with quite different semantic meanings. Thus, the exact scale interpretation is difficult to describe.

Main Reference: Chiew, T. K. & Salim, S. S. (2003). Webuse: Website usability evaluation tool. Malaysian Journal of Computer Science, 16(1), pp. 47-57.

WEQ - Website Evaluation Questionnaire

Application area: Evaluation of websites. Especially designed for governmental websites, but items seem to fit to all types of websites that are built to provide information about organizations or special areas of interest.

Length: 26 items on 8 scales, *Item Format:* Statements with a 5-point answer scale

Scales and their interpretation:

- *Completeness:* Is the information provided by the website is precise and sufficient?

- *Comprehension:* Is the information provided by the website easy to understand?

- *Ease of use:* Is the website user friendly and easy to use?

- *Hyperlinks:* Do the hyperlinks point to the expected information?

- *Layout:* Is the design of the website attractive and appealing?

- *Relevance:* Is the information provided by the website useful?

- *Search Options:* Are the search capabilities of the website useful?

- *Structure:* Is the structure of the website clear and supports to detect relevant information?

Main Reference: Elling, S., Lentz, L. & De Jong, M. (2007). Website Evaluation Questionnaire: Development of a research-based tool for evaluating informational websites. Lecture Notes in Computer Science, 4656, pp. 293–304.

WOOS - Wahrgenommene Orientierung in Online Shops (German)

Application area: Restricted to web shops. Measures orientation of the user in the shop.

Length: 7 items on one scale, *Item format:* Statements with a 7-point answer scale

Scale interpretation: Is the structure of the shop clear? Is it easy to navigate? Is it easy to find the desired products?

Main Reference: Yom, M. & Wilhelm, T. (2004). WOOS – Ein Messinstrument für die wahrgenommene Orientierung in Online-Shops. In: R. Keil-Slawik, H. Selke, G. Szwillus (Hrsg.): Mensch & Computer 2004: Allgegenwärtige Interaktion, pp. 43–53. München: Oldenbourg Verlag.

Appendix 3: Assignment of Items to UX Aspects

Questionnaire	CQ	CU	PE	IN	EF	CO	CL	US	NO	ST	IM	BE	ID	VA	LO	TR
UEQ	0	0	3,5	0	3	3,5	1,5	0	4	3	0	0,5	0	1	0	0,5
Attrakdiff2	0	0	2	0	2	2	0	0	4	4	0	1	3	4	0	0
SUMI	0	0	15	1	6,5	14	0	0	0	2	0	1	0	0	0,5	0
SUS	0	0	5	1	1	1	0	0	0	0	0	0	0	0	1	0
ISONORM	0	5,5	14	1	5	10	0	0	0	0	0	0	0	0	0	0
meCue	0	0	2	0	0	0	0	3	1	5	1	1	3	2	7	0
VISAWI	0	0	0	0	0	0	0	0	2	3	0	9	0	4	0	0
PSSUQ	0	0	2	0	3	2	1	0	0	0	0	0	0	0	0	0
WAMMI	0	0	4,5	3	4	1	0,5	1	0	0	0	1	0	0	0	0
PUTQ	0	9	25	0	17	39	3,5	0	0	0	0	0	0	0	0	0
USE	0	1	5	1	2	2	0	8	0	1	0	0	0	0	0	0
PUEU	0	1	2	0	1	1	0	6	0	0	0	0	0	0	0	0
QUIS	0	2	8,5	0	1	5,5	3	0	0	1	0	0	0	0	0	0
CSUQ	0	0	4	0	3	3	1	1	0	0	0	0	0	0	0	0
SUPR-Q	0	0	0	0	0	1	1	0	0	0	0	0	0	0	2	2
WEBQUAL	2	0	1	2	4	3	2	6	3	3	0	3	0	0	0	3
UMUX	0	0	0	0	1	0	0	1	0	0	0	0	0	0	0	0
ISOMETRICS	0	7	24	1	11	33	0	0	0	0	0	0	0	0	0	0
MSPRC	0	3	8,5	2	6,5	10	2,5	7	6,5	11	0	2	4	12	0	3,5
Quesi	0	0	1	8	0	2	0	1	0	0	0	0	0	0	0	0
UXNFQ	0	1	1	0	2	3	0	1	0	5	0	0	9	0	0	1
WOOS	0	0	5	0	1	0	1	0	0	0	0	0	0	0	0	0
NRL	8	0	3	0	2	2	4	0	0	0	0	1	0	1	0	0
WEBLEI	20	2	1	0	2	9	0	2	0	3	0	0	1	0	0	0
Upscale	0	0	3	0	1	0	0	3	0	0	0	0	0	0	1	0
UFOS	11	0	23	1	5,5	19	10	3,5	0	1	0	0	0	0	0	0
AttrakWork	0	0	3	2	2	1	0	8	0	7	0	0	4	1	0	2
e4	0	6	1	0	2	2	0	4	0	0,5	1	0	0	0	1,5	0
UES	0	0	1	0	0	0	0	1	0	1	3	3	0	0	0	0
DEEP	4	0	1	0	2	5	6	0	0	1	0	0	0	0	0	0
SUISQ	0	0	1	4	3	1	0	1	0	0	0	0	0	0	2	2
SASSI	0	1	4	0	4	10	0	1	0	1	0	0	0	0	1	2
WEBUSE	3	0	2	0	4	9	2	0	0	0	0	2	0	0	0	0
WEQ	6	0	4	0	3	1	2	3	0	0	0	3	0	0	0	0
EUCS	7	0	0	0	1	0	1	0	0	0	0	0	0	0	0	0
HARUS	1	0	1	0	1	3	3	0	0	0	0	0	0	0	0	0
HED/UT	0	0	0	0	2	0	0	7	0	4	0	0	0	0	0	0
INTUI	0	0	0	10	0	1	0	0	0	4	0	0	0	0	0	0
Web-Clic	3	0	0	0	0	0	0	2	0	2	0	0	0	1	0	2
UEQ+	7,5	4	3	4	3,5	3,5	1,5	4,5	4	4	0	4	0	4	0	4,5

Table 5: Assignment of items to UX aspects. Please note that some items could not be assigned.